# THE SHOCK OF THE OLD

# THE SHOCK OF THE OLD

Technology and Global History Since 1900

**DAVID EDGERTON**

OXFORD
UNIVERSITY PRESS

2007

# OXFORD
### UNIVERSITY PRESS

Oxford University Press, Inc., publishes works that
further Oxford University's objective of excellence
in research, scholarship, and education.

Oxford   New York
Auckland   Cape Town   Dar es Salaam   Hong Kong   Karachi
Kuala Lumpur   Madrid   Melbourne   Mexico City   Nairobi
New Delhi   Shanghai   Taipei   Toronto

With offices in
Argentina   Austria   Brazil   Chile   Czech Republic   France   Greece
Guatemala   Hungary   Italy   Japan   Poland   Portugal   Singapore
South Korea   Switzerland   Thailand   Turkey   Ukraine   Vietnam

Copyright © 2007 by David Edgerton
The moral right of the author has been asserted.

First published in Great Britain by Profile Books, Ltd., 2007.

Published by Oxford University Press, Inc.
198 Madison Avenue, New York, NY 10016
www.oup.com

Oxford is a registered trademark of Oxford University Press

Library of Congress Cataloging-in-Publication Data
Edgerton, David.
The shock of the old : technology and global history since 1900 /
by David Edgerton.
p. cm.
Includes bibliographical references and index.
ISBN-13: 978-0-19-532283-5 (cloth)
1. Technology—History—20th century.
2. Technology—Social aspects—History—20th century.
I. Title.
T20.E3275 2007
609'.04—dc22
2006026435

1 3 5 7 9 8 6 4 2
Printed in the United States of America
on acid-free paper

*For Andrew*

# CONTENTS

*I stood on a hill and I saw the Old approaching, but it came as the New.*

*It hobbled up on new crutches which no one had ever seen before and stank of new smells of decay which no one had ever smelt before.*

Bertolt Brecht (1939), from 'Parade of the Old New', in *Bertolt Brecht: Poems 1913–1956*, John Willett and Ralph Manheim (eds) (London: Methuen, 1987), p. 323

# Introduction

Much of what is written on the history of technology is for boys of all ages. This book is a history for grown-ups of all genders. We have lived with technology for a long time, and collectively we know a lot about it. From economists to ecologists, from antiquarians to historians, people have had different views about the material world around us and how it has changed. Yet too often the agenda for discussing the past, present and future of technology is set by the promoters of new technologies.

When we are told about technology from on high we are made to think about novelty and the future. For many decades now the term 'technology' has been closely linked with *invention* (the creation of a new idea) and *innovation* (the first use of a new idea). Talk about technology centres on research and development, patents and the early stages of use, for which the term *diffusion* is used. The timelines of technological history, and they abound, are based on dates of invention and innovation. The most significant twentieth-century technologies are often reduced to the following: flight (1903), nuclear power (1945), contraception (1955), and the internet (1965). We are told that change is taking place at an ever-accelerating pace, and that the new is increasingly powerful. The world, the gurus insist, is entering a new historical epoch as a result of technology. In the new economy, in new times, in our post-industrial and post-modern condition, knowledge of the present and past is supposedly ever less relevant. Inventors, even in these post-modern times, are 'ahead of their time', while societies suffer from the grip of the past, resulting in a supposed slowness to adapt to new technology.

There are new things under the sun, and the world is indeed changing radically, but this way of thinking is not among them. Although the emphasis on the future itself suggests originality, this kind of futurology has been with us a long time. In the nineteenth century the idea that inventors were ahead of their time and that science and technology were advancing faster than the ability of human society to cope was a commonplace. By the early twentieth century this notion was made academically respectable with the label 'the cultural lag'. In the 1950s and even later, one could claim without embarrassment that scientists 'had the future in their bones'. By the end of the twentieth century, futurism had long been *passé*. The technological future was as it had been for a long time. Intellectuals claimed there was a new kind of future, one prefigured by 'post-modern' architecture. Yet this new kind of future was to be brought about by an old-style technological or industrial revolution which would change everything.

In the case of technology reheated futurism has held its appeal long after it was declared obsolete. The technological future marched on as before. Consider the case of the first successful flight of NASA's X-43A space aeroplane on 27 March 2004. Although it lasted all of ten seconds, it made the news the world over. 'From Kitty Hawk to the X-43A has been a century's steady advance', wrote one newspaper; from 'seven miles an hour to Mach Seven is a striking indication of how far powered flight has travelled in a hundred years'.[1] Soon we would be enjoying, yet again, almost instant travel to Australia from London.

Just below the surface was another history, which blew great holes in this old-fashioned story. Every few weeks between 1959 and 1968 B-52 aircraft took off from Edwards Air Force Base in California, with one of three X-15s under their wings. Once high up the X-15s fired their rocket engines and were actively flown by twelve 'research pilots', clad in silver pressurised space suits, reaching speeds of Mach 6.7 and touching the edge of space. These hard-drinking engineer-pilots, mostly combat veterans (among them Neil Armstrong, the first man to set foot on the moon), looked down on mere 'spam in the can' astronauts, as Tom Wolfe observed in *The Right Stuff*. While the astronauts became famous, the elite X-15 pilots were left to lament, as one did, that in the early 1990s he was still 'one of the fastest airplane pilots in the world. I am too old for that. Someone younger should have that honor.'[2] Past and present were connected even more directly. The B-52, which took the X-43A and its booster rocket up, was one of the same B-52s used on the X-15 programmes and was now the oldest flying B-52 in the world.[3] It was built in the 1950s. Not only that, but the key technology of the X-43A was the scramjet, a supersonic version of the ramjet. A technique decades old, it was used in a 1950s-designed British anti-aircraft missile, the Bloodhound, which was itself in service into the 1990s. In short, the story might well have been '1950s aeroplane launches unmanned ramjet plane which flies a little faster than 1960s Right Stuff pilots'.

By thinking about the history of technology-in-use a radically different picture of technology, and indeed of invention and innovation, becomes possible.[4] A whole invisible world of technologies appears. It leads to a rethinking of our notion of technological time, mapped as it is on innovation-based timelines. Even more importantly it alters our picture of which have been the most important technologies. It yields a global history, whereas an innovation-centred one, for all its claims to universality, is based on a very few places. It will give us a history which does not fit the usual schemes of modernity, one which refutes some important assumptions of innovation-centric accounts.

The new history will be surprisingly different. For example, steam power, held to be characteristic of the industrial revolution, was not only absolutely but relatively more important in 1900 than in 1800. Even in Britain, the lead country of the industrial revolution, it continued to grow in absolute importance after that. Britain consumed much more coal in the 1950s than in the 1850s. The world consumed more coal in 2000 than in 1950 or 1900. It has more motor cars, aeroplanes, wooden furniture and cotton textiles than ever before. The tonnage of world shipping continues to increase. We still have buses, trains, radio, television and the cinema, and consume ever-increasing quantities of paper, cement and steel. The production of books continues to increase. Even the key novel technology of the late twentieth century, the electronic computer, has been around for many decades. The post-modern world has forty-year-old nuclear power stations as well as fifty-year old bombers. It has more than a dash of technological retro about it too: it has new ocean-going passenger ships, organic food and classical music played on 'authentic' instruments. Aging, and even dead, rock stars of the 1960s still generate large sales, and children are brought up with Disney films seen by their grandparents when they were children.

Use-centred history is not simply a matter of moving technological time forward. As Bruno Latour has aptly noted, modern time, where this behaved as moderns believed, has never existed. Time was always jumbled up, in the pre-modern era, the post-modern era and the modern era. We worked with old and new things, with hammers and electric drills.[5] In use-centred history technologies do not only appear, they also disappear and reappear, and mix and match across the centuries. Since the late 1960s many more bicycles were produced globally each year than cars.[6] The guillotine made a gruesome return in the 1940s. Cable TV declined in the 1950s to reappear in the 1980s. The supposedly obsolete battleship saw more action in the Second World War than in the First. Furthermore, the twentieth century has seen cases of technological regression.

A use-based history will do much more than disturb our tidy timelines of progress. What we take to be the most significant technologies will change. Our accounts of significance have been peculiarly innovation-centric, and tied to particular accounts of modernity where particular new technologies were held to be central. In the new picture, twentieth-century technology is not just a matter of electricity, mass production, aerospace, nuclear power, the internet and the contraceptive pill. It will involve the rickshaw, the condom, the horse, the sewing machine, the spinning wheel, the Haber-Bosch process, the hydrogenation of coal, cemented-carbide tools, bicycles, corrugated iron, cement, asbestos, DDT, the chain saw and the refrigerator. The horse made a greater contribution to Nazi conquest than the V2.

A central feature of use-based history, and a new history of

*1. A mule hauling equipment on a track in the building of the Berlin–Baghdad railway near Aleppo between 1900 and 1910. Mules, and railways, were vitally important technologies of the twentieth century in both rich and poor countries.*

invention, is that alternatives exist for nearly all technologies: there are multiple military technologies, means of generating electricity, powering a motor car, storing and manipulating information, cutting metal or roofing a building. Too often histories are written as if no alternative could or did exist.

One particularly important feature of use-based history of technology is that it can be genuinely global. It includes all places that use technology, not just the small number of places where invention and innovation is concentrated. In the innovation-centric account, most places have no history of technology. In use-centred accounts, nearly everywhere does. It gives us a history of technology engaged with all the world's population, which is mostly poor, non-white and half female. A use-perspective points to the significance of novel technological worlds which have emerged in the twentieth century and which have hitherto had no place in histories of technology. Among them are the new technologies of poverty. They are missed because the poor world is thought of as having traditional local technologies, a *lack* of rich-world technologies, and/or has been subject to imperial technological violence. When we think of cities we should think of *bidonvilles* as well as Alphaville; we should think not just about the planned cities of Le Corbusier, but the unplanned shanty towns, built not by great contractors, but by millions of self-builders over many years. These are worlds of what I call 'creole' technologies, technologies transplanted from their place of origin finding uses on a greater scale elsewhere.

A consequence of the new approach is that we shift attention from the new to the old, the big to the small, the spectacular to the mundane, the masculine to the feminine, the rich to the poor. But at its core is a rethinking of the history of all technology, including the big, spectacular, masculine high technologies of the rich white world. For all the critiques, we do not in fact have a coherent production-ist, masculine, materialist account of technology and history in the twentieth century. We have big questions, and big issues to address, which are surprisingly open.

A use-centred account also refutes some well-established conclusions of innovation-centric history. For example, it undermines the assumption that national innovation determines national success; the most innovative nations of the twentieth century have not been the fastest growing. Perhaps the most surprising criticism that arises from the use perspective is that innovation-centric history gives us an inadequate account of invention and innovation. Innovation-centric history focuses on the early history of some technologies which became important later. The history of invention and innovation needs to focus on all inventions and innovations at a particular time, independently of their later success or failure. It needs to look too to invention and innovation in all technologies, not just those favoured by being well known and assumed to be the most significant. Traditional innovation-centric histories have space for Bill Gates,

*2. The United States became one of the richest agricultural nations in the world partly by creating highly mechanised, but animal-powered, agriculture. Here a farmer drives a team of twenty mules pulling a combine harvester through the wheat fields of Walla Walla County, Washington in 1941. By this time the tractor had been displacing horses and mules in some areas for twenty-five years.*

but a history of invention and innovation would also include Ingvar Kamprad, who made his money from mass-producing and selling wooden furniture. He founded IKEA and is, some think, richer than Gates. More importantly, our histories need to have a place for the majority of failed inventions and innovations. Most inventions are never used; many innovations fail.

The innovation-centric view also misleads us as to the nature of scientists and engineers. It presents them, as they present themselves, as creators, designers, researchers. Yet the majority have always been mainly concerned with the operation and maintenance of things and processes; with the uses of things, not their invention or development.

Given the importance of innovation-centric futurism in discussing technology, history can be an especially powerful tool for rethinking technology. History reveals that technological futurism is largely unchanging over time. Present visions of the future display a startling, unselfconscious lack of originality. Take the extraordinary litany of technologies which promised peace to the world. Communications technologies, from railways and steamships, to radio and the aeroplane, and now the internet, seemed to make the world smaller and bring people together, ensuring a perpetual peace. Technologies of destruction, such as the great ironclad battleships, Nobel's explosives, the bomber aircraft and the atomic bomb were so powerful that they too would force the world to make peace. New technologies of many sorts would emancipate the downtrodden. The old class system would wither under the meritocracy demanded by new technology; racial minorities would gain new opportunities – as chauffeurs in the motor age, pilots in the air age, and computer experts in the information age. Women were to be liberated by new domestic technologies, from the vacuum cleaner to the washing machine. The differences between nations would evaporate as technology overcame borders. Political systems too would converge as technology, inevitably, became the same everywhere. The socialist and capitalist worlds would become one.

In order to be at all convincing these arguments had to deny their own history, and they did so to a remarkable extent. The obliteration of even recent history has been continuous and systematic. For example, in the middle of 1945 the bomber ceased to be a peace-creating technology; the atomic bomb took its place. When we think of information technology we forget about postal systems, the telegraph, the telephone, radio and television. When we celebrate on-line shopping, the mail-order catalogue goes missing. Genetic engineering, and its positive and negative impacts, is discussed as if there had never been any other means of changing animals or plants, let alone other means of increasing food supply. A history of how things were done in the past, and of the way past futurology has worked, will undermine most contemporary claims to novelty.

We need to be aware that this futurology of the past has affected our history. From it we get our focus on invention and innovation, and on the technologies which we take to be the most important. From this literature, the work of low- and middle-ranking intellectuals and propagandists, ranging from, say, the books of H. G. Wells to the press releases of NASA's PR officials, we get a whole series of clichéd claims about technology and history. We should take them, not as well-grounded contributions to our understanding, for they rarely are that, but as the basis of questions. What have been the most significant technologies of the twentieth century? Has the world become a global village? Has culture lagged behind technology? Has technology had revolutionary or conservative social and political effects? Has new technology been responsible for the dramatic increase in economic output in the last hundred years? Has technology transformed war? Has the rate of technical change been ever increasing? These are some of the questions this book will try to answer, but they cannot be answered within the innovation-centric frame in which they are usually asked.

These questions become much easier to answer if we stop thinking about 'technology', but instead think of 'things'. Thinking about the use of things, rather than of technology, connects us directly with the world we know rather than the strange world in which 'technology' lives. We speak of 'our' technology, meaning the technology of an age or a whole society. By contrast 'things' fit into no such totality, and do not evoke what is often taken as an independent historical force. We discuss the world of things as grown-ups, but technology as children. For example, we all know that while the use of things is widely distributed through societies, ultimate control of things and their use has been highly concentrated, within societies and between societies. Ownership, and other forms of authority, on the one hand, and use on the other, have been radically separated. Most people in the world live in houses that do not belong to them, work in workplaces belonging to others, with tools that belong to others, and indeed many of the things they apparently own are often tied to credit agreements.

Within societies, states and/or small groups have had disproportionate control; some societies have much more stuff than others. In many places of the world much is owned by foreigners. Things belong to particular people in ways which technology does not.

# 1

# Significance

Is the condom more significant in history than the aeroplane? We all know that technology has made an enormous difference to the history of the twentieth century. But just how important is difficult, perhaps impossible, to assess. When it had the greatest effect is also difficult to assess. Can one distinguish between technological and other changes? What is the appropriate measure of significance? Is it a quantitative measure, perhaps of economic impact, or some qualitative estimate of social or cultural effect? Is cultural significance to be measured by the presence of a technology in the movies, the pages of newspapers, and the works of intellectuals? Or can we detect it even when a technology hardly resonates at all at these levels? The aeroplane is by this measure very culturally significant, the condom insignificant. Once we start thinking seriously about these questions we will open up the history of twentieth-century technology to many fresh insights.

Our world abounds with seemingly authoritative stories of which technologies have been most significant, and when. They focus on a small number of cases. For the years up to around 1940 electricity, motor cars and aviation are conventionally deemed to be the most important. The period of the Second World War and later is seen as the age of nuclear power, computers, space rockets and the internet.[1] Sometimes biotechnologies, including new foods, medicines and contraceptives (the Pill), are part of these narratives, as are chemicals.[2] To be sure there are variants. Thus in one account 1895 to 1940 was the

3. *Rocketry was, from the very beginning, a very public technology. Its public prominence has led to an exaggerated idea of its significance to history, especially for the 1940s and 1950s. Here photographers record the first launch from what was later known as Cape Canaveral on 24 July 1950. The rocket was a 'Bumper V-2', a modified V-2.*

period of *electrification*; 1941 to the late twentieth century was the era of *motorisation*; and this was followed by the age of *computerisation* of the economy.[3]

These accounts bear an uncanny resemblance to claims for significance made long before any historical analysis could be carried out. One analyst, writing in 1948, thought that the world had already gone through three industrial revolutions associated with particular technologies. The first depended on iron, steam and textiles; the second on chemistry, large industries, steel and new communications; and the third, still under way in 1948, was 'the age of electrification, automatic machinery, electric control over manufacturing processes, air transport, radios and so on'. A fourth was on the way: 'with the coming of intra-atomic energy and supersonic stratospheric aviation we face an even more staggering fourth Industrial Revolution,' he claimed.[4] In the 1950s some believed that there had been a 'scientific revolution' which followed the original industrial revolution. This had started in the early- to mid-twentieth century and was associated with aeroplanes, electronics and atomic power. For others a third industrial revolution, of which the 'warning signs' appeared in the 1940s, was based on nuclear energy and electronically controlled automation.[5] In the Soviet Union the idea of a 'Scientific–Technical Revolution', centred on automation, became Communist party doctrine from the mid-1960s.[6] More recently, analysts have tended to highlight what they see as a radical transition from an industrial society to a post-industrial, or information, society brought about through the actions of the digital computer and the internet. In this context, some economists have developed the idea that economic history has been shaped by a very few 'general-purpose technologies'. The central ones are successively steam power, electricity and now information and communication technologies (ICT).

How seriously should we take these claims for these technologies, and for their significance in these particular periods? The answer is that such accounts, for all that they reflect what we think we know, are not as well founded as might be supposed. They are clearly innovation-centric in their chronology, implying that the impact of the technologies comes with innovation and early use. That is not the only problem. What is the basis for the choice of the general-purpose technologies, and how solidly does it rest? Why the steam engine, for example? Why not the heat engine, ranging from the reciprocating steam engine to petrol and diesel engines, to the gas and steam turbines? Similarly, what does electricity mean? It clearly includes lighting and traction, and perhaps industrial uses. But does it include electronics, where there is hardly a substitute? Can we think of telephony, telegraphy, radio, radar and television without electricity? Yet if 'electricity' is to include these, how does one differentiate 'electricity' from ICT? Which leads to the question, what exactly is meant by ICT? Just as importantly we need to ask why other technologies are not on the list. There are many other pervasive technologies to choose from, from the working of metal (the lathe or the milling machine might be good cases), to synthetic organic chemistry or metallurgy.

While there is enough consistency of choice to suggest a common understanding, there is enough variation in dates and arguments to suggest no detailed analysis of significance lies at the root of these choices. The lack of any surprises in the standard lists of technologies chosen suggests that what they are linked by is high cultural visibility and that they have long been claimed to be central to the history of the twentieth century. The technological boosterism of the past has too often been turned into the history of our material world.

Occasionally radio programmes, magazines or newspapers ask their publics or experts for their choice of the most important invention in history. The results are invariably quirky, easily challengeable and often silly. Part of the British radio-listening public responded to an old-fashioned techno-boosterist series of lectures with a vote that made the bicycle easily the most significant technical innovation since 1800. Water-treatment and supply systems topped the list of most beneficial technologies, and the washing machine was the most significant domestic technology.[7] Such polls have the virtue of forcing us to think and to challenge the consensus views about which technologies have been the most significant.

### Assessing technologies

How should claims for technological importance be assessed? First, it is essential to distinguish between the innovation itself and use. In most cases the choice of significant technology is not only highly selective, but dating of significance is highly innovation-centric. The process of invention, development and innovation is sometimes enormously expensive. *Sometimes* these costs are recovered and indeed surpluses made, but the benefits (and sometimes increased costs) come only from *later use*. The time of maximum use is typically decades away from invention, or indeed innovation. For example, electricity and car usage are still increasing, more than a century from innovation. This issue was partly recognised in response to an intriguing problem. The rate of growth of the economies of the rich countries was slower in the 1970s, 1980s and indeed 1990s than it had been in the long boom of the 1950s and 1960s, yet everyone was saying that new technology was changing things radically. As an economist put it, information technology was everywhere except in the productivity data. One reaction was to claim that the data were wrong, they could not capture the transformations wrought by information technology; statistical offices – long used to taking account of quality changes – looked closely at their assumptions and techniques, but decided they were recording the effects. Another response was that the impact of ICT, like that of electricity, would be felt much later than an innovation-centric approach suggested. In other words, the timing of the revolution was all wrong, perhaps by many decades. But the dates are just the beginning of the problem, for it is not just a matter of when, but of which technology, and how big the effect is.

## Use is not enough

Significance is not the same as pervasiveness or usefulness. Understanding the difference between use and usefulness, between pervasiveness and significance, is essential. Economic historians of technology have done just this. They argue that the significance of a technology for an economy is the difference between the cost or benefit of using a technology and that of the best alternative. Thus Robert Fogel assessed the importance of nineteenth-century US railways not by assuming that without them people and goods would be impossible to transport, but by comparing railways with other means of transportation, including canals and horse-drawn wagons. He found, in a rough calculation, that railways increased the output of the US economy as it stood in 1890 by less than 5 per cent of GDP. Since the American economy was growing very fast at the time, this was the equivalent of saying that without railways the US economy would have had to wait until 1891 or 1892 to achieve the output it reached with railways in

1890.[8] Twentieth-century motorisation, or electrification, or the role of civil aviation, has not been subject to such detailed assessments, yet we can imagine productive worlds without the motor car or the aeroplane, (though a world without electricity, in some respects only, is a different matter). Rockets and atomic power, so beloved in the 1950s and 1960s as world-transforming technologies, are as likely to have made the world poorer rather than richer once all the costs and benefits have been computed.

Many object to this kind of counterfactual history – one which invokes something which did not happen – as unsatisfactory. And so it is. Yet it is inescapable if we want to assess significance sensibly. For most assessments already have an implicit, hidden counterfactual assumption which is usually critical to the argument.

The hidden counterfactual assumption which lies behind the equation of use and significance is that there was no alternative. Two anecdotal examples illustrate this: an article in the press imagined what the world would have been like without computers; the conclusion was that it would barely work at all, and therefore that computers were extraordinarily significant.[9] This is the equivalent of asking what would happen if all existing (electronic digital) computers suddenly stopped working. The second example is a television programme of the last years of the twentieth century about a Japanese management guru who believed that the internet was bringing about a new era of global citizenship.[10] This was put to the test by interviewing him in San Francisco, but using the internet. The link kept breaking down, and was in any case of low quality. The presenter poked some mild fun at the unfortunate sage, but missed the real joke. The capacity to communicate with someone in San Francisco has existed for a long time. As far back as the late nineteenth century one could have communicated by telegraph; the long-distance telephone was available from the early twentieth. The message about citizens of the world, the borderless market and so on, would have been the same.

One of the most dramatic changes in price over the twentieth century was that of electronic communication, resulting in drastic reduction in the real costs of telephone calls (some 99 per cent), and making possible the mass transmission of other data (as in the internet). Similarly, the case of the computer-less world assumes no alternative to computers, but we would use alternatives and do things differently. Of course, computers do things better than alternatives, and for many uses of computers there may well be no alternative, but that is exactly what one needs to catch hold of. The question is not what computers do, but how well they do it, and what they can do that cannot be done otherwise.

Precisely because of the fecundity of invention there usually have been comparable alternatives. There were computing machines before electronic computers. Punched-card machines were used for large-scale data processing, mathematical calculations were done with teams of 'computers' calculating with machines, often electric ones. Slide-rules were important tools in the design workshop – the large industrial versions were far removed from those for school use. Digital electronic computers were preceded by mechanical analogue computers, from tide predictors to differential analysers. Electronic analogue computers played a vital role, along with digital computers, in the design of complex systems for decades after the Second World War. Telecommunications existed before the internet: the telegraph continued to carry large amounts of long-distance traffic into the years after the Second World War. The telephone and the radio were widely used. Television by cable and by high-frequency radio transmission has been around for decades. There was sound reproduction before the CD: wax cylinders, shellac and vinyl records, wire and tape recorders all worked. There is more than one way to skin a cat, to fight a war, to generate energy. Yet, these alternatives are often difficult to imagine, even when they exist. I remember asking engineering students in the mid-1980s what alternatives there were to satellites for long-distance telecommunication but they could find none. This was exactly the moment when the world was once again being girdled with cables – not the copper cables with repeaters of the great era of telegraph, but with fibre-optic cables. Alternatives are everywhere, though they are often invisible. Invention, and human ingenuity in using inventions, means that we should compare with alternatives, but because the world changes in so many ways it is extremely difficult to compare with past or alternative worlds.

The hidden counterfactual assumption that there was no alternative is an extreme one; the more common assumption is that there was no comparable alternative: the newest was radically more effective, efficient, powerful and generally better than what it superseded. But to become widely used, a thing does not have to be massively better than what preceded it; it need only be *marginally* better than alternatives (assuming for the moment that better technologies will replace worse ones). In some cases, often taken to be trivial, we understand this without difficulty. The paper-clip is ubiquitous not because it is an earth-shatteringly important technology. Indeed its very ubiquity, simplicity, its unchanging design over decades, the fact that it does not move at huge speed or consume vast quantities of energy, all seem to point to it being a minor technology. Crucially we know we can do without paper-clips. As a result of invention we have a remarkable repertoire of paper-collating technologies, each adapted to very particular uses. There are many ways of holding paper together: pin it, staple it, punch holes and secure it with 'Treasury tags', use Sellotape, put it in a ring-bind or other sort of folder, or bind it into a book.[11] We use paper-clips so much because they are, for many uses, marginally better than alternatives, and we know this.

### Technological choice

The assumption that the new is much superior to older methods is widespread. Thus alternating current (AC) electrical systems were assumed to be superior to direct current (DC) systems in the so-called battle of the electrical systems in the late nineteenth century. So they were, in some respects, but not all. In any case, the big choice lay not in an irrefutable demonstration of the superiority of one over the other, but the belief that AC would be better in the long run, a belief that became a self-fulfilling prophecy. Although, in fact, not entirely:

DC systems remained in operation for many years, and new ones were installed. They were also continuously developed in specialist areas. One of the major advantages adduced for AC was the lower cost of transmission, yet in particular cases, for example underwater transmission, high-voltage DC has been used, including in the first and second English Channel electric links between Britain and France, dating back to 1961.

The assumption that the new is clearly superior to what went before has an important corollary: failure to move from one to the other is to be explained by 'conservatism', not to mention stupidity or straight-forward ignorance. 'Resistance to new technology' becomes a problem to be addressed by psychologists, sociologists, even historians.[12] But the idea of 'resistance' makes sense only if there are no alternatives. It is absurd to talk of resistance to technology or innovation in a world where individuals or societies simply could not accept every innovation, or indeed product, on offer. Resistance is required. In choosing one technology, society was necessarily resisting *many* 'old' and 'new' alternative technologies. In that sense, many, perhaps most, technologies fail. However, some new technologies were indeed often additions to existing, alternative technologies. The bomber did not do away with armies and navies; the digital computer did not spell the end of the analogue computer until the 1960s.

Historians who have focused on the issue of technological choice point again and again to the availability of competing technologies. For example, in the USA in the early years of the twentieth century, the petrol-powered car was, briefly, less common than either the steam or electric-powered car; indeed in Chicago the electric car dominated. In later years electric cars found niche markets: they accounted for around 20 per cent of motor taxis in Berlin between 1907 and 1918.[13] Before the Great War German fire departments had a strong tendency to choose electric fire engines to replace horses. In mid-century, with the growth of industrial electric vehicles, came the unique British milk float, delivering milk to nearly every household in the land. Yet, while representing a plausible alternative, the electric vehicle generally lost out to the petrol-powered car. Among the many reasons for this was the problem of use outside the range of electrical networks, and the particular problems encountered with battery maintenance.[14] In the world of cars there have been different kinds of internal combustion engine – diesel, petrol and two-stroke; different kinds of body material, including the use of a great deal of wood as late as the 1940s in the USA, and synthetic materials too. A nice example, developed and kept in production for many years in the particular conditions faced in the German Democratic Republic was the Trabant – a car with a resin/wool body and a two-cylinder two-stroke engine. There have been many types of competing road material in the twentieth century, for example, including tarmacadam and cement.[15]

In aviation too there have been many different types of engine and of aeroplane. There were petrol engines and diesel engines and the Soviet Union devoted huge effort to the *steam* aero-engine in the 1930s.[16] Petrol engines came in many varieties: rotary, radial and inline. Jet engines would develop into turbo-prop, turbo-jet and turbo-fan variants. The transition from wood to metal in aircraft construction in the interwar years provides an interesting case of how choices were made. Moving to metal was often taken as an index of technical progress – metal was obviously better, and the quicker designers switched to metal the more advanced they were made to appear. Conversely, late use of wood was seen as the result of some eccentricity. But the assumption that wood was inferior to metal does not hold. What drove the shift from wood to metal was the *belief* that metal was the material of the future and thus inherently more suitable for aircraft, an ideology later subscribed to by historians of aviation. Nevertheless successful wooden aircraft, notably the British Mosquito of the Second World War, continued to be made.[17] Note too that electric cars are making a comeback, and indeed that aircraft structures are now being made of 'composites', similar in principle to the plywood-glue composites used in aircraft in the interwar years.

One other way in which alternatives remain visible once we look for them is in what might be called reserve technologies, to be used if the technology of choice breaks down. They are much less common now in rich countries than in the past because of the increasing reliability of systems. However, even in rich and stable countries houses with electric light would have had paraffin lamps, and indeed candles, in reserve, and a Primus stove for cooking, in addition to an electric or gas range. Ships had hand-powered reserve steering gear, in case the main gear failed; they carried lifeboats with sails and oars. Cars will carry spare tyres, often more primitive than the usual tyres. Typically, but not necessarily, these reserve technologies are older, simpler technologies. This reversion in time of crisis to an earlier, more robust and perhaps lower stage is an interesting reflection perhaps of an evolutionary pattern of thinking about technology. In many societies older technologies, or rather what are seen as old technologies, have a particular place in ceremonial occasions – from the use of candles at dinner, to the parading of troops in nineteenth-century uniforms and sometimes weapons, and the use of horse-drawn hearses in funerals.

Sometimes circumstances forced the use of a reserve technology. For British men around 1960, the preferred method of committing suicide was poisoning using domestic gas, which contained carbon monoxide. From the early 1970s this was no longer possible as methane replaced coal-gas. Partly as a result, use of car-exhaust fumes grew increasingly popular, and in 1990 this briefly became the most common method. The rate then fell sharply, partly because of the spread of catalytic converters, which made exhaust fumes far less lethal. Hanging and strangulation became more commonly used – and by the end of the century were easily the most important methods. This was not by necessity: women preferred solid and liquid poisons.[18]

## Assessing aviation and nuclear energy

Private and public bodies have long wanted to assess projects, often in advance of undertaking them. Thus the US Army Corps of Engineers, responsible for water works in America, were instrumental in developing cost-benefit analysis to justify their projects in the early part of the last century.[19] The clinical trial has long been important to doctors and to medical systems, but so have cruder assessments. One interwar doctor claimed that Britain could save 1.67 per cent of its annual national income if instead of treating the common complaint of leg ulcers with bed-rest, a new product, an elasticated plaster (Elastoplast), was used. It is not known whether this saving was realised, but if it was this was surely one of the most important British technologies of the century.[20]

Twentieth-century warfare provides some important cases of the assessment of significance of technologies. In waging war against societies, assessments were made of the significance of particular systems, raw material supplies, industries and so on. What would most effectively incapacitate an enemy, the destruction of its transport, its energy supply, its industry in general or particular industries? What means should be selected to achieve such destruction? Two central cases of such assessments involved the most celebrated and supposedly world-transforming technologies of the century – aviation and nuclear power.

Before the Second World War airmen believed that the new war from the air would be devastating and decisive. The strategic bombing of continental Europe by the RAF and the US Army Air Force, and that of Japan by the USAAF, was the result of such beliefs. A central argument was that modern societies would collapse under the impact of even mild bombing (an argument later transferred to rockets and nuclear weapons). During the war it became clear to some that air power was not necessarily devastating or decisive, leading to acrimonious disputes over the whole bombing effort and/or which targets should be attacked. Sometimes the discussions highlighted the strategic significance of particular industries. Thus there were arguments for attacking ball-bearing production, highly concentrated in a few plants, and manufacturing a product without which motor vehicles could not work; or attacking synthetic oil plants, because without fuel Germany could not fight; or electricity plants and so on. On the eve of the Normandy landings there was a particular debate about how best to help the advancing armies. What should be attacked? German

*4. A B-29 bomber drops bombs in the mountains of Korea, early 1951. Although the USA did not use B-29s to drop atomic bombs against what they called the 'communist hordes' in Korea, they devastated the country. Regrettably, more attention is given to the non-use of atomic bombs in this war than the terrible effects of the bombing. Yet, for all the destruction the USA did not win the Korean War.*

industry as a whole, the oil industry or transportation? If the latter, how should it be attacked? Should one attack road and rail bridges or marshalling yards and repair depots? The former were difficult to destroy, but remained so, the latter were easily hit, but were quickly repairable.[21] The commander of the British bomber forces between 1942 and 1945, Sir Arthur 'Butcher' Harris, dismissed precision attacks on particular plants and industries as 'panaceas'; he argued that the only effective targets were whole cities.

There was a broader question: how significant was the bomber? In 1945 Sir Arthur Harris claimed that 'the heavy bomber did more than any other single weapon to win this War', adding that, while the key technologies of a future war would change, the 'quickest way of winning the War will still be to devastate the enemy's industry and thus destroy his war potential'.[22] In his final despatch the British commander used a series of tables and graphs of tonnage of bombs dropped to make his case. He showed that nearly 1 million tons of bombs were dropped by the RAF, some 45 per cent on 'industrial towns'. The index of success was the 'total acreage of devastation' in the target built-up areas of Germany; by the end of the war 48 per cent of them were 'devastated' or 'destroyed' by RAF bombs alone. Harris produced practically no graphical information or data on the effects of bombing on industrial production, or on the effects of attacking synthetic oil or transportation, both of which he had been against. Nor did he consider alternative strategies, except in two cases. He claimed that between April and September 1944, when Bomber Command was, in his view, distracted from 'its proper strategic role', that is diverted to attacking transportation and the German army around D-Day, Germany was able to reorganise war production and increase the supply of armament, particularly of new weapons.[23] Secondly, he claimed that, without bombing, Germany could have used the 2 million workers in anti-aircraft forces and engaged in repairing bomb damage to make arms instead. Relying on the evidence of the captured German armament minister Albert Speer, he claimed Germany could have increased production of anti-tank and field guns by around 30 per cent.[24] In his interrogation Speer claimed that in 1944 30 per cent of output of guns was for anti-aircraft use, as were 20 per cent of heavy shells, 50–55 per cent of the 'electrotechnical industry' and 30 per cent of the optical industry.[25]

However, Harris's claims were to be subject to devastating attack as a result of one of the greatest ever retrospective technology assessment exercises. As the land armies moved in to the bombed areas, they were joined by investigators from the US Strategic Bombing Survey. The survey was led by the head of the Prudential Insurance Company: the monstrous effort involved 350 officers, 300 civilians and 500 enlisted men.[26] The USSBS came out against the RAF and its predominant practice of area bombing, but particular reports supported the attacks on transportation and synthetic oil. They claimed that the bombing of cities had a negligible impact on production, whereas the crippling of transport and synthetic oil production had effects felt right across the German war machine.[27] Everywhere was evidence which contradicted important claims. For example, in 1944 only some 13 per cent of Germany's heavy guns (over 75mm) were anti-aircraft guns. Furthermore, compared with 1943, the proportion of anti-aircraft guns was falling, contrary to the confident assertions of the bomber and the bombed.[28]

The assessment made by the USSBS of the bombing effort against Japan was specially striking. The bombing of the Japanese home islands was much less heavy than that of Germany: 160,000 tons of bombs were dropped rather than the 1,360,000 tons which fell within Germany's borders.[29] Yet, the damage was similar because the bombs were more concentrated in time and more accurately delivered. Some 40 per cent of the built-up area of the sixty-six cities attacked was destroyed. And yet, the effects on the economy were not clear cut because of the repercussions of another form of attack on Japan – blockade. 'Japan's economy was in large measure being destroyed twice over, once by cutting off of imports, and secondly by air attack', reported the USSBS. Even *without* any bombing, war production would have been halved by 1945.[30]

The USSBS also made a devastating comparison between the two instances of atomic bombing and conventional bombing, as it came to be known later. They estimated that the Hiroshima bomb did the same damage as '220 B-29s carrying 1,200 tons of incendiary bombs, 400 tons of high-explosive bombs, and 500 tons of anti-personnel fragmentation bombs', while the Nagasaki bomb was the equivalent of '125 B-29s carrying 1,200 tons of bombs'.[31] In another measure they concluded that the atomic bomb 'raises the destructive power of a single bomber by a factor of somewhere between 50 and 250 times'.[32] That gives an effective TNT equivalence of an atomic bomb at something in the range of 500 to 2,500 tons, rather than the usually quoted 10–20,000 tons of TNT. The difference arises because most of the huge explosive power of an atomic bomb was not directed at the target. What the report was suggesting was that an atomic raid did the same sort of damage as a standard large conventional one, a few per cent at most of the destruction meted out to Japan from the air. The designers of the bomb would not have been surprised. In May 1945 a key committee meeting at Los Alamos was told that 'one atomic bomb on an arsenal would not be much different from the effect caused by any Air Corps strike of present dimensions'.[33] This knowledge was critical in target selection, since potential atomic targets had to be 'likely to be unattacked by next August'; the meeting was told of a 'list of five targets which the Air Forces would be willing to *reserve for our use* unless unforeseen circumstances arise [emphasis added]'. Four were selected – Kyoto, Hiroshima, Yokohama and Kokura Arsenal – and 'reservations for these targets' were requested.[34] Atomic bombs showed their destructive capabilities only because alternatives were kept out of play. We should not, however, underestimate the point that they were weapons of mass terror as well as mass destruction.

The atomic bombs were the product of an industrial effort which cost just under $2bn ($20bn in 1996 dollars). One billion dollars to destroy a city which would have been destroyed at minimal additional cost by one conventional raid represented an awful lot of 'bucks per bang'. Another way to look at it is that it cost $3bn to manufacture the 4,000 or so B-29s which were used exclusively in long-range operations against Japan, including as atomic bombers. This figure included their spare parts, but excluded maintenance, fuel, weapon and staffing costs, as well as the cost of building and running airfields.[35] Another index was that the total cost of the atomic bombs was the equivalent of making one-third more tanks or five times more heavy guns.[36] It is not difficult to imagine what thousands more B-29s, one-third more tanks or five times more artillery, or some other military output, would have done to Allied fighting power. Might it not have shortened the war considerably? In other words, by reducing the conventional material available, the atomic programme, it could be argued, lengthened the war and this cost lives. That we do not see this is partly the result of a carefully fabricated myth put about after the war, that the bomb brought the war to a quick end and *saved* no fewer than 1 million US lives.[37] This myth depended on the dubious counterfactual argument that the Japanese would have fought on and on had they not suffered atomic bombing, and that the only other way of defeating them involved an invasion that would cost 1 million lives. In other words, this argument assumed that blockade and conventional bombing were ineffective by comparison with the atomic bomb. Yet Japan was very close to surrender before the bombs were dropped. The crucial factors which led to surrender were the entry of the Soviet Union into the war against them, and the change in the terms of surrender being offered, a change which came *after* the atomic bombs were dropped. The bombs may have made surrender easier, but not more likely. They did not end either the war, or war in general.

The German V-2 project, another huge wartime undertaking, was also economically and militarily irrational, and this too was obvious to some at the time. British scientific intelligence suggested the Germans were building a rocket of around 10 tons, with a warhead of around 1 ton. This estimate, which proved correct, was controversial because it was not cost-effective to build missiles that could fly 200 miles and deliver one ton of explosive once, when you could build aeroplanes which could deliver ten times that, again and again, over greater ranges. And yet, that is exactly what the Germans did.[38] In October 1942 the V-2 was successfully tested. Two years later, the first V-2 was fired in anger, and around twenty were being built a day. The V-2 'was a unique weapon', says its historian, Michael Neufeld, in that 'more people died producing it than died from being hit by it': at least 10,000 slave labourers perished in the course of production and around 5,000 from it.[39] Nearly 6,000 V-2s were made so that, very crudely, it took two human lives to make a V-2 and each killed one person. It is estimated that instead of V-2s Germany could have built 24,000 fighter aircraft.

The total cost of development and production of the V-2 was around $500m, about a quarter of the US atomic bomb project. Yet the destructive power of *all* the V-2s produced amounted to less than could be achieved by a single raid on a city by the RAF or the USAAF. The 'United Nations', as twenty-six and then more, anti-Axis Allies were known from 1942, should have been grateful to Werner von Braun, Albert Speer and Adolf Hitler for supporting a technology this draining to their own war effort. However, the Axis should have been even more grateful to General Groves and the atomic scientists for coming up with the most expensive explosive ever created. There is a terrible symmetry here since the US produced only four atomic bombs during the war, each of the destructive capacity of a conventional raid – in other words, the bang per buck was identical at $500m per destroyed city. Of course, had the war continued longer, the economics would have made a little more sense, as the capital cost had been spent. Nevertheless the costs per bomb or rocket were still huge. Had the war extirpated militarism from the world and had the development of weapons stopped, the rocket and the A-bomb would not have been seen as harbingers of the future, but more likely as the last dreadful examples of the irrationality of war and military technology.

Within the context of the unprecedented peacetime militarism which followed the Second World War, both the rocket and bomb were *later* to make a certain sort of sense. For the combination of the rocket and the *hydrogen* bomb, which was in a quite different class of destructive power from the A-Bomb, was to make sense in bang-per-buck terms, simply because destructive power increased so much. To that extent the atomic bomb and V-2 cases illustrate the short-sightedness of focusing only on the early stages of a technology (though both were put into production on a huge scale in wartime). We have, in other words, an example of the distinction to be made between what is efficient at a given time and what may be more efficient over time, what economists call static and dynamic efficiency.

Yet the post-war US atomic programme, including bombers and missiles, although capable of immense destruction, was not cheap: nearly $6,000bn (in 1996 prices) were spent between 1940 and 1996.

That was about one-third of all defence expenditure and just under the total spent on social security by the United States.[40] So powerful was this arsenal that it could not be used, so at this point we have to throw away our use criterion of significance. Its utility, to the extent it had any, was in preventing certain actions by others. Yet, for the Chinese Communists, famously, atomic weapons were 'paper tigers', although they too built them.

## Spin-off

One of the most common responses to claims that a particular technology has not had the powerful positive effect it was claimed to have has been to suggest that there have been significant secondary effects not captured by the direct assessment. Thus one response to the claim that railways were not *that* important to economic development was to point to the stimulating effect they had on other industries such as engineering, iron and steel, and telegraphy. The term 'spin-off' is used to describe this effect. The significance of spin-off has not been properly assessed, for it was a propagandistic argument which few in the know took seriously. One important feature of spin-off arguments is that they tend to be associated, with no convincing evidence, with technologies which are already for other reasons regarded as fundamental. Aviation, rockets and nuclear power were all key cases.

One of the most famous examples, even if regarded with some derision, was that the US space programme spun-off Teflon, a new plastic which found an important use in coating frying pans to make them non-stick. Such arguments were important since there was no economic utility in civil space missions until quite recently. Of course, the civil space programme had other purposes, such as providing entertainment, propaganda and a welcome distraction from more pressing and tedious problems, but these were not aims the promoters would have emphasised. Teflon was hardly enough of a justification for its enormous cost.

Interestingly the origin of Teflon, or PTFE, had nothing to do with the space programme. It had been known and used for decades before

*5. Building the Shippingport nuclear reactor, the first commercial reactor in the United States, on the Ohio River, around twenty-five miles from Pittsburgh, Pennsylvania. Based on a reactor designed for an aircraft carrier, it was classic spin-off technology: a military technology applied to civil uses. A long-lived machine, it was built in 1957 and remained in use until 1982. However, the 'atomic age' never materialised.*

the 1960s, and was even used for coating frying pans. The DuPont company invented it in 1938; it was given its name and first sold in 1945.[41] Its main wartime use had been in the bomb-production programme. The Teflon non-stick frying pan was invented in France in 1954 by Marc Grégoire, and launched by a new French company called Tefal (TEFlon + ALuminium) in 1956; by 1961 Tefal was selling 1 million a month in the USA alone.[42] NASA maintains a website and publishes a magazine called *Spin-off* yet Teflon is nowhere mentioned, though NASA claims parentage of cordless power-tools, ribbed swimsuits, and important improvements in pacemakers, laser angioplasty, digital signal processing, smoke detectors, bicycle helmets, baby formula and much more besides.

Remarkable as it might seem, some spin-offs have themselves had negative effects on the wealth of nations. In 1956 the British started generating electricity using power from a nuclear reactor the main aim of which was producing plutonium for atomic bombs. This was misleadingly hailed as the first commercial nuclear reactor in the world.[43] Britain already had the most ambitious civil nuclear power plans in the world, and would generate more nuclear power than any other country for the next decade. The first British programme was based on the Magnox reactors. Some are still in operation today, with the last due to close in 2010, giving these machines lives of around forty years. As early as 1965 a decision had to be taken on the next generation of reactors, and the advanced gas-cooled reactor was chosen. Construction started in the 1960s; the first was completed in 1976, the last in 1989. They all still operate, and the last will be decommissioned in 2023. The AGR programme was enormously expensive and led to a net loss to Britain, compared with the costs of using other nuclear, and indeed non-nuclear, technologies. Compared to a hypothetical pressurised water reactor (PWR) programme the total loss was predicted to be around £2bn in 1975 prices.[44] When the electricity industry was privatised, the Magnox reactors could not be sold; the AGRs were effectively given away free.

A second great project of the 1960s derived from military precedents, the Anglo-French supersonic airliner Concorde, was also, according to cost-benefit analysis, a dreadful waste of money. The prototype flew in 1969, and commercial, if that is the right term, flights started in 1976. Would there be any returns? The airlines said that they could not fly Concorde profitably even if it was given to them for nothing, as effectively happened in the cases of British Airways and Air France, who operated them for around thirty years. Worthwhile spin-offs from the Concorde project or the civil nuclear programme are hard to find.

It is significant that these are big, controversial technologies, funded, organised and deployed by states. One result is that many associate the state with horrendously bad technological judgement, while civil society, and markets in particular, it is assumed, will make better decisions. In civil society the question of significance is left to anonymous and multiple calculators. Yet large corporations have great powers of decision and it does not follow that lots of competing decision-makers will give better results. For they make their judgements on the basis of givens which they might not themselves control. The outcome of many such small decisions can add up to an overall negative outcome by comparison with the alternatives. The effect is much harder to calculate, and there is less incentive to do so. Yet it is often claimed, for example, that the motorisation of the world through mass car ownership is not the optimal use of resources. Public transport could, it is argued, yield a better outcome.

## Small technologies and big effects

At first blush contraception is associated, at least when we think of technologies of contraception, with the oral contraceptive Pill. The Pill is regarded as important not just because it is a powerful contraceptive, but because it is often held to have initiated a sexual revolution. In the rich countries of the world that sexual revolution was real enough, so the claim that it was brought about by the use of synthetic steroidal hormones is a striking case of how something small and mundane can trigger extraordinary change. What exactly the Pill did is far from clear. When the Pill is linked directly with the sexual revolution, one can easily detect the assumption that either there were no alternatives to the Pill as a contraceptive or that the alternatives were much inferior. The history of these alternatives is, by comparison, hardly known. While the Pill is the subject of a vast literature, the condom and the many other mundane birth-control technologies are rarely made central to the history of contraception.[45] Yet contraception provides a wonderful example of the long existence of many alternative means, the significance of declining and disappearing technologies, and of re-emerging 'old' technologies.

Fertility control, birth control and contraception have all been practised by different means for a long time. In the twentieth century there were several birth-control techniques from abortion to sterilisation, withdrawal, many forms of rubber contraceptives and chemical ones too. Several of them were, for much of the century, illegal in many parts of the world, and nearly everywhere were hidden from public view. Knowing what went on, having any indication of the use of the various methods, is extremely difficult.

One of the most important forms of contraception appears to have been the condom. The condom was associated with the barber shop and the barracks, and the prevention of disease, and was for many decades the product of a semi-underground industry. From the 1930s condoms could be mass produced by dipping glass moulds into latex solution. They could be turned out by the billion, and made cheaply and thinly enough to be disposable. US condom production was 1.4 million daily in 1931 and increased rapidly, so that in post-war America they were widely used. After the Second World War, helped doubtless by the issuing of condoms to troops, contraceptive condom usage went up strongly. For example, annual British sales increased steadily from around 43 million in 1949, to 150 million in the late 1960s.[46] Clearly condoms were not used in the majority of sexual encounters.

Condoms were, however, just one of many contraceptive technologies. Alongside them there were all sorts of feminine contraceptive technologies available from a semi-underground market – products such as abortificients, spermicides, douches and more besides, including sterilisation. In the USA in the 1930s sales of such technologies were about the same as those of condoms. The famous birth-control campaigners operating in interwar Britain and the USA, Marie Stopes and Margaret Sanger, promoted a particular kind of feminine rubber technology, the diaphragm and the cap. They were under the control of women, and were respectable in ways in which condoms were not; they also required medical intervention. The aim of these campaigners was to medicalise and feminise contraception. Margaret

Sanger went on to be a key figure in promoting the research that led to the contraceptive Pill, which would be manufactured by the pharmaceutical industry and prescribed by doctors. It was available in the USA from the late 1950s, and licensed for contraceptive purposes in 1960.

The Pill had enormous success. It did not just add to contraception technology but led to the decline of other barely visible contraceptive technologies. In the USA condom sales were falling rapidly in the early 1960s, and by the late 1960s the Pill was a more common form of contraception than the condom. In Britain condom use fell from the early 1970s. The Pill was more effective than previous contraceptives, did not involve the intercession of vulcanised rubber in the mingling of body fluids, and crucially its use was separated in time from sex, all vital qualities which did not affect its contraceptive power, but had a huge impact on its desirability. Also important was the fact that the Pill was the only contraceptive technology that could be, and was, talked about in public.

The Pill made contraception public and respectable in ways unimaginable before it burst on to the scene, and therein lay at least part of its power to help transform sexual relations. The link between Pill availability and sexual behaviour is the subject of debate: there is no clear-cut conclusion to be drawn about its relationship to the sexual revolution; the main novelty was sex between people who did not intend to marry each other, rather than pre-marital sex per se. Its relationship to the use of other techniques in relation to sexual behaviour is unexplored.[47] It is implausible, however, to suggest that the contraceptive Pill was the only available technical means which could have brought about the sexual revolution.

Suggestive is the fact that in the post-sexual revolution era pre-Pill contraceptives did not disappear. After the Pill, there was more research than ever in contraception, leading to the development of competing technologies, including the IUD.[48] The condom is an example of a growing, disappearing and reappearing technology. Sales increased rapidly from the 1980s in the wake of AIDS, a phenomenon which made the condom, for the first time, as mentionable as the Pill. World condom production capacity increased from 4.9 billion in 1981 to 12 billion per annum in the mid-1990s. There was, as one might expect, technological innovation in condoms, with the first anatomically shaped one produced in 1969, the spermicide-lubricated in 1974, and more since. In 2004 the Durex brand celebrated seventy-five years of history with the slogan '75 years of great sex'.

## Malaria

The control of malaria, like birth control, has been done in many different ways. As in the case of the Pill, the significance of any particular method needs to be looked at in relation to other methods, not a hypothetical world where malaria was uncontrollable. The re-emergence of diseases thought to have been mastered, like malaria, or cholera or TB, has led to renewed use of old techniques of dealing with them, as well as new ways.[49] Malaria was, and is, one of the most serious diseases on a world scale. It was not, as it now is, confined to tropical regions, but endemic in many temperate areas (for example southern Italy) in the first half of the twentieth century. Malaria was treatable, and it could be controlled with prophylactic doses of treatments, or by eliminating the mosquitoes which carried it. The standard treatment used a natural product, quinine, which the Dutch empire came to control through ownership of plantations in their colony of Java. Synthetic alternatives began to be explored, particularly in Germany. In the 1930s Atebrin (mepacrine) was developed, but because it made the skin go yellow was not much used. However, the loss of the Dutch East Indies to the Japanese in the Second World War forced the Allies to use it, as a prophylactic and treatment. There was a large programme of anti-malarial research during the war which led to three drugs which would be widely used post-war in treatment and as prophylactics: chloroquine (already made and dismissed by the Germans in the 1930s), amodiaquine and proguanil (paludrine). In Syria and in former French colonies in Africa, chloroquine was used in mass prophylaxis in the 1970s in an attempt to eradicate the disease, but the result was increased levels of resistance.[50]

But drugs are just part of the story. Insecticides and the elimination of insect-breeding grounds by controlling water flows and ensuring good drainage had proved to be effective too. Indeed just such multiple measures had already succeeded in eliminating malaria from many parts of the world. But malaria control is particularly associated with DDT. DDT was developed by Ciba-Geigy in Switzerland but taken up on a huge scale by the Americans, not just to deal with malaria, but also with the lice that transmit typhus, notably during the Second World War. Its inventor, Dr Paul Müller, was awarded the Nobel prize for medicine and physiology in 1948. The British developed another powerful new insecticide, Gammexane, though this was less used. In 1944 it was announced that in the Pacific General MacArthur had won 'one of the greatest victories ... a victory by Science and discipline over the anopheles mosquito', not surprisingly, since before this malaria had accounted for about ten times as many casualties in soldiers as combat.[51] After the war DDT was widely used to try to eradicate malarial mosquitoes. What DDT offered was not malaria-eradication, but a cheap, quick means of killing mosquitoes, which did not require such detailed and prolonged intervention: it was a low-maintenance option.[52]

But precisely that lack of depth of intervention was probably critical in allowing malaria to survive, and indeed later to expand, as systems of surveillance were weak and further weakened. The late 1950s saw the start of a global programme to eradicate malaria from the areas in which it was still found, excepting sub-Saharan Africa. The programme was based on a 'spraygun war' with DDT, but, though initially successful, it lost momentum in the late 1960s. In India in 1951 there were 75 million cases, and 800,000 people died of the disease. DDT spraying starting in 1953 and the army of spraymen brought malaria cases down to 50,000 in 1961. But new outbreaks were not policed or dealt with, leading to an increase later. By 1965 cases had doubled to 100,000, rising right through the 1960s and early 1970s, to reach perhaps 50 million in the late 1970s. As a result 'WHO began to resurrect older tactics that had been superseded by miracle pesticides … the whole rusty arsenal reappeared.'[53] The production of old drugs had to be stepped up and new variations brought in, with renewed attention given to netting.

In the world as a whole, the motor vehicle is just behind malaria in the list of killers, a sobering measure of the significance of a technology. Three times as many people (nearly 200,000 out of a world total of around 1 million a year) die in Africa from car accidents as in the whole of Europe. In Africa the death rate per car on the road is up to forty times greater than in the rich countries. Even though there are many fewer cars in Africa than Europe, they kill nearly three times as many people, corrected for population, than in the rich countries of Europe. In Kenya, road accidents are the third cause of death after malaria and HIV/AIDS. But this linking of malaria and the motor car tells us that our sense of technological time needs adjusting, and it is to that topic that we now turn. For malaria has been increasing in Africa, not because Africa is reverting in time, but because it has been entering a new future, one not envisaged in the old models.

# 2

# Time

An Imperial Airways aeroplane flies over a camel caravan in the 1920s; a donkey cart carries the remains of a motor car through Bombay. This juxtaposition of what is taken to be old and new has long been a common photographic genre. The first represented technological optimism, the second a much more ambivalent attitude. These seeming clashes of technological time arise from a particular understanding of old and new. We see technologies such as the camel, the donkey cart, the wooden plough or the hand-loom as technologies of previous historical eras. Yet they, just like the aeroplane and the motor car, were made, maintained and used throughout the last century; they existed in the same, interconnected world. What better example of this is there than that shown in some startling photographs which appeared at the end of the twentieth century: poor Indians and Bangladeshis were dismantling giant ocean-going ships, not in some state-of-the-art dry-dock, but with minimal equipment on the beaches of the Bay of Bengal and the Arabian Sea.

While donkey carts and hand-looms belong in folkloric museums, aeroplanes and motor cars belong in science and technology museums. Very occasionally they are combined. The Science Museum in Bangkok, which opened in 2000, brought together the usual displays of science and technology with those more characteristic of a folk museum: it had a section on 'traditional technology', including carving, pottery, metallurgy, wickerwork and textiles. These were not technologies to be left behind, but were displayed to help preserve and *revive* traditional handicraft skills. In the rich world, science museums and folk museums are usually separate, and each has a different sense of time. Science and technology museums want, and do, tell a story of novelties, firsts and of the future.

The London Science Museum has a showcase gallery, grandly entitled 'The Making of the Modern World'. This has a timeline inscribed on its floor, but it is an innovation timeline. Thus steam power appears only in the eighteenth- and nineteenth-century parts of the display. Yet, on entering the main hall of the museum the visitor had, until recently, to pass by a triple-expansion reciprocating marine steam engine. Most adult visitors confidently dated this machine to the mid nineteenth century, for it looked like something from 'the industrial revolution'. Yet the labels told a different story: the engine was built in 1928 for a British fishing boat. Converted to a pleasure yacht the boat and engine were in use for decades, long enough indeed to become of historical interest: a museum piece, as the expression goes. In fact, the museum is full of twentieth-century steam engines; they are just not part of the story it sets out to tell its mostly young visitors. Such machines are more likely to be highlighted in folkloric industrial museums, or in those devoted to old forms of transport or warfare. 'Useful things disappear more completely than meaningful and pleasurable things,' noted a brilliant analyst, who recalled how we keep old paintings, jewels and suchlike, but not tools.[1] They disappear as soon as they no longer have practical use. Yet many things we think of as old remained in practical use for longer than our future-oriented accounts of technological history allow. Our industrial, scientific and technological museums testify to the long life of many machines, and yet, at the same time, many deny the significance of this point for our thinking about technology.

Many of the most important technologies of the twentieth century were invented and innovated long before 1900. Some, but not all, declined during the twentieth century. Their importance should not be underestimated, for even as technologies disappear they remain significant. It is not until they are nearly completely gone that they

*6. A new technology in the early twentieth century. Rickshaws on Benten-Dori Street, Yokohama, Japan, on a feast day in 1906. The rickshaw spread to the rest of South and South East Asia from Japan in the twentieth century. Its use was still increasing in certain places late that century, and it is still in use in the twenty-first.*

become as insignificant as when they first appeared. Indeed the history of twentieth-century technology usefully starts with technology usually seen as old, perhaps even obsolete, merely persisting anachronistically, like camel caravans and donkey carts, or better still horsepower.

## Times are changing

Traditionally technological timelines date technology by invention or innovation. Timelines imply that *time* is a key variable, that it is the march of time which shapes history. That is the assumption behind graphing so much economic data against time. Yet things do not spread like a contagious disease, with a few people getting new technologies early, followed by increasing numbers learning from those who have them, until the rate of adoption falls as most people have them. The international spread of ownership of things shows that the diffusion of things works differently – the rate of take-up has varied enormously between countries, irrespective of how long the technology took to arrive in the first place.

New technologies appeared in every corner of the world very soon after innovation. Cars appeared in Barcelona by 1898. The famous firms of Hispano-Suiza and Elizalde were formed in the city in 1904 and 1911, respectively. By 1912 the Dutch East Indies (now Indonesia) had 1,194 automobiles.[2] The Argentine city of Salta, in the foothills of the Andes, had more than 200 motor cars by 1915. The first aeroplane flight in Barcelona was in 1910, and the first locally produced aircraft to fly was built in 1916. The first plane to fly in Japan did so in 1910 and in 1914 Japanese forces used aircraft against German forces in China. Aeroplanes were used in war in North Africa and the Balkans, before the Great War. Colombia's first airline started operations in 1919.

Television provides another rich example of rapid initial adoption around the world. Before 1939 only Britain and Germany had TV; the rich countries established or re-established broadcasting in the late 1940s and early 1950s, as did Argentina (1952) and Japan (1953).[3] Much of Africa was not far behind. Morocco, Algeria and Nigeria got television in the 1950s; in the early 1960s it arrived in many more African nations, Korea, Singapore, Malaysia, China, India, Pakistan, Indonesia, and most of the Middle East.[4]

The time it took for a new technology to reach a particular part of the world tells us little about the rate at which its use was to be taken up, and thus its impact, in different countries. This was not a matter of

31

time but of money. Crudely speaking the uptake of new technologies was determined by income. In the United States there was a profusion of consumer goods such as cars and washing machines in the 1920s at levels which were some thirty years in advance of even the richest *European* countries. Europeans were poorer than Americans; once they became as rich as the Americans had been they bought them in similar quantities. And that process is repeating itself: as other countries become richer they too see more and more of their people buying these standard goods which have been around for a long time. Many countries have not reached the levels of income per head or motorisation or electrification that the United States achieved in the 1920s. Although much of Africa first got television in the 1950s and 1960s there were only around twenty-five TV sets per 1,000 population in the 1980s, well below the level of countries now richer who first got television at the same time or later.

Yet while technological replication over time, driven by economic development, is a crucially important element in the history of the twentieth century, it can mislead us. The replication over time is far from exact. Thus at the end of the twentieth century places such as Colombia, Morocco, Mexico, Thailand, China and Brazil had roughly the same level of income per head as the richest countries of the world and the great imperial powers had in 1913. Clearly they had different technologies for transportation, communication, health care and so on. Part of the reason was that new technologies became available; technological time is a factor. But, equally, 'old' technologies came into use in ways which were not prefigured in the past. As poor countries became richer they expanded the use of technologies that form no part of the usual schemes of modernisation.

## Horses, mules and oxen

The use of the horse for human purposes was invented thousands of years ago. The breeding, rearing, training and maintaining of horses was expert work that created beasts which did not exist in the wild. If we were to date the age of horsepower by its maximum use, it would be much more recent than one might think. Twentieth-century horse-power was not a left-over from a pre-mechanical era; the gigantic horse-drawn metropolis of 1900 was new. In Britain, the most indus-trialised nation in the world in 1900, the use of horses for transporta-tion peaked not in the early nineteenth century but in the early years of the twentieth. How could it be that horse transport expanded at the same time as trains pulled by 'iron horses'? The answer is that economic development and urbanisation went hand in hand with more horse-buses, horse-trams and horse-carriages. In addition, while train and ship carried goods over long distances, over shorter distances horse-drawn vehicles became ever more necessary. Thus visitors to London's Camden Market, on the site of a huge railway yard and interchange with the canal system, will note that many of the old buildings were stables.[5] These were not there to house animals used for riding in nearby Regent's Park, but for draught animals. In 1924 the largest and most progressive British railway company, the London, Midland and Scottish, had as many horses as it had locomo-tives – 10,000. By contrast it had just over 1,000 motor vehicles. In 1930 the London and North Eastern Railway railway had 7,000 steam locomotives and 5,000 horses, and only about 800 motor vehicles.[6] There is no doubt though, that by 1914 in the great rich cities of the world, horse transport was giving way to the motor-powered buses, lorries and cars, and electric-powered trams.

In agriculture, the horsepower peak was to come later. For example, in Finland the horse population peaked in the 1950s because they were used in logging. The United States provides the most graphic example. Agricultural horsepower peaked in 1915 with more than 21 million on American farms, up from 11 million in 1880, a level to which it had returned by the mid-1930s.[7] The US case is particularly interest-ing because at the beginning of the twentieth century it had highly mechanised agriculture, but this was horse-powered agriculture. We are apt to underestimate the implications of relying on horsepower in the countryside. At the peak of agricultural horse use in Britain and the USA, about one-third of agricultural land was devoted to the

*7. The horse was vital to all belligerents in the Great War. Here horses destined for the war are taken from Paris. In the Second World War they were crucial to the German army, which marched into the Soviet Union with many more horses than Napoleon did in his invasion of the Russian Empire in 1812.*

horses' upkeep: they were large consumers of grass, hay and grain.[8] Mechanised agriculture helped the US to become the richest large nation in the world, and one that by the 1910s was by far and away the largest producer of motor vehicles.

In one area of twentieth-century life, the use of horses for transport was particularly remarkable. The Great War and the Second World War are seen as industrial wars, as feats of engineering and science and organisation. And so they were. Because of this both involved huge numbers of horses, which, like men, were conscripted. Every belligerent depended on them, as well as on mules and other beasts of burden. Before the Great War, the small British army had 25,000 horses but by the middle of 1917 the great new mass British armies had 591,000 horses, 213,000 mules, 47,000 camels and 11,000 oxen. In late 1917 there were 368,000 British horses and 82,000 British mules on the Western

Front alone, hugely outnumbering British motor vehicles. This was not a question of a deluded commitment to cavalry. Only one-third of the British horses on the Western Front were for riding (and only some of these were in cavalry units) – the great majority transported the vast quantities of materiel required in modern war, particularly from the railheads to the front. The use of the animals was not an exceptional emergency measure to make use of Britain's existing horses. Horses were desperately needed, and Britain bought 429,000 of them and 275,000 mules from the US, and imported vast quantities of fodder too. Britain's ability to exploit world horse markets was crucial to its military power.[9] In any case the British were not unique. The vast American armies pouring into Europe in 1918 equipped each of their very large infantry divisions with 2,000 draught horses, another 2,000 riding horses and no fewer than 2,700 mules: one horse or mule for every four men.

An even starker example of the continuing importance of the horse is provided by the Second World War. The German army, so often portrayed as centred on armoured formations, had even more horses in the Second World War than the British army had in the Great War. The horse was the 'basic means of transport in the Germany Army'. German rearmament in the 1930s involved mass purchase of horses such that by 1939 the army had 590,000, leaving 3 million others in the rest of the country. Each infantry division needed around 5,000 horses to move itself. For the invasion of the Soviet Union in 1941, 625,000 horses were assembled. As the war progressed the German horse army got ever larger as the Wehrmacht pillaged the agricultural horses of the nations it conquered. At the beginning of 1945 it had 1.2 million horses; the total loss of horses in the war is estimated at 1.5 million.[10] Could it be that the Great War and the Second World War saw more horses in battle than any previous war? Could it be that the draught-horse-to-soldier ratio also increased, despite the use of other forms of transport?[11] Certainly the Wehrmacht embarked on its march to Moscow with many times more horses than Napoleon's *Grand Armée*. Indeed, it took longer to get there.

There is no doubt that the global horse and mule population dropped from the early decades of the twentieth century. Horses disappeared from rich cities and from the fields of wealthy countries. Yet in some parts of the world not only did animal traction remain important, but it became *more* important as animals replaced human power. In one dramatic case, animal power replaced tractors. Cuban agriculture was transformed from the early 1960s with Soviet and East European agricultural machinery and supplies, resulting in a downgrading of animal traction. But the collapse of the Soviet bloc in 1989 led the Cuban government to develop an animal traction programme. The agricultural horse population recovered, but the main focus was on oxen. They were bred and trained in large numbers, and the technical infrastructure needed to use them was built up. The recovery in the number of oxen was spectacular. They had fallen from 500,000 in 1960 to 163,000 in 1990 but increased to 380,000 in the late 1990s. They replaced 40,000 tractors.[12]

## The decline of the 'mule' spinning machine

The twentieth century has seen the decline in use of many industrial machines. A good example is the cotton-spinning machine that dominated the most important cotton industry existing in 1900 – the 'mule' spinning machine of the British cotton industry. The 'mule', invented in the early nineteenth century, was so-called because it was a hybrid of two different types of spinning machines – it used the stretching motion of the spinning 'jenny' and the roller action of the 'water-frame'. Each twentieth-century mule had around 1,500 spindles, and each pair of mules was operated by the male spinner and his two assistants, called the 'big piecer' and the 'little piecer'.

The spinning mule was at the centre of what was a globalised industry. Cotton was processed thousands of miles from where it was grown and was exported from a few industrial centres to the whole world. The hub of the industry was free-trading Britain, and particularly Cottonopolis itself, the city of Manchester. The peak year of the British cotton industry was 1913 when it was not only the largest, but also the most efficient cotton industry in the world.[13] In the interwar years, as trade de-globalised and Japan emerged as a major competitor, Manchester's exports slumped. In 1931, the worst year of the depression, output was half what it had been in 1913. It was not to recover very much, and from the early 1950s a long steady decline continued, though this declining industry remained important. In the 1930s it had around 30 per cent of world textiles exports, and 15 per cent in the early 1950s. Cotton goods accounted for 25 per cent of all British exports in the 1920s, and still made up 5 per cent in the early 1950s.

The machinery in use in the cotton-spinning industry into the late 1950s was overwhelmingly mule spinning machines, all of which were old. Around 80 per cent of the mules in use in 1930 had been installed before 1910. Hardly any mules were added after 1920, and none after 1930, so that by 1950 a great majority of the mules were well over forty years old, the estimated life of the machines in 1930. In other countries an alternative spinning technology, the ring-spindle spinning machines, had taken over but the peculiarly high proportion of mules in the British industry was not due to resistance to rings. It followed from the fact that after the early 1920s there was little investment in new machines at all. So low was investment that at the rate of re-equipment obtaining in 1948 it would have taken fifty years to replace all the mules with new rings, and another fifty years to replace the old rings.[14] In the mid-1950s too, investment was at a rate at which it would take decades to replace just the existing ring-spindles.[15]

The history of the industry after 1913 was thus one of a shrinking number of increasingly old machines. Many mules were lost simply because they became so old that they were not worth keeping, but many machines were taken out of use when still workable, because there was no market for their product. Some argued that these old machines took work from the new ones which might otherwise be installed. As a result the government went to the lengths of setting up something called the Spindles Board, which bought and scrapped spindles from those firms willing to sell. This is one example of a worldwide phenomenon which shocked progressive opinion in the 1930s – the destruction of machines when people needed work and the world needed clothing. Between 1936 and 1939 the Board scrapped 6.2 million spindles, which compares with 15 million scrapped independently between 1930 and 1939. In the different economic circumstances after the war further scrapping schemes were promoted. The greatest came following the 1959 Cotton Industry Act, which led to the breaking up within a year of nearly 10 million mule spindles, which were by then fifty, sixty and seventy years old. Some lived on and found themselves in folklore museums, or in museums of science and technology.

Our technological museums, with their emphasis on first design, tend to miss out on the extraordinary life stories of the objects they have. But the old stuff still in use now has its own nostalgic journals. There are many specialist publications on old trains, cars and ships still in operation. There are magazines such as *Propliner,* which deals with working old propeller-driven aircraft. That we are nostalgic for twentieth-century technologies, as well as nineteenth-century ones, points to the importance of the disappearance of things which represented the future. The ironer, a machine to iron clothes, diffused to 10 per cent of Canadian households, but rather than being the beginning of a new wave of household automation, promptly disappeared, much as the British tea-making machines would.[16] The airship, a technological wonder of the early decades of the century, went out of use quickly from the 1930s. The miracle insecticide DDT was to disappear faster than the mosquitoes and other insects it was used to kill. Concorde looks like being the first and the last supersonic airliner. Manned hypersonic aeroplanes disappeared in the 1960s. At the end of the twentieth century, nuclear power, once the technology of the future, was set to be phased out in many countries. And in medicine too, many treatments invented in the twentieth century were discontinued, lobotomy and ECT being prominent examples, though the last is still occasionally used.

## Not Alphaville but *bidonville*: technology and the poor megacity

The story of the poor world (a term preferable to the euphemistic 'developing world', and the now irrelevant 'Third World') and technology is usually told as one of transfer, resistance, incompetence, lack of maintenance and enforced dependence on rich-world technology. Imperialism, colonialism and dependence were the key concepts, and the *transfer* of technology from rich to poor, the main process. The crucial measures in play were the stock of rich-world technology in the poor world and its innovative capacity. There is a second line of thought, in which the poor world betrayed its true nature by adopting, even partially, 'western' technology.[17] Dating to at least the interwar years, this view held that modern technology destroyed these local, ancient, alternative and more authentic cultures. More recently 'western' technology has been thought of as spearheading a violent assault on poor societies. Both accounts fail to take into consideration the distinctiveness of the new poor world as it emerged in the twentieth century. In particular, they fail to see the poor world as a distinctive *technological* world, one that was particularly fast-growing, and dependent on local and what are usefully called 'creole' technologies, many of which we think of as 'old'. That distinctive world can be voyeuristically consumed, as in the writings of the architect Rem Koolhaas and his associates, but it also needs to be understood not as the future, but as a distinctive world with its own technology of poverty.[18]

World population trebled in the twentieth century, but Europe's population increased by only about 50 per cent. The significant growth has been in the poor world – Asia, Latin America and Africa. One of the greatest changes was in the *cities* of the poor world, which grew at extraordinary rates. By the end of the century (in stark contrast to the beginning) most of the largest cities of the world were poor places: where once Paris, London and New York led in scale and opulence, the largest cities of 2000 were places few would seek to emulate: São Paolo, Jakarta, Karachi, Mumbai (Bombay), Dhaka, Lagos and Mexico

City. This was a new kind of urbanisation, and a spectacularly fast one, which did not replicate the earlier experience of Berlin or Manchester. These were not cities of horses, or of trains, or spinning mules, or great electrical or chemical industries. Furthermore, large parts of them were built without architects, engineers or building contractors, and without conforming to building regulations. These parts of these cities were not made for cars or trains, let alone the information superhighway.

Central to this new urbanisation was the growth of the slum, or shanty town, though we must be wary of these terms because they describe many different types of housing. For example, the *favelas* of Rio de Janeiro are connected to electricity and water, while the *asentamientos* (settlements) of Guatemala City are dark at night. At first sight, the term slum might refer, as it generally did in the rich world and in many parts of the poor world, to decayed old parts of cities where the poorest lived. But in the later twentieth century in particular a new kind of slum, a newly built – one might say purpose-built – one, arose. The optimistic term *pueblos jóvenes*, or young towns, used to describe the slums of Lima says something important about them even though many are decades old.

We need to be particularly wary of definitions of slums in terms of the *lack* of facilities characteristic of rich cities, such as permanent structures, particular forms of sanitation or electricity. We need to ask not what technology the shanty town lacks, but what it has. For poor cities had particular and often novel systems of building, of sanitation, or supply of water, of food and all the other necessities of life, which were not traditional but new. They proved capable of sustaining a new kind of rapidly expanding urban existence on an enormous scale, even if usually a miserable one. One modern technology of the slum was the Kenyan 'flying toilet'. A plastic bag, that ubiquitous product of the post-Second World War chemical industry, was used not only to defecate into, but to dispose of what was once quaintly called 'night soil': the bag was tied, taken outside, swung around, and hurled away as far as possible from one's patch.[19]

The modern materials from which many slums are built are sometimes inscribed in their very names. The early temporary slums of North Africa were known as *bidonvilles*, for the buildings were made from opened-up and flattened-out oil drums (*bidons*). The term is now generic in French. The Arabic term for *bidonville* in Morocco is *mudun safi*, 'metal towns'. The Durban slum dwellings are called *imijondolos* in Zulu, possibly derived from the use of wood from crates that had carried John Deere tractors in through the port in the 1970s.[20]

One material stands out in the development of the poor world, rural and urban, and that is corrugated iron or galvanised iron used for making 'tin roofs'. In the nineteenth century, it spread around the world to areas of British army operation as transportable housing. It also became a key material for building roofs and walls of white settler communities in Australia, New Zealand and the Americas, where it is now of interest as a vernacular architecture. It was hugely important in the twentieth century as a truly global technology. Its cheapness, lightness, ease of use and long life made it a ubiquitous material in the poor world in a way it never had been in the rich world. A visitor to West Africa in the Second World War noted of 'Ibadan, then the largest town in black Africa ... [it] had grown in less than a century from a local market into a city with nearly 100,000 inhabitants – though alas, as so often in Africa, the houses were mostly roofed with galvanized iron.'[21] Today Ibadan is at one end of a shanty-town corridor of 70 million people.[22] Its roofs, to judge from aerial photographs, are still of rusted corrugated iron.

Corrugated iron was not just an urban technology; it was used to replace thatch roofs on traditional rural buildings as well. In Rwanda corrugated iron was first used by the Belgian colonisers for their public buildings. By the end of the twentieth century a lighter type was the standard roofing material of even the poorest homes. Farmers' houses built of adobe had corrugated iron roofs, and were called *terres-tôles* (earth-sheets). As the only part of the house villagers cannot make, the iron roof became a prized possession; it was looted from Tutsis' homes in the genocide of 1994. As the tables turned, Hutu refugees trudged to the Congo bearing sheets on their backs, others buried them in their fields.[23]

As in other technologies, there has been innovation in corrugated iron, in both shapes and materials. It has become lighter and stronger, available in many more grades and types. New shapes of corrugations have been used, and new coating introduced. Yet the long-established sinusoidal corrugations still dominate the cheapest grades.

A second crucial cheap material was asbestos-cement, especially corrugated asbestos-cement. Asbestos-cement was patented in 1901 by an Austro-Hungarian, Ludwig Hatschek, an asbestos producer. He called his invention 'Eternit', and the material and the name have both been long lasting. Production started by a Swiss company of the same name in 1903, which became a major multinational with branches all over the world. Eternit still means asbestos-cement in many places; in others it was called 'Uralite' or 'Uralita'. Although this is not always clear, by far the main use of asbestos – a fibrous mineral – has been for the manufacture of asbestos-cement (also known as fibro-cement), mainly used to produce corrugated roofing, sheets for building work, and water and sewage pipes. It has been a key material in modern urbanisation. At the beginning of the century it was primarily utilised in North America; after the Second World War its use boomed there, and particularly in Europe, but growth took off in Asia, South America and Africa in the 1960s and 1970s.[24] Unfortunately asbestos was found to be a serious carcinogen, and its use was progressively banned in the US, Europe and elsewhere. As a result, world production fell from the mid-1970s. But at the end of the century production was still at the levels of the 1950s. Even in the 1990s in South Africa, 24 per cent of new subsidised housing had asbestos-cement roofing.[25]

The Martinican/French writer Patrick Chamoiseau, in his book *Texaco*, the great novel of the shanty town, reflected a new understanding of the poor city that was emerging in the 1960s and 1970s. In *Texaco* the history of Martinique is divided into the age of the *ajoupas* (shelters) and longhouses, the age of straw, the age of crate wood, the age of asbestos (fibro-cement) and the age of concrete, reflecting the key materials of the shanty towns.[26] In the age of asbestos, asbestos-cement sheet was used for walls; the roofs were of corrugated iron. Thereafter the people bought the occasional bag of cement to make their world more stable and secure. One of the characters in the book is a new model urbanist who began to understand this new kind of city. Indeed, 'self-help housing' and '*auto construcción*' became terms of art in urban planning, recognising that houses were being built in vast numbers, well outside the standard networks of modernity.

Corrugated iron, asbestos-cement and cement were not invented in the poor world, they were first exported to it, and then locally produced. The growth of the poor world went along with a massive increase in use of these 'old' technologies from the rich world, and yet also, importantly, it was a story of the spread of distinctive technologies often adapted from 'old' technologies. One can usefully describe them as 'creole' technologies. 'Creole' is a complex term with a long history and many variant meanings. It most commonly means local derivatives of something originally from elsewhere (typically the white and black populations of the Americas). The term also carries the sense of earthy, local, genuine, vulgar, popular, in contrast to the sophistication of the metropolitan. Creole means derived, but different from, the originating case. It sometimes carries the sense of hybrid between the incomer and the existing, though this is not the common form.[27]

## Creole technology

One important aspect of creole technology is that the basic imported technology acquired a new lease of life in the poor world. There were many cases of late adoption and long use in the poor world of rich-country technologies. A small example would be that carrier pigeons were introduced to the police services in Orissa (India) in 1946 and were phased out only in the 1990s. The Indian motor-vehicle industry provides some better-known examples. From the mid-1950s the 1955-

model Royal Enfield Bullet motorcycle was manufactured in India. Production of the same model continues to this day at the rate of 10,000 a year in the original Madras factory, and with methods which still involve little assembly-line work. Hindustan Motors in Uttarpara, West Bengal, still make the Ambassador, based on a mid-1950s Morris Oxford Series II motor car. Production started in 1957 and to date 800,000 have been produced. The history of the Volkswagen Beetle is a particularly notable case given the scale of its production. By the early 1970s it had overtaken the Model T Ford as the car most widely produced in the world (15 million), and it would continue to be manufactured, reaching a total of 21 million. The end of production came in Mexico in 2003, where it had been made since 1954. Brazilian production stopped in 1986, restarted in 1993 and finally came to an end in 1996, long after production finished in Germany.

Communist China had its own distinctive attitude to old technologies of production. It pursued a 'walking on two legs' policy of industrialisation that has been called 'technological dualism'. The first leg was large-scale, urban, factory production, using models brought from the Soviet Union. This was a huge effort of transfer of technical skills, models, designs and factories. China long remained a producer of Soviet technology: till the end of the 1980s it was making Soviet trucks and steam locomotives from the 1950s. Steam-train buffs flocked to the sidings and marshalling yards of China, for only in the mid-1980s did diesel and electric locomotive production overtake that of steam locomotives.

The second leg was locally run, small-scale industry, reliant on local raw materials and supplying local needs, usually in the agricultural sector. These industries were based on centrally-supplied designs of technologies, usually themselves based on 'old' technologies that had gone out of use elsewhere in the world. From the late 1950s 'backyard iron and steel' production, together with small-scale cement kilns, fertiliser plants, agricultural machinery workshops, food-processing works, power generation and mining boomed under the Great Leap Forward. Fertiliser production was a rare example of a novel technology, for local plants made a fertiliser used nowhere else in the world – ammonium bicarbonate.

The Chinese people paid an enormous price for what was by any measure the profoundly unsuccessful Great Leap Forward. Millions of lives were lost to famine, and there was also a cruel waste of technological and natural resources in a desperately poor country. With the collapse of the Great Leap many local enterprises closed. But many did not, and survived till the next great expansion phase for these industries, the Cultural Revolution. By 1971 60 per cent of fertiliser production came from small plants; 50 per cent of cement; 16 per cent of hydro-generating capacity; overall around 10 per cent of Chinese factory output.[28]

## Transport

The idea that the technologies of the poor world simply lag behind those of the rich world in time is not generally applicable, as the case of the fabric of the poor megacity illustrates. Transport provides a second example, since the poor megacities had different transport patterns from those of the great rich cities of 1900, or even of 1930. These rich cities did not have the bicycle or motorcycle densities of the megacities of late twentieth-century Asia. Indeed bicycle and motor-bicycle production boomed in the world, particularly in the poor world, from the 1970s. For the first time in many decades bicycle production surged ahead of motor-car production. In recent years around 100 million bicycles were produced every year and only about 40 million cars. In 1950 there were around 10 million of each, and they remained about equal to 1970. The great change was the expansion in Chinese production to 40–50 million bicycles from a few million in the early 1970s.[29] In addition Taiwan and India between them were, at the end of the century, making more bicycles than were produced in the world in 1950. Bicycle-derived technologies of the poor megacity provide an instance of a creole technology.

In 2003 it was reported that the city of Calcutta was still trying to get rid of the hand-pulled rickshaw, long gone from most of the rest of Asia. These rickshaws were deemed old-fashioned even by the standards of hand-rickshaws: Calcutta's had spoked wheels, but not ones derived from bicycle technology; they were made of wood and were rimmed with solid rubber rather than pneumatic tyres. Surely these were survivals from the distant past?

In fact the hand-pulled rickshaw, far from being an ancient invention, was apparently devised in Japan in the 1870s, though similar things had been in use in Europe on a small scale. The rickshaw replaced the palanquin/sedan chair. Use boomed from the very late nineteenth century, first in Japan, where numbers peaked around 1900 and quickly spread in Asia. In Singapore the total was highest in the early 1920s, while Calcutta saw hand-rickshaw growth in the 1920s and 1930s. In most places the hand-rickshaw went out of use after the Second World War, condemned as a barbarous machine humiliating the poor pullers.

The cycle-rickshaw (sometime called a trishaw) was, as an invention, almost as old as the rickshaw; yet as a thing-in-use it peaked even more recently.[30] Developed in the 1880s, it found hardly any use until around 1929 in Singapore, where by 1935 cycle-rickshaws outnumbered hand-pulled rickshaws. They appeared in Calcutta around 1930, Dhaka about 1938, and Jakarta around 1936. By 1950 they were present in every country in south and east Asia. Japan had never had many. There were variations in design across countries but relatively little within countries. The most common was that with the passenger sitting behind the driver (India, Bangladesh, China, the Macao 'triciclo'). But the version with the passengers forward of the driver was also common, for example the Indonesian 'becak', the Vietnamese 'cyclo' and the Malaysian 'trishaw'. Others had the passenger to the side, as in the Philippines 'sidecar', the Burmese 'sai kaa' and the Singapore 'trishaw'.[31]

Far from disappearing after the Second World War, the cycle rickshaw continued to expand rapidly in the 1960s and 1970s. It was estimated in the late 1980s that there were 4 million in the world, and that the number was still increasing overall though in some countries there were decreases. Dhaka was the capital of the cycle-rickshaw with some 300,000 at the end of the twentieth century. A subsequent creole technology, unknown in the rich cities of the world, is the scooter-based taxi. From the 1950s these 'auto-rickshaws' appeared in India, and similar designs have spread all over Asia (for example, the Thai 'tuk-tuk' and the Bangladeshi 'baby-taxi').

The cycle-rickshaw was an urban, not a rural, machine. It followed, rather than preceded, seemingly newer transport techniques. Rickshaws needed the metalled roads which were built for cars and buses and lorries. Yet in the great expanding cities of Asia they were seen as demeaning technologies of poverty and as technologies of the past that needed to be got rid of. The city governments of Asia, whether colonial or post-colonial, wanted to control them, restricting licences, and indeed in places banning them outright. Yet if governments had success in getting rid of machines such as the spinning mule in the middle of the century, they failed miserably in the case of the rickshaw, for numbers, as we have seen, continued to rise. They have now appeared in places they had never been before, including central London, where they operate regularly from the Soho entertainment district.

## Remodelling the boat

Water transport provides some good examples of creole technologies, particularly in the sense of hybrids. In Bangkok the great river which runs through that megacity is home to a remarkable breed of craft. Long, thin, wooden boats have been converted to a species of powerboat by the addition of a large car engine mounted on gimbals which powers a propeller on the end of a long shaft. The operator controls the boat by moving the whole engine and associated propeller. A brilliant invention, these 'long-tailed boats' first appeared in Bangkok, but have since spread through Thailand, not just for the tourist trade, but as a standard means of powering a boat. The tails are made in Bangkok and cost $100; engines can be bought for around $600, compared with a motorbike at $500. They are also present on the Mekong, in Cambodia and Vietnam, and some say on the Amazon in Peru.

*8. Collecting hay in the Carpathian foothills in the Ukraine on the eve of the twenty-first century. Although it might seem to be a relic from the past, the wheels of the cart seem to be from a car, and there is an electricity or telephone connection. Furthermore, Ukrainian agriculture was forcibly modernised decades ago.*

Another case of a creole technology is the rejuvenated 'country-boat' of Bangladesh, a country where millions depended on water transport. These boats, hand built by itinerant and miserably poor boat carpenters (*mistri*), increasingly lost out to land transport. It was in the north-west of Bangladesh that they were transformed in the early 1980s. New wells, powered by petrol pumps, were installed there, but these were idle most of the year. An anonymous engineer used one of these engines to drive a boat; by the late 1980s many were used in the wet season and on market days in the dry season. Increasingly engines were permanently fitted, but irrigation-pump engines remained the most popular since they were subsidised. In the 1980s iron sheet started to be used to make boats, and for bigger boats, recycled steel plates from the shipbreakers on the coast.[32]

The cycle-rickshaws, the motorised country-boats, the long-tailed boats, as well as the buildings of the shanty towns, combine the products of large-scale industry – the car engine, the bicycle, cement, asbestos-cement – and the local and small scale. These were derivative, adapted technologies. But they were more than that – for they were local adaptations that gave new life to older, more traditional forms. This hybridity was common. In many parts of the world donkey carts were made using motor-car axles and especially wheels. Wooden fishing boats of the most primitive sort were made much more efficient by synthetic fishing nets; larger wooden boats of craft construction were fitted with engines, with radar and with sonar, as a visit to any number of the world's small fishing ports will confirm.

## Retro and reappearance

In the rich world there have also been many reintroductions of 'old' technology. Cable TV was a disappearing technology in the 1950s and 1960s, yet returned with a vengeance in the 1980s, as a seemingly new form promising ever more TV channels. Indeed cables in general returned, though often in the form of fibre-optic cables which carried many times more traffic than copper ones. The use of condoms expanded massively through the twentieth-century, then declined with the introduction of the Pill and other new contraceptives, but growth resumed following the appearance of AIDS. Acupuncture, known in Europe from the seventeenth century, had a boom in the early nineteenth, from which it slowly declined in Europe till it re-emerged in the 1970s. The passenger liner gave way to the airliner in the late 1950s and early 1960s, yet many were converted to cruise ships in the 1960s and 1970s, developing an industry which at the end of the twentieth century carried more passengers than ever before. Cruise ships take over 8 million passengers on holiday; the greatest passenger port in the world is now Miami. The biggest liners ever built were no longer the interwar behemoths such as the *Normandie* or the *Queen Elizabeth*, but a new generation dating from the last years of the twentieth century. One company has built the largest sailing ship ever made, based on the *Preussen* of 1902, for the luxury cruise market.

The *Royal Clipper*, delivered in 2000, was built at the former Lenin Shipyard in Gdansk and the Dutch Merwede yard. The Harland and Wolff shipyard in Belfast gets regular enquiries about rebuilding the ill-fated *Titanic* as a cruise liner. Airships are used for televising major events, and for taking tourists over great cities.

The Ambassador and the Bullet were sold back into the rich world from whence they came decades earlier. Old treadle sewing machines made for the poorest markets are also sold as replicas in the rich world.[33] Luxury mechanical watches, such as those of Patek Philippe, are still made. Before 1988, when it converted to making diesel locomotives, the Datong Locomotive Works in China, exported steam locomotives to the USA for use on tourist lines.[34] Among gun aficionados in the USA an industry grew up making working replicas of nineteenth-century rifles. Antique cameras and replicas of classics, notably Leicas, sell to a discerning clientele, and vinyl records have a distinct niche market.

One of the most important novelties in food production and consumption has involved, according to Tim Mondavi of the California wine-maker Mondavi, 'moving forward to the past'. Mondavi introduced oak fermentation barrels and other 'old' technology to their high-tech winery and vineyards.[35] The production of 'organic' foods has a special relationship with the past. Part of the claim of the organic movement is that organic production is less damaging to the environment and more conducive to animal and human health. Central to the practice is the abandonment of the use of synthetic fertilisers, pesticides and fungicides. Yet organic certification rules allow for the use of many of the materials which were standard in late nineteenth-century agriculture, such as mined and crushed phosphate rock as fertiliser. Guano use is permitted under certain circumstances, as are nineteenth-century copper-based fungicides such as Bordeaux and Burgundy mixtures, though allowed quantities are being restricted.

Sailing cruise ships and other manifestations of retro take place in a world which is radically different from the one in which sailing ships dominated sea transport and where synthetic fertilisers were not available. Corrugated iron roofs and the bicycle were the products of modern industries, of a world whose productive capacity was transformed in the twentieth century. Yet in that remarkable story too, the seemingly old was much more important than we sometimes care to recognise.

# 3

# Production

The output of the world economy has increased much faster than a rapidly growing population through most of the twentieth century. One period stands out for particularly rapid growth and change: the three decades after the Second World War. These years saw output increases which were unprecedented in world history and have not been seen since then in the rich countries. As important historical transition periods go, it is rather modestly named. It is called the 'long boom', or the 'golden age', terms which do not conjure up revolutionary change. In technological history – if considered at all – it tends to be relegated to a third or fourth industrial revolution. But in many parts of the world, including much of Europe, this was the period of the first industrial revolution, as employment shifted decisively from agriculture into industry and services. It was an era when productive processes increased very rapidly in efficiency, turning out long-known products at ever lower prices. That process has continued since, with unprecedented rates of growth, in the poor world.

The usual story of production goes like this: there has been a shift in employment and output from agriculture to industry and then to services. The first is labelled the industrial revolution. The second is called a transition to post-industrial, knowledge or information societies, linked to what many called post-modernism, what some Marxists called 'new times', and, what capitalist Wall Street gurus called the 'new economy'.[1] In one version peddled in the 1990s, modern economies are becoming 'weightless' and 'dematerialised'. Such accounts resurrect an old argument, as if it had never been made before, that in future it will not be land or capital which will have power, but knowledge. They promise, again, a world where 'intellectual property' and 'human capital' rule.

Yet this stage theory of history, focusing on *shares* of employment, easily misrepresents the whole. In the twentieth century the output of agriculture expanded enormously and it continues to do so. The long boom saw the most radical revolution in the history of rich-country agriculture: productivity increase was so rapid that employment decreased even as output increased. Industrial output expanded enormously and continues to do so, even as employment in industry started to fall in the rich countries in the 1970s. Services too have long been growing. The expansion of employment in services is in part the extension of services that can be provided only by employing more people. To a very crude and counter–intuitive first approximation, falling employment is not necessarily a measure of failure or backwardness, but of rapid technical change. We should recognise too that the boundaries between these artificial categories are not as clear cut or revealing of underlying trends as they are made to seem. The killing of animals is usually classified under manufacturing industry, not agriculture; publishing as well as printing are manufacturing industries; some maintenance activities come under services, together with transport.

The tripartite division into agriculture, industry and services also misses a vitally important dimension – the non-market productive activities of households, a fundamental part of total production, whether in agriculture, industry or services. It has long been recognised that the standard national income (GDP) data in use since the 1950s has not included non-traded goods and services.[2] Because there are no wages for most housework, it does not figure in most national accounts. Most unpaid work in the rich world is done by women, though by no means all. The one area where men do more than women is maintenance and repair.[3] We know this from use-of-time

*9. Mrs Mary Faust of Anderson County, East Tennessee, with a spinning wheel, around 1910. Even in the United States, where the Model T Ford was already being mass produced and which had the most efficient industry in the world at that time, was the spinning wheel in use.*

studies and the 'satellite' national accounts including household work created in recent years. For the rich countries the figures vary between 30 and more than 100 per cent of the conventionally measured GDP. In many parts of the world the household remains a key economic unit, both for subsistence and for production for the market, particularly in agriculture, as in the 'peasant' household, that great neglected economic and cultural unit of the twentieth century. The household is a good place to start.

## Household production

The 1922 *Encyclopaedia Britannica* entry on 'mass production' noted of the 'factory system' that its first effect was 'to emancipate the home from being a mere adjunct to the loom or bench, and its later effect was to provide the home with means to develop the dignified status which it has now attained'. Siegfried Giedion, a pioneer of the study of the mechanisation of the rich household wrote in 1948, that 'One can hardly speak of household "production".[4] There is much to be said for the rich household as a place where machines are used for consumption rather than production.

Indeed domestic technologies of leisure deserve more serious consideration than they usually get in the history of technology. In the rich world the household was to take up technologies of leisure such as the radio, TV and video recorders much faster than washing machines or vacuum cleaners. The car and the telephone have behaved more like radio and television than washing machines and both were, at least at first, primarily leisure technologies.[5] Cars were for visiting and going on trips rather than travelling to work. The telephone, though first sold as a business tool, was very quickly taken up by women, for what telephone engineers saw as frivolous use – socialising and gossiping.[6] In largely family-run US farms in the 1920s the motor car diffused much faster than the truck or tractor.[7] By 1920 there was the extraordinary total of 2 million cars on US farms, compared with 250,000 tractors and 150,000 trucks; by 1930 the number of cars reached about 4 million, where it stayed into the late 1950s.[8] In 1920 roughly half of all mid-western farms had cars, well over that had telephones, while less than 10 per cent had tractors, running water or electric lights; for 1930 80 per cent had cars, 60 per cent had telephones, 30 per cent had tractors, and 15–20 per cent had electric lights and running water.[9] Around 40 per cent had radios in 1930.[10] This pattern of acquisition by households would endure, however much some complained that slum dwellers bought televisions before sewing machines, or Japanese farmers of the 1950s bought gaudy tiles and kimonos rather than washing machines.

Yet production remained a key role of the household. From at least the interwar years the wealthier households of rich countries were seen as places requiring new domestic technologies and a new scientific organisation of domestic work, devoted to the production of food, cleanliness, order. The seemingly private world of the domestic kitchen now had its own experts, pioneer social researchers interested in the impact of modernity, students of budgets and of time use, activist promoters of new kinds of hygienic living, and proponents of 'home economics', 'domestic science' and 'household engineering'.[11] Many of these studies were promoted by interested parties, for example the Rural Electrification Agency in the USA, the electric appliance manufacturers and industry-funded bodies such as the British Electrical Development Association. They would not have recommended one-woman domestic production for the manufacture of domestic appliances.

One of the hoariest old clichés of the advertisers and the sponsored researchers was that new technologies in the home had relieved rich-world housewives of drudgery and given them leisure. Yet in the United States middle-class women had seen an increase in domestic work earlier in the century, with a decline only in the 1960s, long after the widespread use of new domestic technologies. Machines replaced domestic servants, changing the role of the middle-class housewife from supervisor of workers to machine-operator. The labour productivity of domestic work increased, but this led not to a decrease in work, but rather to increased domestic production. By how much domestic productivity and production have increased, and how this compares with large-scale industry or with agriculture is unclear, for the outputs of this sort of domestic production are not measured. Despite its importance in the provision of so many quickly changing outputs from increasingly clean clothes to many new types of domestically prepared food, this vast world of production is hardly charted.

But we can say something about the tools of household production. The machine tools of the rich home were very different, generally, from those of industry, as were the non-machine tools. These tools were called 'consumer durables' and not 'producer durables'; they were not an 'investment' but 'consumption'. The tools of the household were the product of large-scale industry and scientific investigation, and many were cheapened very considerably by mass production.[12] So dominant did some firms become that trade names were not just familiar, but sometimes became the generic name: we have only to think of Singer or Hoover to make the point.

Even seemingly old-fashioned tools were remade by large corporations. One particularly long-lived, though not widely diffused, type of cooking range which is now associated with nineteenth-century domesticity, provides an interesting case. The AGA range was launched in 1929, the product of a very large and inventive Swedish firm (AGA – or, in English, 'gas accumulator company') that in the interwar years made, among other things, cars, radios and film equipment. The president of the company, who oversaw its growth between 1909 and 1937, was Nils Gustav Dalén, winner of the 1912 Nobel prize in physics,[13] for his work on inventions concerning the storage and use of acetylene, and the related automatic lighthouse, which launched the company on its path to success. Dalén personally developed the AGA range, making it the most fuel efficient ever made, in the sense that it converted a high proportion of fuel into usable heat. By 1934 it was being sold worldwide and was later manufactured in some ten countries. AGA stopped making them in 1957, but production continued in Britain; indeed still does.[14] Another long-lived technology, it acquired the patina of retro-chic in an era when the major expansion was in gas and electric ranges.

Gas and electric ranges, like the AGA, did not change radically from their introduction in the late nineteenth century to the present. The novelties in domestic production technology have been few. Baths, showers, sewing machines, cooking ranges, vacuum cleaners, washing machines, electric irons, refrigerators, freezers and dishwashers were all available in the interwar years, and most long before that. Most have remained much the same for many decades. The extent of use has been a story not of time and innovation, but economics, and the availability of inputs, such as electricity, gas and piped water. As countries became richer they acquired more of them. And they became richer by producing more and more of them. The levels of consumption of motor cars, washing machines, telephones and the like which were seen in the United States in the 1920s were not to be found in the rich parts of Europe until the 1950s and 1960s. They would spread to the rest of the world later still.

## The sewing machine and the spinning wheel

A particularly good example of the complex history of household technology, not least because of its global diffusion, is provided by the sewing machine. In the rich countries the watch, bicycle, piano and sewing-machine industries were very much in the vanguard of the new consumer-durable industry in the years before the Great War.[15] The sewing machine was produced on a huge scale by essentially one global enterprise, the Singer Sewing Machine Company, a pioneer not only in mass production but in mass selling through credit. In 1905 Singer had the then very large number of 30,000 workers making sewing machines in eight factories round the world, but they were dwarfed by the global sales force of 61,444 in more than 4,000 branch offices.[16] Singer, with perhaps 90 per cent of world market (outside the USA) was selling around 2.5 million machines before the Great War, with around 1.3 million coming from the Clydebank plant in Scotland.[17]

Through the twentieth century sewing-machine production would increase. In the late 1960s Japan, by then a leading producer, made 4.3 million, mostly for export.[18] Thereafter production was to fall: by the mid-1990s it was down to 4 million worldwide: 2.3 million came from China, followed in order by Taiwan, then Japan, USA and Germany.[19] In China in the 1960s, 1970s and 1980s the sewing machine was one of 'four big belongings'; the others were the wristwatch, the radio and the bicycle.[20] In the Chinese countryside in the mid-1980s, each farm family had '1 bicycle, about half had a radio, 43 per cent owned a sewing machine, 12 per cent had a television set, and about half the rural adults owned wristwatches.'[21]

Essentially the same sewing machine was employed in various different contexts. Most went to homes, where they were used to make and mend family clothes, and to produce for the market, in vast putting-out systems. They were also installed in small sweatshops and packed into gigantic clothing factories as they developed from the 1930s.[22]

The sewing machine also provides a wonderful example of very long-lived models not only being kept in use, but continuing in production for a long time. Treadle-powered machines, not so different from those made before 1914, were, in the 1960s, 'by far the most important modern appliance' in a small town of the district of Huaylas in Andean Peru.[23] In Mae Hong Son, northern Thailand, in April 2002, treadle-operated Singers decorated with a sticker celebrating 150 years of Singer machines were on sale alongside white goods, next to an internet café. At the other end of the world, an expensive (male) tailor working alone making men's suits in Lecce, Italy, also used a treadle-operated Singer.[24] Treadle-powered sewing machines feature regularly in discussions of micro-credit initiatives supported by international development agencies.

The sewing machine had a very particular place in the thinking of Mahatma Gandhi, as exemplary of an alternative approach to production. Gandhi was a strong opponent of the machine-based industries and famously argued not for mass production, but for production by the masses. Yet, he made what he called 'intelligent exceptions' to this hostility to industrially-made machines. 'Take the case of the Singer Sewing Machine,' he said. 'It is one of the few useful things ever invented ...' His interviewer responded that he could not object to the factories that made them, to which Gandhi replied that he was 'Socialist enough to say that such factories should be nationalized, or State-controlled'. He claimed that the sewing machine was 'but one of the exceptions I have in mind … I would welcome any day a machine to straighten crooked spindles' so that 'when the spindle gets wrong every spinner will have a machine of his own to get it straight.'[25] The key machine in Gandhi's ideal world was not the sewing machine, but the spinning wheel, already a defunct technology in India. 'The spinning wheel represents to me the hope of the masses,' claimed Gandhi. 'The masses lost their freedom, such as it was, with the loss of the *charkha* [spinning wheel]. The *charkha* supplemented the agriculture of the villagers and gave it dignity. It was the friend and the solace of the widow. It kept the villagers from idleness. For the *charkha* included all the anterior and posterior industries – ginning, carding, warping, sizing, dyeing and weaving. These in their turn kept the village carpenter and the blacksmith busy.'[26] He *reintroduced* the hand spinning wheel or *charkha* to India; and it became part of the Indian National Congress flag.

## Tools and small trades

Production by the masses characterised a great deal of productive activity by the poor in the twentieth century. It is perhaps not surprising that the symbol of the world Communist movement was not Henry Maudslay's lathe, so celebrated by Marx, nor the spinning mules or the looms of the textile industry, also familiar from Marx, or the Model T. It was instead the hammer and the sickle, the first the key tool of the forge one might find in the countryside, and the second, a key instrument of unmechanised agriculture.

All through the twentieth century small enterprises operated with the simplest of tools. Even in manufacturing trades, between one quarter and a third of workers in Germany and France around 1900 worked alone.[27] Family-owned and run restaurants were serving 1 million meals a day in Paris in 1939, a figure which fell to 250,000 in 1950, due to the rise of factory and office canteens, though growth then resumed.[28] A Sicilian farming family in 1931 lived in two rooms and a stable – they owned a mule and chickens and few possessions apart from some 'rudimentary' agricultural implements.[29] In a proclamation issued in June

10. *Wilbur Wright working in his bicycle shop in Dayton, Ohio, around 1900. It was representative of millions of small engineering enterprises the world over. With his brother, Orville, he was later famous for pioneering controllable and powered heavier-than-air flight.*

1944 a commander of the Greek resistance movement ELAS described the means of production of his community. He spoke of 'The butcher with his knife, the grocer with his weights, the café owner with his chairs, the greengrocer with his scales'.[30] In the 1980s the country-boats of Bangladesh were made by itinerant boat carpenters, traditionally Hindus (in a Muslim nation), so poor they could not buy the materials to make the boats, or sometimes even their own simple tools.[31]

Travelling through the poor world it is hard to miss, today, a tiny metal-working shop, in both country and city districts, where the most complex bit of machinery may well be an oxyacetylene, or electric, torch for welding. At dusk bright intermittent light from welding illuminates streets all over the world, issuing from maintenance workshops which might also make simple equipment. Or think of the tiny businesses repairing electronic equipment based on the pavements of Bangkok, or the recyclers of tyres into shoes and many other goods, to be found in many poor cities.

## Family farms in the USA and the USSR

The family farms of the North American Midwest were among the richest in the world at the beginning of the twentieth century. These farms were immensely productive, not in terms of land (for here European farmers were well ahead), but in terms of labour. From the 1920s enormous numbers of Fordson tractors appeared: they could replace five horses, and plough three times as fast. A recent large tractor can plough thirty times faster than the horse team.[32] A key effect of the tractor was to reduce the amount of hired help on the Midwestern family-owned farm; this had the consequence too that the farmer's wife was saved the work of feeding large numbers of hired workers, a standard practice, illustrating the blurred line between the home and the farm.[33] Interwar Midwest farm women were very heavily engaged in other non-domestic activities, tending gardens and raising poultry, and smaller but still significant proportions milked cows, did the bookkeeping and worked for a small part of the year in the fields.[34] Even after the Second World War well over 60 per cent of Midwest farms engaged in gardening, dairying and butchering; egg production was also still high. Farm women increasingly had off-farm employment, and work in the fields, rather in these small-scale enterprises.[35]

How different the conditions in the Soviet Union! Consider the Volga German agricultural settlement of Brunnental in the mid-1920s. The farmers here were much poorer, and lived extraordinarily self-sufficient lives. Harvesting was done with the scythe, and for some farmers with reapers and binders; threshing was carried out with horse-powered machines, rarely with a motor-powered one. There was at least one Fordson tractor, but the settlement had to supply much of its own agricultural equipment. Horse-drawn wagons were built by hand, with the help of a lathe, by a cartwright and his two teenage sons. It took four weeks of heavy labour to make; the same process with modern power tools might take twenty hours. Significantly the chronicler who told the above story listed the occupations in the settlement by families not individuals: there were families of cabinet makers, shoemakers, tailors, plumbers, felt-makers, tanners, blacksmiths and millers.[36] There being no ready-made clothes, farmers' wives and daughters made them at home, often sewed entirely by hand, though the richer farmers' wives had sewing machines. Clothes were made from raw wool; most houses had spinning wheels. Tailors were used only for heavy clothes.

This world was brutally torn apart by collectivisation in 1929. The richer farmers were dispossessed of all their property and sent into internal exile and often death. The rest became semi-employed; some worked for the new central Machine Tractor Stations owned by the state which served three collective farms. Years of famine followed, until recovery came in the late 1930s. In 1941 all these Volga Germans were sent into internal exile in Siberia.

By 1930 the very poor USSR had about a quarter of all Europe's tractors, and two-thirds by 1939. There were many more tractors than cars in the countryside, where there was no electricity and no consumer goods of note. Collectivisation was not, however, driven by tractorisation, but by a political imperative to change the class structure in the countryside, and to extract grain from farms to feed the cities (and its new factories) and for exports to pay for tractors and other capital goods. Collectivisation went much faster than the provision of tractors. In fact, it almost certainly reduced the power available on farms, as farmers killed their animals, including draught animals, which would otherwise have been collectivised. The total number of Soviet agricultural horses collapsed from 33 million at the beginning of 1929 to 15 million at the beginning of 1934.[37] Rural crafts, including clothes making also fell, partly because skilled workers moved to the city, were dekulakised or were too poor.[38] In many villages collectivisation brought about a retrogression in living standards and mechanical equipment.

Before the Second World War, collective farms had an average of seventy-five households. After it, Soviet collective and state farms would grow even bigger. These vast farms of thousands of hectares and hundreds of households were stunningly unproductive and failed to increase Soviet agricultural output much at all. Production did increase in the 1960s and 1970s but only at a huge cost in investment and labour. Paradoxically collectivisation ensured the continuation of the garden plot that had disappeared from US agriculture. From 1935 collective-farm households could operate a small plot to produce their own food, and could sell the surpluses. These family plots of approximately one acre would be very important indeed in meat, egg, vegetable and fruit production, right up to the present day.

## The agricultural revolution in the long boom

The phrase 'green revolution' is applied to the introduction of new varieties, irrigation and fertiliser to agriculture in the poor world in the 1960s. Partly because agriculture is associated with poverty and the past, and because of the focus on novelty, the even more significant agricultural revolution in the rich world was missed.

In the rich world agriculture in the long boom saw much greater rates of labour productivity change than industry or services, and at much greater rates than before.[39] In high land-productivity Britain, yields doubled in the post-war years from a very high base. New regimes of intensive agriculture through irrigation, and addition of artificial fertiliser (especially nitrate, largely produced by the Haber-Bosch process, innovated before the Great War) made plants grow fast and large. Plants were changed too. The introduction of hybrid corn (maize) in the US corn belt in the late 1930s and 1940s was just one example, though an important one, of new varieties being grown.[40]

While traditional rice-production systems in Asia yielded around 1 tonne per hectare, at the beginning of the twentieth century Japanese farmers were getting 2.5 tonnes; Japanese farmers had doubled yields through irrigation in the nineteenth century; and in its colonies of Korea and Taiwan in the interwar years. Yet in the 1950s, though the Japanese countryside was still routinely regarded as 'feudal' and backward, human excrement, night soil, was still used as fertiliser. Very quickly new housing, running water, washing machines, televisions, and then refrigerators were brought in. Agricultural machinery became plentiful on small farms, giving a unique combination of highly mechanised and very intensive output of rice.[41] Japan was to continue to lead the way in Asia in high productivity.[42] By the early 1960s it was getting 5 tonnes per hectare, when the Asian average was around two. Even after the green revolution had long passed, Japan still led. Today it produces 7 tonnes per hectare, compared with half that in Bangladesh.

The green revolution in rich countries made a huge impact on patterns of global trade, belying the standard image of a poor agricultural world exporting food to a rich industrial world. The USA remained, for example, a major wheat exporter, but increasingly to the poor world. It exported wheat to the USSR in the 1970s and 1980s on a huge scale. It remains a major producer of raw cotton, whose principal export market was once Britain, but is now the poor countries of the world where the cotton-spinning industry is concentrated. China imports cotton from the USA, and sells it textiles. Government policy in rich countries protected land and labour-efficient agriculture from the cheaper but less efficiently produced products of the poor world.

The gap in agricultural labour productivity between the rich world and the poor world, already large, widened after the Second World War.[43] The green revolution in the poor countries mitigated a growing divergence between the agriculture of the rich world and that of the poor, but probably at the price of increasing inequalities within the poor world. A short Japanese wheat variety, the Norin No. 10, was the key to making the short wheat plants that could take intensive applications of water and fertiliser. The IR8 rice variety was derived from dwarf strains developed in Taiwan in the interwar years by the Japanese.[44]

In the rich world animal husbandry was industrialised in the long boom, particularly in the case of chickens and pigs. The extreme example is that of chickens. In 1960 there were around 4 billion chickens in the world, whereas at the end of the twentieth century there were 13 billion. But the number killed for meat in a year has increased from 6 billion to 45 billion. Chickens lived much shorter lives.[45] That was just one dimension to the industrialisation of the chicken. Since the 1930s the US broiler (eating) chicken has become bigger (nearly twice as heavy), younger (about half the age), and has taken much less feed to bring it to the size needed (less than half).[46] This was done by making significant changes in both the nurture and the nature of chickens. A key series of steps was taken in the 1930s, among them bringing the chickens indoors, which required supplementing their diet with vitamin D, the use of electric lighting and artificial incubation. The intensive study of chicken feed resulted, by the 1950s, in a standard corn-and-soybean-based diet. The 1950s saw the breeding of hybrid chickens adapted to these artificial nurturing regimes. Many had been winners of 'The chicken of tomorrow contest'.

Pig production too was industrialised. Although the keeping of single pigs had disappeared in Britain by mid-century, even in the early 1960s half of all pigs were in herds with fewer than twenty breeding sows; by the 1990s 95 per cent were in herds of more than 100 breeding sows. Most lived, like broilers, indoors, and were, like the chickens, new sorts of fast-growing hybrids.[47] At the end of the century million-pig installations were being developed. Yet the greatest expansion in the number of pigs since the 1960s was in fact to be in non-industrialised pigs, kept in small numbers by farming households and fed with a variety of foods. In 1960 China had a quarter of the world's pigs, but today it has around half of the world's one billion pigs, not surprisingly because pork remains the staple meat in China, and meat eating has increased markedly. More than 80 per cent are still produced on a small scale, by non-specialist producers.

## Industry and mass production

We have told the story of production in terms of household production, agriculture, and small firms. Yet the standard image of twentieth-century production is centred on mass production. The central idea is that the twentieth century, especially during the long boom, saw production dominated by the large-scale production of standard parts. As a result of this mass production, efficiency of production increased dramatically. This led to unprecedented rates of economic growth and material well-being for the working classes now employed in gigantic factories and firms.

Mass production has had extraordinary effects, which are difficult to grasp.[48] At the beginning of the twentieth century one could build a house for the price of a car. Today, in the rich world, one would get little more than a small extension to a house for the price of an immensely more complex motor car. This is despite the decrease in costs of bricks, concrete, doors and windows, and any number of fittings, which are now mass produced. To take a biological example: the price of chicken has fallen much faster than beef. This observation suggests we should not equate mass production with modern production as a whole, even in rich countries since houses and beef are still produced. Even within manufacturing industry mass production accounted for a small proportion of production. In 1969 75 per cent of US industrial production was batch produced, even though in engineering mass-produced components were ten to thirty times cheaper.[49] Yet there were very important increases in efficiency which did not come from the sort of mass production we associate with the car industry, or the making of refrigerators. Across the board productive processes were becoming more efficient.

For example, the scale of Haber-Bosch ammonia plants increased, and the inputs, such as hydrogen, were produced in cheaper ways too. The result was ever larger quantities of cheap nitrogen fertiliser, which had a dramatic effect, combined with other inputs, in increasing the productivity of land. Another powerful example might be the increasing efficiency of the use of fuel, labour and capital in power stations.

*11. The construction of fast, motor torpedo boats out of wood for the US Navy in the Second World War. They were built undercover, of pre-fabricated sections. Production techniques for seemingly old products and materials were changing just as they were in 'new' industries.*

The key was larger power stations operating at higher temperatures. Another would be the explosion in the efficiency of ships after the Second World War, particularly oil tankers and similar vessels. Growth in the size of ships was crucial to the sustained reduction that took place in freight rates. In the case of crude oil, for example, transport costs decreased rapidly as a proportion of crude-oil prices. World steel production trebled between 1950 and 1970, with plants becoming much larger. In other sectors production increased radically in efficiency, but without necessarily needing increases in scale. Agriculture is a good example.

### Cars in the long boom
The mass production of motor cars was pioneered in the United States

by one company and one car, Ford and the Model T. At its peak in the 1920s the Model T was produced at an annual rate of 2 million, and by the time production ceased in 1927 15 million had been built. Ford was at this time easily the largest car manufacturer in the world, and had made America easily the most motorised nation in the world. Even the richest parts of Europe would not reach 1920s' levels of US motorisation until the late 1950s, let us recall.

The great boom in car production after the Second World War was largely an American and European affair, with the European makers growing faster, though from a much lower base. In each nation the great car firms were regarded as powerhouses of the booming economies. Even in a poor country such as Italy, car ownership went up more than ten-fold in the fifteen years between 1950 and 1964; from 0.34 million to 4.7 million cars. The number of cars just overtook motorcycle numbers, which increased from 0.7 to 4.3.[50] Between 1955 and 1970, 2.7 million Fiat 500s were made and 3.6 million Fiat 600s between 1957 and 1975.[51] European car workers were not yet able to buy cars themselves, but would be doing so by the late 1960s.[52]

In the long boom the Eastern European economies, like those in the West, grew very fast. Yet, the Soviet Union and its allies, for all the emphasis on standardised production and the possibility at least of plenty for the masses, were places of low consumption. Even in the 1960s the superpower USSR made only 1 per cent of the world's private vehicles, and 12 per cent of commercial ones; in comparison Britain made 10 per cent of the cars, and 9 per cent of the trucks.[53] So committed were the Soviets to mass production that they suffered from 'premature mass production', the putting into production of not properly tested goods.[54] But mass consumption in the richest countries was more typically about the extensive multiplication of firms, styles, types, rapid model change, the pursuit of endless novelty.[55]

The mass-producing car industry informed a whole understanding of modern production. It *was* modern industry, the place where the pace was set. The post-war years were labelled with such terms as 'Fordism', at least when the mass production of cars in Europe and

North America ceased to grow fast from the 1970s. Rapidly expanding Japanese car production became a model for 'Post-Fordism'. But just as the significance of mass production, or 'Fordism', was exaggerated, so were reports of its demise. At the end of the twentieth-century Ford had capacity in Europe to build 2 million cars a year; one factory was making 400,000 Focuses per annum, and another 330,000 Mondeos. In 1996 Volkswagen worldwide turned out over 800,000 Golfs, the car that took over the production record from the Beetle, which itself took over from the Model T. The world's largest car producers in 2000, still Ford and General Motors, were producing around 8 million vehicles each per annum, many times more than in the interwar years. Even in Britain more cars are produced today than ever before, and at world level production is not only increasing, but is still dominated by North America, Europe and Japan.

## Service industries

There is no doubt that the rise of employment in the service industries in the rich countries is one of the major economic changes of the last thirty years. A number of analysts have, perversely, identified this growth in service employment with the rise of an 'information society', with connotations of weightlessness, or indeed the 'dematerialised' economy. This was a fashionable, and misleading, way of saying little more than that service industries now account for very large proportions of GDP and employment.[56] This is partly the result of mis-specification because services include a vast range of activities, many of them far from weightless or indeed new. Services include transportation, by road, rail, water and air, telecommunications and postal services, the retail sector, as well as banking and finance, and small creative industries. That such a sector is weightless is immediately contradicted by the sheer bulk of the things associated with it, the unprecedented weight of stuff in the shops, the piles of paper in any office, not to mention the proliferation of computers, fax machines and Xeroxes. One need only look at homes in the rich world to see they are crammed with stuff, which is why storage is a growth industry and moving house becomes a bigger and bigger affair. In 2003 research for a British insurance company suggested the existence of £3.2bn-worth of unused goods, headed by sandwich toasters, electric knives, soda streams, foot spas, and ice-cream makers. There are 3.8 million unused fondue sets.[57] One source of confusion is that vast quantities of stuff used in service industries and in homes are imported, rather than produced domestically, but that is a different issue. The USA and Britain have large trade deficits in manufactured goods, which means that they use more than they produce; that is not to say that manufacturing ceases to be important to them.

The idea that manufacturing is not important, that what really matters is branding and design, is one of those confusions arising from thinking about only part of a story. The idea arises from the observation that *in rich countries* some giant enterprises are in retailing and control brands – the value is added by these activities, not in production. Yet branding and adding value through design are hardly new – they went along with manufacture, often in the same large company, as in the cases of Singer, or Ford or General Electric. We should not confuse the siting of economic activity with its significance. For the concentration of branding, marketing and design in rich countries, and production in poor countries, does not mean that production is no longer important. Indeed it is precisely because of the radical cheapening of manufactures through mass production and the use of very cheap labour, that they seem so unimportant to the rich. The point about manufacturing and mass production is that the latter produces goods extraordinarily cheaply, and does so all over the world. Massive economies of scale are exploited as never before on a global level to produce cheap mass-produced goods of great complexity. Think of cheap PCs, mobile phones and IKEA furniture. Mass production is now so common it is invisible.

At the beginning of the twenty-first century Wal-Mart is the largest corporation in the world, by annual sales ($300bn in 2005/6) and by employee numbers. With nearly 2 million workers it is vastly larger not only than the biggest firms of 1900, but also than the very largest manufacturing employers of the 1960s. But it is a retailer, not a manufacturer. Indeed it indirectly employs many more millions, largely in China, mass producing all sorts of stuff for the American consumer. IKEA, again principally a retailer and designer, controls the mass manufacture of furniture, indirectly employing an estimated 1 million workers. Indeed IKEA provides a wonderful example of the arguments of this book. First, of the continuing significance of what we take to be old, in this case not just furniture, but *wooden* furniture, supplied, obviously, by forests. In terms of industry it exemplifies beautifully the extension rather than the retreat of mass production, and its globalisation, producing fantastically cheap outputs. In terms of service industries it is an example of mass retailing and mass consumption of identical goods (it has made 28 million Billy bookcases since launch in 1978); it is also an example of the reduction of transport costs by flat-packing, and an example of the concentration of design and marketing activity in a rich country (Sweden). As a domestic industry it is an example of a family-owned firm, and indeed one which provides goods to be transported home by non-paid domestic workers, and assembled by them too. Such products made its founder and owner, it is alleged, the richest man in the world, richer than Bill Gates of Microsoft, who had briefly taken first place following the death of Walton of Wal-Mart.

One of the great novelties of the last quarter or so of the twentieth century was the emergence of poor countries as suppliers to the world not of food and raw materials, but of manufactures. The case of China is all the more extraordinary given its history as a Communist nation and one which had had a very particular approach to modern industry. The Chinese had systematically promoted old small-scale technologies in the 1950s. In the Cultural Revolution of the late 1960s and early 1970s, there was a concerted attack on the division between managers and workers – a distinction central to Taylorism and Fordism, and an attack too on the division of labour itself.[58] Small-scale rural industries were promoted, as during the earlier Great Leap Forward. Although the Chinese economy grew, it did so very unstably and relatively slowly.

After 1976 the Chinese Communist party changed direction, and with the abolition of collective farming and the move to household farming in the 1980s, presided over a productivity surge in Chinese agriculture. In this same period rural industries grew at a phenomenal rate, many times that of the Chinese economy as a whole. Local 'township and village enterprises' were the key to this growth. The transformation of the Chinese countryside in the last twenty years is surely the fastest and deepest in world history, affecting many hundreds of millions of people.[59]

Millions, often women, left the countryside, and, housed in dormitories, toiled for pitiful wages in the factories of the new industrial areas. Chinese growth has been dependent on overseas investment, primarily from Japan, Taiwan and from overseas Chinese elsewhere. Multinational enterprise, Japanese included, has also been important. In these respects the industrialisation of China has been very different from that of Japan. Market Stalinism and foreign investment were critical in China's drive to industrialise. Despite its scale and speed and its impact on the global economy, the growth of China is not the product of a profoundly new economy. It has a distinctly old feel to it.

At the beginning of the twenty-first century China was sucking in vast quantities of heavy raw materials, from oil to copper, driving up world prices. It became easily the largest steel producer in the world, with rates of growth comparable to those of steel in the long boom. The 'new economy' was being replaced by a very old economy driven by commodity prices. Far from the information superhighway being the conduit for all this new production, it was none other than the ship that carried the great bulk of Chinese production, and indeed world trade as a whole. In the year 2000 the world merchant fleet was rated at 553 million gross registered tonnes (a measure of the carrying capacity of ships), up from 227 million in 1970, 85 million in 1950 and 45 million in 1914. As its scale suggested, it carried more material than ever before in history, and so cheaply that the price of manufactures was hardly affected by freight rates. This industry employed some

1 million seamen, with a majority of officers from rich countries and a majority of ratings from poor countries, largely in Asia.

Most shipping still transports fuel and bulks such as ore and grain, yet manufactures were very important too, largely carried in that great invention of the 1950s, the container. Since then global container traffic, which now dominates all sea traffic excepting bulks, has continued to increase. At the beginning of the twenty-first century the largest container ships, at 90,000 GRT, could carry over 8,000 containers, with a crew of just nineteen. The majority of the vessels were manufactured in the East. Wal-Mart is the largest single importer of containers in the USA, bringing in half a million every year, mostly from China.

The great long boom and the more recent boom in the East, China in particular, far from being primarily cases of successive technological revolutions, are in many ways inflexions of the same technological and industrial revolution happening in succession. Of course it is far from identical, but the similarities are striking: the huge increase in agricultural productivity, the expansion of industry – not least the old classics such as steel making – and the expansion of ship-borne international trade. In both cases the revolutionary nature of each era is masked by a deep political stability in the growing countries. Politics, the nation and borders matter.

# 4

# Maintenance

Many of the great dystopian novels of the twentieth century look forward to a future society which is more technically advanced than the present, but one that was stagnant. These were technological societies without innovation. Thus the technological societies in Zamyatin's *We*, Huxley's *Brave New World* and Orwell's *Nineteen Eighty-four* were not revolutionary or progressive, even technologically. These are worlds of order without change, which have to be kept going. They are threatened by curious outlaws. Terry Gilliam in his dystopian film of the 1980s, *Brazil*, captured both aspects of this literature. The innovative touch was that to the viewer the technology was no longer futuristic, but clearly an extrapolation to the present of 1940s' technology. So too were the values of the society that used them. There were many references to maintenance, not just of the social order, but the technical order too. Repairmen from a central office appear as hideous agents of the state, and plastic surgery, maintenance for the human body, recurs as a theme. There is also, in the form of Robert De Niro, an outlaw repairman, who not only repairs the system, but is free from it.

One of the most enduring ideas about technology in the twentieth century suggests that the essentially human has been taken over by the artificial. Nightmares about breakdown of the complex world of artifice that makes modern life possible propel deep concerns about the need for discipline, order and stability to keep the system going. As one philosopher of technology noted in the 1970s: 'In almost no instance can artificial-rational systems be built and left alone. They require continued attention, rebuilding, and repair. Eternal vigilance is the price of artificial complexity.'[1] He noted too, that in a technological age we should ask not who governs, but *what* governs: 'government becomes the business of recognising what is necessary and efficient for the continued functioning and elaboration of large-scale systems and the rational implementation of their manifest requirements.'[2]

One particularly striking evocation of such thinking in the post-war years compared the modern condition to ancient dependence on the control of water. Ancient Egypt, Mesopotamia and China depended on constant vigilance over, and maintenance and repair of, complex irrigation systems. It was argued that this required a huge all-powerful state: these ancient 'hydraulic societies' were necessarily not democratic. The implication was that Asiatic and despotic traditions, quite different from those which led to feudalism and capitalism, were crucial in shaping both the Soviet Union and Communist China.[3] Yet similar analogies were also applied to the capitalist West. A famous American student of technology, Lewis Mumford, writing in the early 1960s, regarded the ancient 'pyramid age' as one characterised by 'authoritarian technics', which he saw as a historical alternative to 'democratic technics'. Yet, in the post-Second World War years, particularly in the United States, Mumford saw a new authoritarian technics appearing, a kind of 'occidental despotism'. Mumford was a savage critic of this new manifestation of a world controlled by raw power and systemic technologies.[4]

For many analysts in the twentieth century the nature of technology itself was responsible for this new authoritarianism. It was argued that technology was becoming ever greater in scale, more interconnected, more centrally controlled and more critical for the maintenance of human life. An example might be electricity supply – organised on a massive scale as an interconnected system on which we were all dependent. This led to ever greater danger of failure, since a failure could lead to total breakdown. The consequence was not only the need for greater requirements for vigilance and maintenance of the technology, but a society itself increasingly disciplined to avoid breakdowns. A society with nuclear power stations was, in this view, a society that needed to be heavily policed.

Much of the discourse on technology is a commentary on philosophical and other writings on technology. There is a danger that descriptions of technology turn into realities which are used to explain the nature of modern society. The history of maintenance provides some important insights into the questions of discipline and order in relation to modern technology. It will also force us to rethink some standard economic categories and to reconsider important aspects of the history of work and production, not least that of engineers.

Just like land, buildings and people, things have had to be maintained, repaired and looked after, often for very long periods. Although central to our relationship with things, maintenance and repair are matters we would rather not think about. Mundane and infuriating, full of uncertainties, they are among the major annoyances surrounding things. The subject is left in the margins, often to marginal groups. So low has been the status of 'maintenance engineering' that attempts were made, with some success, to rename it 'terotechnology'.[5] The term 'terotechnology', apparently coined by a British government committee in the 1960s, derives from the Greek *teros*, meaning to watch, observe, guard, and as it happens is singularly appropriate.

That we neglect maintenance when we think and write about our technology is an instance of the great gulf there is between our everyday understanding of our dealing with things and the formal understandings enshrined in, for example, our histories. For in popular culture maintenance is well known. The tale of 'my grandfather's axe' is familiar in many forms. We hear too that the lifetime maintenance costs of an aeroplane will often exceed the cost of purchase. For all that the extraordinary cheapness and 'weightlessness' of computers and software are celebrated, we know there is no escape from the

*12. Even ruins need maintenance. An ancient Greek temple in Agrigento, Sicily, in 2005. Note the use of corrugated iron.*

need to pay a fortune for technical support and maintenance. On one estimate, the initial cost of a PC is but 10 per cent of the total lifetime cost, including installation, repair, upgrades, training. Microsoft has certified more than 1.5 million engineers and administrators for their software around the world. One US estimate is that maintenance represents 60 per cent of the total lifetime cost of the more complex military equipment. Maintenance and repair often result in changes; they are closely connected, in some cases, to remodelling.

## How important are maintenance and repair?

The problem of maintenance becomes visible when it is lacking. For example, the United Nations became concerned about bad maintenance in the poor world in the late 1960s, noting that it was particularly bad for capital-scarce countries, since lack of maintenance reduced the life of expensive assets such as tractors or industrial machinery, and also meant that they were under-used.[6] The vitally important, usually invisible, 'routine, repetitive and even tedious work' of maintenance has been ignored in development projects with inevitable consequences.[7] Hand water pumps introduced in India in the 1960s with no provision for their maintenance soon falling into disrepair is one example. Accounts of the history of Soviet agriculture abound with side comments about the terrible waste resulting from poor maintenance of tractors and other farm machinery, noting, for example, that the problem became even worse with the abolition of the Machine Tractor Stations in 1958. More recently, development experts have noted the waste of resources in poor countries resulting from the failure to maintain roads. More has to be spent rebuilding than would have had to be spent maintaining them.

Maintenance has lived in a twilight world, hardly visible in the formal accounts societies make of themselves. In the economic and production statistics, for example, it is invisible. In the standard economic imagery there is investment and then use of capital goods, but no maintenance or repair, except partially and incidentally. Partly for technical reasons, national accounts do not separately identify maintenance and repair since they are often done in-house, and thus do not appear as a separate cost. Spare parts and so on are lost among other purchases of goods. However, Canada does have statistics on maintenance, because for many years an investment questionnaire also asked about maintenance and repair expenditure. Expenditures averaged over the period 1961–93 were about 6 per cent of gross domestic product (GDP). This was a very great deal more than expenditure on invention and innovation, but considerably lower than expenditure on investment, which was about 10–30 per cent of GDP for rich countries. Yet, in the Canadian case, the maintenance of equipment, as opposed to structures, amounted to 50 per cent of investment expenditure.[8] Other estimates are few and far between. An isolated figure for 1934 US manufacturing and mining suggests that maintenance and repair cost as much as investment in new plant and equipment.[9] In Switzerland, from the 1920s into the late 1950s, spending on improvement and maintenance of roads was greater than on the building of new roads.[10] In the mid-1950s some 60 per cent of what non-rural Australian businesses were spending on investment was on maintenance and repair. In New South Wales alone, the rural sector spent 34 per cent of what it spent on investment (including dwellings) on maintenance and repair.[11] In the late 1960s Britain was spending around £3bn on maintenance, under 10 per cent of GDP, at a time when investment accounted for 20 per cent.[12] For the USA in the late 1980s, renovation and rehabilitation of buildings were one and a half times the spend on new building, and came in at 5 per cent of GDP.[13] These are estimates of the direct costs of maintenance only. Further costs arise because for every power station, locomotive, aeroplane, machine tool being maintained, an additional one is needed to maintain output. Reducing maintenance cost and time could have a dramatic impact not just on direct costs, but on capital and investment costs too.

## Maintenance

The inventing of things has been concentrated in a few places; the making of things is much more widely distributed; the using of things is usually much more widely distributed still. (In some cases making is more widespread than use, for example where a ship or a building is made from parts manufactured in many different places.) Maintenance is almost as widely distributed as use. As a consequence, maintenance and repair are the most widespread forms of technical expertise. Maintenance and repair have been the realm of the small trader and skilled workers. They were different from, marginal to and yet interdependent with the great systems of technics. A good example would be the motor car, manufactured on a large scale in a few places in the world, but maintained and repaired in innumerable workshops the world over. More than that, a great deal of maintenance and repair activity takes place outside the formal economy, pointing to the importance of widespread technical skills. Domestic sewing for the repair of clothing, for example, was once a nearly universal female skill, and still is in many parts of the world.

Unfortunately we are not in a position to give an overview of the main trends in the history of maintenance and repair. Has maintenance as a proportion of output gone up or down? Where there has been a trade-off between initial cost and maintenance, what have producers and consumers gone for? How has this changed over time? In some areas it seems there has been a reduction in maintenance, for example in aviation and in trains, perhaps in ships too. But in rich countries, as far as domestic equipment is concerned, and in industry for IT hardware, repair no longer exists – from electric toasters to fridges, repair is hardly worth carrying out – and not surprisingly the networks of retailer/repairers are long gone. A new toaster retails for less than an hour of repair time. More spectacularly perhaps, most bits of domestic equipment operate for their whole lives without even needing oiling or adjusting in any way.[14]

Furthermore, maintenance is itself becoming highly concentrated and controlled. In the case of cars, the complex electronics in the vehicle means that only approved repair workshops with the correct equipment can even begin to work out what is wrong with a car. In poorer parts of the world, the relationship between initial cost and the cost of maintenance and repair appears to be different, and reminiscent in some respects of the position in rich countries earlier in the century. Where maintenance and repair are cheap compared to initial purchase, things will have longer lives. Furthermore, things will move from a low-maintenance regime to a high-maintenance one as they get older. Thus, the movement of second-hand goods – from consumer goods to capital goods – from rich countries, where it is not worth keeping them going, to poor, maintenance-intensive countries. There is a huge trade in old cars, domestic equipment, power stations and clothes from the rich to the poor world. However, there is every possibility that the products of rich countries may no longer be maintainable in poor countries – the modern motor car being an example.

## Mass production and the art of car maintenance

The early motor industry provides an example of the importance of maintenance, and how this differed in various times and contexts. The electric car was popular in the early days of motoring, but battery maintenance required skills and experience very different from the purely mechanical ones needed for petrol engines. The electric vehicle required specialised facilities for recharging and maintaining batteries, while the petrol car could rely on users and already existing workshops. The attractions of the early petrol car were that it could be used out of range and that it was amenable to a do-it-yourself maintenance culture. The latter was a factor in the relative decline of the electric car, except in some cases of centrally-controlled fleets. [15]

The Model T Ford, in production from 1908 to the late 1920s, easily out-produced all other cars in its time, and provides some particularly stark examples of the significance of maintenance. A key feature of the car was that it was made from interchangeable parts. This allowed the assembly to be carried out without fitters, and it also had implications for maintenance. Henry Ford himself noted that the Model T was designed for ease of maintenance; no special skill was required for repair or replacement:

> I believed then, although I said very little about it because of the novelty of the idea that it ought to be possible to have parts so simple and so inexpensive that the menace of expensive hand repair work would be entirely eliminated. The parts could be made so cheaply that it would be less expensive to buy new ones than to have old ones repaired. They could be carried in hardware shops just as nails or bolts are carried. [16]

In an elegy for the Model T published in the 1930s, E. B. White noted something which escapes most factory-based images of the Model T. The American writer's essay was full of references to witch doctors, superstition and horses, pointing to a world of use and maintenance of the Model T very different from that of the factory. According to White 'a Ford was born as naked as a baby, and a flourishing industry

grew up of correcting its rare deficiencies and combatting its fascinating diseases.'[17] So concerned were Ford with maintenance and repair
that they investigated and standardised repair procedures, which
were incorporated in a huge manual published in 1925. They also set
standard rates for their dealers, forced them to purchase standardised
equipment for repair and encouraged division of labour in repair
shops. However, this plan did not work – it could not cope with the
many vicissitudes and uncertainties of the car-repair business. The
Fordisation of maintenance and repair, even of the Model T, did not
work.[18] As the British naval officer in charge of ship construction and
maintenance in the 1920s put it: 'repair work has no connection with
mass-production.'[19]

Car maintenance is a feature of every place where there are cars,
but in some places and contexts it became particularly significant
and interesting. In the west African state of Ghana, there were by the
early 1970s a large number of motor-vehicle repair men, called 'fitters'.
They concentrated in particular areas, sometimes called 'magazines',
working from shacks or in the open air. The largest was the Suame
Magazine, which in 1971 had nearly 6,000 people working in it. Most
of them were directly involved in car repair, while others sold parts,
supplied the magazine itself with food and so on. There was such
enormous growth in the magazine that by the mid-1980s the population had increased to around 40,000 and it became a centre for
making things of all sorts. The tools used in this vast complex were
rudimentary – there were hammers, spanners in incomplete sets, files
and screwdrivers. Adjustable spanners did not last long; anvils were
improvised.[20] The number of machine tools in this vast complex was
in single figures.[21] The most elaborate tool in common use was the
electric welding kit, which would be central to the manufacturing side
of the magazine.

How could such a place maintain and repair the products of an
industry which was all interchangeable parts, precision engineering
and elaborate maintenance manuals? The answer is that in some sense
it did not – these magazines could not maintain such cars, lorries

and buses so that they remained as they had been when made. There was a mismatch between the car or truck as new and the support infrastructure available. New, imported motor vehicles were degraded by accidents, shortages of lubricants and, importantly, *lack of maintenance.* Then something remarkable happened: in the words of a knowledgeable student of these matters, 'as time goes by and the vehicle is reworked in the local system, it reaches a state of apparent equilibrium in which it seems to be maintained indefinitely ... it is a condition of maintenance by constant repair.'[22] There was almost daily repair to the local buses and trucks, which provided extremely cheap transport. One reason is that these transports were eternal in their equilibrium position. No one would think of replacing one, since they lived in constant interaction with a workshop.[23] Here the economics of investment and depreciation simply did not apply – the costs were those of maintenance and repair.

Ghanaian car repairers developed an intimate knowledge of cars and engines and how to keep them going using local materials. In the process they transformed cars. They got to know them much more intimately than any rich-country user, or even a repairman. This is clear in the 'biography' written by two anthropologists, of a Peugeot 504 used as a long-distance taxi in Ghana in the 1990s, by a driver named Kwaku. Maintenance and repair were in Kwaku's mind from the moment he bought his car, for he purchased a second 504 body, and later a second engine, to be used as sources of spares. In its life Kwaku's car broke down repeatedly and went through a process of rebuilding, rewiring and acquiring a new carburettor to consume less petrol. Replacement gaskets were made from old tyres, fuses were replaced by copper wire, nails were used as lock-pins. The car ran for years. As its biographers put it, the 'widespread "tropicalisation" of motor cars in Ghana (as well as in many other African countries) not only rests on a thorough knowledge of how engines work, but also and especially on a rather unique type of knowledge of how one can keep old ones working in a situation of limited goods'.[24] What might seem like dangerous and costly indifference to the rules set out in maintenance manuals was a remarkable example of extreme technical artifice brought within human understanding. This was a particular form of the creolisation of technology.

## Maintenance and large-scale industry

Increasingly automated motor-car producing plants in the rich world needed extraordinary amounts of maintenance to keep working. Indeed maintenance needs severely constrained the development of automation. A particularly good example is the use of transfer machines in the 1950s. In classical mass production parts were transferred between machines, by hand or by conveyors. Attempts were made, some successful, to develop machines that would take a piece of work from one machine and transfer it to another, where it would be worked, and so on from machine to machine. It was not an assembly line, both because it did not involve assembly and because the machine brought work not to the worker, but to various parts of the machine. These machines, called transfer machines, were at the heart of 1950s' 'automation' in the motor industry. Indeed there was an automation scare – there were visions of jobs disappearing into factories without humans.

Transfer machines had been experimented with in the car-engine industry in the 1920s, but they came back in the USA aero-engine industry during the Second World War. Transfer machines were given a particular boost by a new machine built to make part of the Wright-Cyclone aero-engine during the war, reducing the direct labour for making cylinder heads from fifty-nine to eight man-minutes. After the war, there was a boom in installation of transfer machines in the US car-engine industry. Particularly noteworthy was the new Ford engine plant in Cleveland built to produce around 1.5 million engines per annum. It was, some commented, a single giant transfer machine, since its transfer machines were themselves linked by automatic handling equipment.

But 'Detroit automation', as the large-scale use of transfer machines was called, required rapid and effective maintenance of the whole system and easy replacement of tools on each machine tool. For, if any part of the whole complex of machines interconnected by the transfer machine was not working, the whole machine had to be stopped. 'Downtime' remained a major problem, even with programmed maintenance. These transfer machines demanded not only a lot of maintenance but particularly strict surveillance over the plant and the maintainers. At Ford's Cleveland engine plant, a 'police force' was created to clean and maintain it, a process that required accurate and extensive record keeping. In order to make transfer machines work, the amount of maintenance labour had to increase radically, greatly reducing the saving achieved by reducing direct labour. Sometimes, the cost of the additional maintenance labour was greater than the savings in direct labour. To a significant extent the transfer machine did not eliminate labour, but transferred it from production to maintenance, away from the tedious work of manning machines to the skilled and more varied work of maintenance. Yet maintenance was so big a problem that machines were disconnected, to return to some of the flexibility of the pre-transfer machine era. In any case the promise of the machines was somewhat dented by the horsepower race in engine size, which demanded new plant for ever increasing size of engines. The lines had to be made more flexible than anticipated.[25]

In the history of industries one gets other glimpses of the significance of maintenance and repair. Maintenance costs were an important part both of running and capital costs of railways, accounting for about four times the initial purchase cost of trains.[26] In railways, as in cars, repair and maintenance are not so easily rationalized as new production of new locomotives, since 'the repair activity in railway works is more complex than the production of new vehicles.'[27] There were lots of types to deal with, and one did not know how much work each would take. Already in the interwar years, standardisation of types and rationalisation of repair reduced repair times a great deal. At its Crewe workshops the LMS railway built repair lines which operated at different speeds depending on the size of the repair. Yet as the complexity of locomotives grew, so did the time taken for maintenance and repair. It took twice as long to repair the new diesel locomotives of the 1960s as the steam locomotives they replaced.[28] However, the amount of repair and maintenance needed by the new diesels was much lower, and the reduced maintenance and repair bill was an important point in their favour. Yet railway maintenance continued to be very important, if unglamorous. Following the privatisation of British railways in the 1990s, existing maintenance regimes were disrupted, with the consequence that essential maintenance procedures were no longer followed, resulting in serious accidents.

## Aviation

Although the aeroplane was often associated with freedom, its operation was characterised by exceptional attention to discipline, routine and maintenance. Thus the airport was generally a highly organised and disciplined environment (for passengers) in the way a railway station was not. Aircraft which cease to work fall out of the sky, while cars or ships or locomotives can break down without such dire consequences. Therefore airlines and air forces devote a huge proportion of their resources to maintenance. Promoting the image of flying as safe was vital. It had an important consequence for an otherwise predominantly male industry (not least because of its connection to the military). In the interwar years the 'aviatrix' was a staple of the newspapers. These women flyers, who engaged in all sorts of long-distance flights, became national heroines, supported by the aircraft industry, because they showed that aviation was safe. In most countries 'air stewards' attended to passengers in flight, yet in the USA, air stewardesses or 'air hostesses' took to the air from the early 1930s, setting what was going to be the dominant pattern after the war.

Maintenance was expensive. For example, US domestic airlines, from the 1930s into the 1960s, had a ground-based mechanic for every two flight crew members (including air hostesses).[29] Maintenance accounted for 20 per cent of total costs of airline operation in America in the early 1960s, compared with 27 per cent for crew and fuel costs, 10 per cent for depreciation and 43 per cent for all ground costs. Maintenance took up 35 per cent of flying costs.[30] It was around 25 per cent of flying costs, including depreciation, for the Ford Trimotor in the late 1920s, 20 per cent for a DC-8 jet in the early 1960s and around 30 per cent for a piston-engined DC-6 in 1961.[31]

In the 1920s one of the major advances in the economics of aviation was the decreased need to maintain engines. Between 1920 and 1936 costs fell by about 80 per cent, and represented the main cost saving in engine operation.[32] A good measure of maintenance cost was the time an engine could safely operate before being overhauled, the 'time between overhaul' (TBO). In the early 1920s engines in airline service were operating at around fifty hours between overhaul; by late 1920s engines were achieving up to 150 hours, and 1930s' engines around 500 hours. These were the figures for new engines; once they were in service for two to three years the intervals increased as people got used to them, typically doubling or trebling. Thus the widely used Bristol Jupiter engine was rated at 150 hours when introduced in 1929, but was up to 500 hours in 1932. The Pratt & Whitney Twin Wasp of 1936, which powered the DC-3, was going for 1,500 hours by the late 1950s. The new large piston engines introduced during and after the Second World War started life with TBOs of around 600–800 hours, by the late 1950s these engines were being rated at well over 1,000 hours, with the best, the Pratt & Whitney Double Wasp reaching 3,000 hours. Airlines could count on 2,000–2,500 for their best large engines.

The early jet engines, despite their seeming simplicity compared to the mammoth piston engines of the time, at first needed even more maintenance. The important US military engine, the General Electric J-47, achieved fifty hours on launch in the early 1950s, though this improved to 650 hours by the mid-1950s. When the first jet engines were routinely used in civil airliners in the late 1950s and early 1960s, the TBO was set at the same level as for piston engines (2,000–2,500 hours), but as confidence increased the time was stretched to 8,000 hours.[33] The jet engine became, through intensive effort, a very reliable machine. Today TBOs can be as high as 50,000 hours.[34]

*13. The 0.5 inch guns of a Republic F-24 Thunderjet fighter-bomber are tested by its maintenance crew in Korea, 1952. Air forces have typically had many more maintenance personnel than pilots.*

This dramatic fall in engine maintenance has taken place for very interesting reasons. First, it was due to improvements in the design of engines to make them much more inherently reliable. For example, through reduction in numbers of moving parts, and by using harder-wearing materials. But costs of engine maintenance fell dramatically with length of service of a particular engine type. Typically, there is at first a slight rise (because of unanticipated problems) and then a fall over ten years to 30 per cent of the original maintenance cost. This is due to increasing confidence in the engine itself and increasing knowledge of what needs maintenance. In other words, the maintenance schemes, programmes and costs are not programmable in advance. In these complex systems a great infrastructure of documentation, control and surveillance is needed, and yet informal, tacit knowledge remains extremely important. People and organisations 'learn by using' or 'learn by doing'.

Learning by doing was noticed first not in aircraft maintenance, but in aircraft manufacture, and as long ago as the 1930s. The effect is this: the greater quantity of a good produced, the lower the costs of production. This is the origin of the expression 'going down the learning curve'. This was not the result of conventional economies of scale, spreading of overheads or the mechanisation of methods of production. It applied to a given system of production and a given level of managerial and worker skills. The effect was significant: if output doubled, then costs per aircraft fell by about 20 per cent. Thus the hundredth aircraft produced – of a given type – was 20 per cent cheaper than the fiftieth. The effects are large enough to give much-produced aircraft a distinct cost advantage. For example, in the early 1960s it was 5–15 per cent more expensive to produce the hundredth aircraft in the USA than it was in Britain. But because the number of aircraft made of a given type was higher, America was able to move down the learning curve, with the result that average costs of production were actually 10–20 per cent lower there. This calculation ignored the further beneficial effect to the USA of the fact that a longer production run meant R&D costs were spread over more aircraft.[35]

This effect occurs because managers and workers learn, typically in an informal way, how to make or maintain the aircraft more easily. Extreme dependence on the reliable operation of machinery involved significant costs, and coping with complexities which seemed to dwarf formal human understanding. But humans learn to cope, and reduce the costs of maintenance. The best way of making or maintaining a particular aircraft was not known or calculable at the beginning because of the complexity of the aeroplane; it had to be learned. People were building and maintaining something they had designed which was more complex than they could formally understand. But they learned by experience how to build and maintain significantly more efficiently than could be programmed in advance.

## The battleships and bombers

Sailing ships were very maintenance intensive. The crew were not there just to sail the vessel but to keep it in being. Sail-makers and carpenters formed part of a crew that was constantly patching and repairing, and indeed pumping out the water that streamed into even the best-kept hull. Ships of steel and steam were less maintenance intensive, at least while at sea, but even today maintenance and repair are still carried out at sea. As ships get older they need and get bigger crews to deal with the increased maintenance load. Warships and bombers too, were very maintenance intensive.

Peacetime armed forces are usefully thought of as maintenance and training organisations. After the Second World War some hugely complex systems required extraordinary amounts of maintenance – some aircraft were dubbed 'hangar queens'. But maintenance intensity was not new. The Royal Navy, the great navy of the first decades of the twentieth century, had a global system of dockyards for maintenance and repair of ships in, for example, Malta, Gibraltar and later Singapore. Even in peacetime these dockyards employed thousands of workers, and significant proportions of the fleet were in dock at any one time. The practice before the mid-1920s was that warships were refitted for two months or so every year, in one of the royal dockyards. This was changed in the late 1920s so that ships' crews maintained ships for two and a half years; after that the crews refitted the ships for two months, with dockyard assistance. This programme of 'self-maintenance' and 'self-refit', required more skilled seamen, but 'many thousand dockyard men were discharged.'[36] In Malta, under the new scheme, November and December were devoted to 'self-refit', when the 'main engine, auxiliary engines, capstan and steering engines, boilers, gun-mountings, dynamos, etc' were stripped down and refitted, where possible by the ship's own technical staff. At the same time the ship was 'scraped and painted'.[37] Over longer periods, around seven years for a cruiser and ten years for a battleship, a longer refit of around one year was needed to re-tube boilers and re-wire (as well as make other changes deemed desirable), giving planned lives of twenty and twenty-seven years respectively.[38]

A ship was not necessarily a stable entity. Ships were often radically changed, often more than once, in the course of their lives. The modern battleship provides some fascinating cases of long-lived, long-maintained and much-changed machines. The first modern-pattern battleship, the *Dreadnought*, was launched in a royal dockyard in 1905. By 1914 the numbers already built or under construction were astounding: twenty for Britain, fifteen for Germany, ten for the USA, four for Russia, four for France, three each for Italy, Austro-Hungary and Spain, two each for Japan, Turkey (none of which was delivered), Chile (only one delivered, after war), Argentina and Brazil. Building continued through the war and beyond, but from 1922 to 1936 there was a moratorium (with a few exceptions) on new construction, as part of a process of multi-lateral naval disarmament. As a result most of the battleships of the three great naval powers used in the Second World War were built in the decade 1911–1921 so that by 1945 nearly half the world's battleships were over thirty years old.

The South American states already had a long tradition of keeping warships going for extraordinary periods. Argentina's two pre-First World War US-built dreadnoughts, were used into the 1950s, as were the two British-built battleships of Brazil's Navy, the *Minas Gerais* and the *São Paulo*, and the single Chilean one, the *Almirante Latorre*. Perhaps the most astonishing case was the Turkish battleship *Yavuz*, which had been given to the Ottoman Empire by Germany in 1914 and served the remainder of its life with the Turkish Navy, being broken up only in 1971.

But few, if any, were as they had been when completed. They were not only maintained and repaired, but they were also refitted and reconstructed. The Japanese Navy reconstructed nearly all its interwar battleships, and they changed shape and engine power particularly dramatically. In the British case a nice example is provided by some

14. *The Brazilian dreadnought battleship* Minas Gerais, *ready for maintenance and repair work in a floating dock Affonso Penna, Rio de Janeiro, in 1910. Battleships, like all warships, required very regular maintenance. Brazil had to buy not only the battleship but also the floating dock from Britain.* Minas Gerais *was reconstructed in the 1930s and scrapped in the 1950s.*

of the five Queen Elizabeth class battleships which were launched in Britain between October 1913 (the *Queen Elizabeth* itself) and March 1915. All except *Barham*, sunk by a U-boat in November 1941, survived two world wars, to be broken up in the late 1940s. What a Queen Elizabeth battleship was and looked like in 1918 was pretty clear, but by 1939 they were different ships. Between 1924 and 1934 they were given substantial refits, a process which included trunking the funnels into one, and fitting huge anti-torpedo bulges on their sides, as well as changes in the smaller armament. Then, in the 1930s, all except *Barham* and *Malaya* were 'reconstructed', which meant that they were given new engines, major changes were made to the guns and mountings, and much of the superstructure was rebuilt. In the Second

World War the *Queen Elizabeth* would have had a decisive advantage in combat against *Barham*. Reconstruction cost about half the price of a new battleship. However, it took longer than expected: it was harder to predict how long it would take to reconstruct, in comparison with building from scratch.

Most battleships were scrapped quite soon after the Second World War, but the US kept four Iowa class battleships, designed in the late 1930s, in reserve, meaning they were kept on a care and maintenance basis. They were put back into service in the 1960s and the 1980s and again in the early 1990s. The USS *New Jersey* was briefly recommissioned in the Vietnam war, when it bombarded the land with 3,000 16-inch shells. All four were recommissioned by President Ronald Reagan in the 1980s and became platforms for launching cruise missiles. USS *Wisconsin* also fired 300 tons of 16-inch shells during the 1991 Gulf war. Not since the early nineteenth century had ships this old been in action.

The Falklands war of 1982, immortalised by Jorge Luis Borges as 'two bald men fighting over a comb', certainly involved some balding equipment. In 1951 Argentina acquired two Brooklyn class cruisers which had entered into service with the US Navy in 1939. One, the former USS *Phoenix*, was renamed *17 of October*, a key date in the rise of General Perón, the Argentine President. The ship took part in the coup of 1955 which toppled Perón and was renamed the *Belgrano*. In 1982 she was sunk by a British submarine as she sailed away from the Falklands with 21-inch Mk8 torpedoes, a type that had been in service in the Royal Navy for longer than the life of the *Belgrano*. The *Belgrano* and the torpedoes which took her to the bottom were not the only veterans. Britain bombed an airstrip on the Falklands with a 1950s-built Vulcan bomber, which was refuelled in the air by a converted 1950s bomber of another type, the Victor.[39] Argentina's one aircraft carrier, the *Veinticinco de Mayo*, was appropriately enough the former HMS *Venerable*, a Colossus class British carrier built in 1945. She was sold to the Dutch in 1948, and on to Argentina in 1969. Taken out of service in 1986, she appears to have been scrapped in India around

2000, though there had been plans to modernise her. Another ship of the class, the former HMS *Vengeance*, was still in service in 2001 as Brazil's *Minas Gerais*. She was broken up on Alang beach in Gujarat in 2004 (see plate 27 on p. 208). Another British wartime carrier, HMS *Hercules*, of a very similar class, went to India and became the INS *Vikrant*, decommissioned only in 1997.[40]

Similar stories can be told about aircraft of the nuclear age. The B-52 bomber, one of the first, and certainly the most produced nuclear bomber, had a particularly extraordinary record. It first flew in 1952, and was last manufactured in 1962. Not only is it still in use, it is expected to continue in service to 2040 though, of course, much changed. Stories are told of grandchildren of early B-52 pilots now flying them. Another example is the KC-135, an air-refuelling tanker, which was manufactured between 1956 and 1966. More than 600 of the 732 tankers built were still in service in the mid-1990s. At the end of the twentieth century, with new engines and many other modifications, they remain the main refuelling aircraft of the US Air Force. Odd as it may seem, the KC-135, ordered by the US Air Force, was turned by its maker, Boeing, into the much more famous 707 passenger jet, which is long out of service.

More prosaic things than battleships and bombers have been kept in use for long periods by constant maintenance and repair. The last large sailing ships for commercial service were built in the 1920s, among them the *Padua*, built in Germany in 1926. She survived after the Second World War as a Soviet training ship, and latterly an Estonian one. The last big fleet of sailing ships was operated in the 1930s by Gustaf Erikson, flying the Finnish flag, mostly on the Australian grain trade. The last square-rigged ship in commercial operation, the *Omega*, was engaged in carrying guano to the mainland of Peru between the 1920s and her sinking in 1948: she had been built in 1887. More recent ships have also had long lives. The SS *France*, launched in 1960, was laid up in the 1970s but was then taken over, rebuilt and renamed *Norway*, becoming a huge success as a cruising ship. Indeed she pioneered modern cruising in specialist and large ships and remained in service until 2003, after a number of further important changes. The *QE2*, built in the late 1960s, is still going after major refits; it was given diesels instead of its original steam turbines in the mid-1980s, and had a big refit in the mid-1990s. In parts of the world some old locomotives were in use for long periods. The Shakuntala Express, which operates in a remote part of Maharashtra, was pulled by a steam engine built in Manchester in 1921, from 1923 to 1994.[41] In Uruguay one can still see on the roads a few American built motor cars of the 1920s; Cuba retains many US models from the 1950s, and extraordinary effort is made to maintain car batteries. London's Red Routemaster buses – first used in 1954 and in production till 1968 – were withdrawn from regular service in 2005 but are still used (though of course refurbished and re-engined) to ferry tourists on sightseeing tours of London. Malta has many British buses from the 1950s and 1960s on its roads. Many London Underground trains had lives of many decades, and London suburban services use rolling stock built in the early 1960s. A notable example was a type of underground train introduced in the late 1930s and not replaced until the 1970s. Even then, fifty-eight were given an 'extra-heavy overhaul' in the early 1970s; they were used to the mid-1980s on London underground, and some continued in service on the Isle of Wight into the 1990s. For nearly one hundred years an electric power station in Lots Road, Chelsea supplied the underground with electric power. The station opened in 1904, got new turbo-alternators in 1908–1910, in the early 1930s and again in 1963. These last sets remained in use until after 2001.[42]

Concorde provides another example. Having been in service for a quarter of a century, the Concorde fleet was grounded following a serious accident in July 2000. After important alterations on safety grounds, the fleet returned to service, with the expectation that it would be around for many more years. But, the reduction in air traffic following 9/11 2001, and the rise in the cost of spare parts, made operation unviable. In October 2003 the last Anglo-French Concorde commercial flight flew into Heathrow airport, riding a wave of technological nostalgia, an odd outcome for something so futuristic.

A correspondent to a British newspaper noted: 'Sadly, we are about to witness the premature death of Concorde, an aircraft whose structure still has no finite life.'[43] He meant of course that, with maintenance, the structure could be kept going indefinitely.

In many cases maintenance, refurbishment and overhaul have resulted in improvement over time. One case of particular interest is the improvement in efficiency of steam locomotives, the life work of an Argentine railway engineer, Livio Dante Porta.[44] He was able to increase the efficiency of existing steam engines, as were others using his ideas (for example in South Africa). Despite some investment in new designs for steam locomotives, prompted by the oil crisis of the 1970s, the move towards diesel and electric traction was too powerful for steam to compete.

## From maintenance to manufacture and innovation

Maintenance sometimes also means a significant remodelling as with battleships and bombers. Similarly, small-scale maintenance workshops could be and were used to change things, sometimes as soon as they were bought. For example, in the 1920s a Ford Model T buyer 'never regarded his purchase as a complete finished product. When you bought a Ford you figured you had a start – a vibrant, spirited framework to which could be screwed an almost limitless assortment of decorative and functional hardware.'[45] Many things could be bought by mail order, another great American invention, but the first thing E. B. White, the author of this recollection, did with his new car was to take it to a blacksmith to have brackets fitted to hold an army trunk. One could acquire everything from mirrors to devices to stop rattling. The United States itself has the most extreme forms of modification of cars. For some white males souped up 'hot-rod' cars are a passion, for 'chicanos' elaborate 'low-riders' with hydraulics to raise and lower the body and elaborate internal decoration are a product of a culture of 'customisation' of cars dating certainly to the 1940s, perhaps even the 1930s.[46] This process of remodelling and decorating cars, lorries and buses is common to many poor countries, from Mexico to Afghanistan to the Philippines. Surely nothing would have horrified Ford more.

There are many examples in the history of twentieth-century technology where enterprises started by maintaining a technology, moved on to manufacture components or the whole thing, and then to innovate. But equally there are others where maintenance did not lead to such a development. The case of railway locomotives is particularly interesting because the facilities needed to maintain and manufacture steam locomotives were essentially the same. Thus British railway workshops not only maintained but made engines. Since steam locomotives required intensive maintenance and repair, everywhere they operated they needed significant industrial facilities. In India, for example, a whole network of maintenance workshops had to be established. But, the Indian railway workshops did not, on the whole, develop manufacture, in order to reserve orders for British-based firms. Indeed, before the Second World War Indian engineering was largely concerned with maintenance.

A very different case is the Japanese bicycle industry. Bicycle production started in the repair shops for imported (largely British) bicycles. First replacement parts were made for imported cycles, then these parts were assembled into complete cheaper bicycles. Bicycles were made by a system of small-scale parts makers and small-scale assemblers, as well as some bigger integrated operations. In the 1920s the industry started exporting and by the 1930s exports accounted for half of all production. Exports went to China and South East Asia and were overwhelmingly of replacement parts (90 per cent) for British-made bicycles.[47] South East Asia was awash with semi-British, semi-Japanese bicycles, and indeed entirely Japanese copies of British bicycles. This extraordinary success, due to a flair for copying and the existence of vast numbers of small firms, is echoed down to the recent past, when Japanese firms still dominated the production of high-quality bicycle parts.

Another industry Japan found great success in, this time after the Second World War, also came out of repair workshops. In the radio industry in the early years after the war a majority of radio sets were made by small enterprises which were not subject to tax. These businesses were repair organisations at a time when repair and replacement of parts in radio sets was very common. Televisions were produced in kit form in the 1950s and often assembled by these repair shops. This close relationship, not wholly unique to Japan, was critical in establishing close links between producers and users.[48] Out of this came a new electronics industry after the Second World War.[49]

In some cases temporary shortages of imports led to repair organisations branching out into manufacture and even design. This happened in many countries during the Second World War, as industrial capacity was developed by imperial powers to produce armaments, and because many countries could no longer buy manufactures. For example, the Indian railway workshops started making armaments and that great Parsi enterprise, Tata Iron and Steel, greatly expanded its operations.[50] In South Africa, Australia, Argentina and many other places, the war led to great expansion in domestic production, often out of repair and maintenance facilities. There were notable cases after the war too. In Ghana the 'magazines' developed into centres for making things of all sorts at a time of severe shortage of imports from the 1970s. Among these products are two standard types of vehicle bodies made of wood – the 'trotro' or 'mammie wagon' passenger vehicle, based on a Bedford truck chassis, and the 'cocoa-truck' transport, based on a bigger chassis.[51] A nice example of a maintenance organisation turning to manufacture and innovation concerns the giant electric supply company for São Paulo in Brazil, the Companhia Energética de São Paulo, one of the largest such enterprises in Latin America. The electronics maintenance division was faced with an enormous problem in the 1980s and 1990s as economic crises led to restrictions on imports of the parts and equipment needed to maintain and replace existing equipment. They responded by devising alternative means of maintenance and devising new ways of controlling parts of the supply system.[52]

## Engineers and the maintenance of society

Although we separate people from things very readily, things cannot exist without maintenance. This imposes a particularly intimate relation with things, which goes well beyond use. To be able to maintain and repair involves different and often greater skills from operating (there are obvious counter-examples, for example the case of a concert pianist and a piano tuner). Few could maintain and repair things. The maintenance man is, however, widespread enough to be instantly recognised as one of the most common forms of technical expert. So much so that professional engineers in the USA and Britain resent the use of 'engineer' for such lowly figures as the TV repairman. Neither do professional engineers relish the association made between the engineer, the oily rag and the spanner, tools of the maintenance man. Professional engineering, they rightly insist, is something else. In recent time engineers have stressed their role in innovation, design and creation of new things. Engineers, in this view, are concerned above all with the future; they are optimistic and progressive; they send new things out into the world.

The image of the professional engineer as creator and reformer is as misleading as the conflation between him and the lowly repairman. Only a small minority of engineers are concerned with design and development, even among the most academically trained. A survey of professional Swedish engineers of 1980 noted that 72 per cent of them worked on the maintenance and supervision of existing things.[53] If most doctors and dentists maintain and repair human bodies, then similarly engineers are concerned with keeping things going, with diagnosis and repair of faults, as well as operations. It is little wonder that as the number of things to be kept going has increased, so has the number of professional engineers. Men who know about ships, buildings, machines, roads, canals, motor cars, have been needed more and more. Their number has increased much more than the population, and much more than the number of doctors, dentists and lawyers. In the United States today there are over 2 million engineers, double the number of either doctors or lawyers.

The extraordinary masculinity of engineering is related closely to what engineers do, not what they know. Expertise in things, whether in the home, or industry or in the fields has been deemed a masculine activity. Thus maintenance and repair have been an almost wholly masculine activity. It is the one domestic task at which men in rich countries devote more time than do women. There was one great exception to these trends and levels in the twentieth century, the Soviet Union, where it seems that a majority of engineers were women (as were the doctors). This hardly went unnoticed in the capitalist world, as can be seen from the comedy film *Ninotchka* (1939), directed by Ernst Lubitsch and written by Billy Wilder. Greta Garbo is Ninotchka, a dour Soviet engineer on a mission to Paris, where she is interested in the Eiffel Tower only from a technical point of view. She is converted to love, luxury and femininity by the class enemy, a French aristocrat, and does not, of course, go on to a career in engineering under capitalism.

That engineering is not primarily about creation and invention is also attested to by the case of state engineers. These men are concerned with the administration of state technologies. The model case is France with its tiny centralised elite corps of state engineers, though it has been replicated in Spain, Greece, Mexico and elsewhere. Among them were the state energy corps (*corps des mines*) or the state transport corps (*corps des ponts et chaussées*), and the many other lower-ranking technical and non-technical corps of the higher administration of the French state. First trained at the Ecole Polytechnique and then at the specialist schools for each corps – for example the Ecole des Mines and the Ecole des Ponts et Chaussées – these men were the dukes and barons of the state nobility. Under the fifth French Republic (1958–) in particular, these 'technocrats' became very important in politics as well as administration, a key case being President Valéry Giscard d'Estaing, a graduate of the Ecole Polytechnique and the ENA (the elite administrators' school). These were engineers concerned with the maintenance of the state. Giscard was a conservative. So was the 'great engineer' Herbert Hoover, President of the USA 1929–33, who was lost in the new world of the depression. Engineers were to be found on the Soviet politburo in the 1970s and 1980s: among them were Leonid Brezhnev and Boris Yeltsin. In 2005 all the members of the Chinese politburo were engineers.

# 5

# Nations

The celebration of the inventive citizen has been an important part of modern nationalism. This invention-chauvinism is, like nationalism, a global phenomenon. Curators of national traditions overestimated the significance of inventors that shared their particular nationality, overemphasised national connections, and made too much of the significance of making things first. 'No we do not have pasteurized milk in France, but we do have Pasteur', said a Frenchman to an American in the 1960s.[1] Juan de la Cierva (1895–1936) is regarded as one of the greatest Spanish inventors, but although he invented and developed the *autogiro* (a flying machine with rotating wings, a little like a helicopter) in Spain, he set up an enterprise in Britain. Or consider Ladislao José Biro (1899–1985), 'without doubt the most important Argentine inventor there has been'.[2] But the context for his invention of the ballpoint pen, or biro, was the increasingly anti-semitic Hungary from which László Jozsef Bíró emigrated in 1938. Famously, in its most nationalist phase, the Soviet Union was able to find Russian inventors for many important technologies, thus Alexander Stepanovitch Popov (1859–1906) invented radio.

In Britain, France and the United States people laughed too easily at what they saw as techno-nationalist excesses in other countries. For here too very similar excessively nationalistic emphases were at work – it would have been hard for a British person to know that radar, the jet engine or even television were not uniquely British inventions. The great technological and scientific museums of the rich world, such as the Science Museum in London, the Deutsches Museum in Munich and the Smithsonian Institution in Washington, are not replicas of each other, or complements, but in some senses competitors too. As a result of this emphasis on national inventiveness, the relations of nations and technology are particularly prone to being discussed in terms of invention and innovation.

Techno-nationalism takes other forms too, for example in claims that this or that country is best fitted for the technological age. The creation of new national identities suited for a technological age was happening around the world. There was hardly a nation that did not have intellectuals who thought his or her nation was best fitted for the 'air age'. Interwar French writers argued that as a vital and aesthetic people the French were particularly suited to be aviators.[3] Hitler thought war in the air was a particularly Germanic form of battle.[4] Sir Walter Raleigh, Professor of English at Oxford and official historian of the Great War in the air, claimed in the 1920s that Britain 'had a body of youth fitted by temperament for the work of the air, and educated, as if by design, to take risks with a light heart – the boys of the Public Schools of England'.[5] Soviet record-breaking pilots, dubbed 'Stalin's falcons', were closely associated with the 'New Man' and with Stalin himself.[6] The Russian-born aircraft manufacturer and propagandist Alexander de Seversky claimed that 'Americans are the natural masters of the aerial weapon ... more than any other people Americans are the natural children of the machine age'; 'Air power is the American weapon.'[7] Yet the inverse problem is just as significant: the attribution to *another* nation of extraordinary technological powers which elude one's own. For example, the feeling in Britain that Germany, then the United States and the Soviet Union, and latterly Japan, does technology better, and that there is always one country which does it best. Thus Lindberg's transatlantic flight of 1927 was hailed in Europe as well as America as evidence of the vigour of the New World.[8] Communists everywhere saw in 'Stalin's falcons' evidence of the superiority of Soviet society.[9] Fascists, and indeed some anti-fascists, saw Nazi

Germany and Italy as the nations best fitted to aviation. More recently Japan was widely regarded as the nation most suited to the electronic age. Individually such claims might seem credible, and have mislead many into thinking too nationalistically about technology, but collectively they contradict each other.

Techno-nationalism assumes that the key unit of analysis for the study of technology is the nation: nations are the units that invent, that have R&D budgets, cultures of innovation, that diffuse, that use technology. The success of nations, it is believed by techno-nationalists, is dependent on how well they do this. This techno-nationalism is implicit, not only in any number of national histories of technology, but also in many policy studies, for example of 'national systems of innovation'. Particular technologies are associated with particular nations. Cotton textiles and steam power are seen as British, chemicals as German, mass production as American, consumer electronics as Japanese.[10] This is despite the fact that all these countries were strong in all these technologies.

On the other hand, we have techno-globalism, particularly focused on communications technologies, which endlessly repeats the idea that the world is becoming a 'global village'. In this old-fashioned view nations are always about to disappear through the advance of globalising new technology. The steam ship, the aeroplane, the radio, and more recently television and the internet, it is argued, are forging a new global world economy and culture, and the nation is at best a temporary vehicle through which the forces of techno-globalism operate.

Nations are important in ways techno-nationalism cannot capture, and the international and global dimension is crucial in ways which techno-globalism is ignorant of. In any case, politics, multinational firms, empire and race were also crucial factors in shaping the use of technology which cut across the national and global divide in complex and changing ways. The nation and the state are central to the history of twentieth-century technology, but not in the ways the relations are usually understood.

## Techno-nationalism

Nationalism, that great hidden ideology of the twentieth century, has been thought of as a deviant notion compared to more acceptable, and seemingly less ideological, liberal and internationalist ideas. Nationalism is seen as an ideological throwback – like militarism and linked to it – a stirring up of supposedly ancient bonds of blood. It is a dangerous blast from the past. Not surprisingly, the linking of nationalism and technology has not been looked on favourably. Thus the term techno-nationalism is used by Western analysts primarily in relation to Japan and now China, to describe a potentially, perhaps actually, dangerous thing.

To suggest that techno-nationalism applies only to such countries would be a great mistake. Intellectuals were very nationalistic about science and technology, particularly in mid twentieth century, in nearly every nation. Indeed nationalism is not only present but very similar in many different nations. Every country had it, at much the same time and in much the same way, even though its central claim was for the uniqueness of each nation. One reason for this is suggested by Ernest Gellner's account of nationalism. For Gellner, nationalism was a way of adapting to a modern, industrial and globalising world. It was a global response to a global phenomenon. The idea is this: in a modern industrial society, where education, bureaucracy, information and communication mattered deeply, to be alienated from all this by linguistic and cultural barriers was intolerable. Hence these functions needed to be carried out in the language spoken by the people. Nationalism, which was something new, was thus vital to modernity. Nationalism in this sense is not a way of escaping from a globalised cosmopolitan modern world, but a means of participating in it while retaining one's dignity, and indeed creating one's capacity to participate.[11]

## National innovation and national growth

An implicit techno-nationalism is found in an extreme and widespread form in the assumption that *national* economic and technological

*15. A national technology. Mahatma Gandhi reading newspaper clippings next to a Charkha (spinning wheel), the great symbol of the Indian National Congress. The spinning wheel was re-introduced into India in the twentieth century as a result of a campaign led by Gandhi to promote 'production by the masses'.*

performance is determined by *national* rates of invention and innovation. It is there in the standard market failure argument, developed in the United States in the late 1950s, for state support of research. The argument was this: individuals in a society would not fund enough research because others could make use of the research just as much as the funder could. This is the famous 'free-rider' problem. The market failed, and thus government should step in to fund research, which would benefit everyone. Of course, states, including the US, supported research long before this argument was put forward, and of course would continue to do so for other reasons. Yet the argument worked only for a closed system, if each nation was insulated from every other one. For the free-rider problem would otherwise also apply to governments – why should the Indian government fund research that would equally be exploited by Pakistani, or US citizens? We should recognise of course that in the 1950s the US dominated world research and development, and thus could be thought of as a closed system.

This implicit techno-nationalism is also found in another justification for national funding of research (and development). It is the idea that to overtake rich countries a nation needs to invent and innovate more, and that if it does not it will descend to the level of the poorest countries. Even casting doubt on the role of *national* R&D can lead the analyst to be accused of being indifferent to their nation becoming like Bulgaria or Paraguay. In such arguments it is often first claimed that invention and innovation is of huge importance to other nations, and then that Britain, India or, say, Thailand spends much less on R&D than the United States and Japan. Thus Spaniards complain that Spain's share of invention has been lower than its share of population, and indeed production. But Spaniards compare themselves to the richest countries in the world, not the world as a whole.[12]

This innovation-centric techno-nationalist understanding is central to national histories of technologies. Historians and others have assumed that Germany and America grew fast in the early years of the twentieth century because of rapid national innovation. They also argued that the British 'decline' (that is slow growth) must have been associated with low innovation, indeed this 'decline' was itself taken as evidence of poor innovation. For example, a recent book on innovation and economic performance, most of it arranged in typical fashion in chapters based on *nations*, expresses surprise that in the case of Japan recent economic performance has not been on a par with the country's huge R&D spending, which is second only to that of the USA in scale.[13] In the 1990s crude versions of endogenous growth theory, which claimed that inputs such as R&D led to growth, globally and nationally, flourished.

So powerful has this innovation-centric view been, especially in its nationalistic versions, that all evidence to the contrary has been studiously ignored. It was known in the 1960s that national rates of economic growth did not correlate positively with *national* investments in invention, research and development, or innovation. It has *not* been the case that countries that innovate a lot, grow a lot. Take, for example, Italy and the United Kingdom. Each was very different in 1900 but not so different in 2000. In the 1980s Italy overtook the United Kingdom in output per head, a shock the Italians named *il sorpasso*. That these countries, such opposites in the usual estimations of national character, had now reached the same level of income per head was unsettling on both sides. In the techno-nationalist world it was literally incredible that Italy had become richer than Great Britain, while spending much *less* on R&D than Britain did. Italian scientists and engineers and research policy experts had long complained that Italy was by no measure a great centre of innovation; it has very few Nobel prizes (one is for the polymerisation of the plastic polypropylene), and its expenditure on R&D has been low by the standards of rich countries. In Britain, so peculiar are the politics of technology that it has been claimed that Italy was spending more on R&D than Britain in order to square this particular circle. What one does not find is the acceptance that Italy has been brilliantly successful in that with little R&D, it has become as rich as Britain.

It is important to stress that this is not a unique case. Spain was one of the most successful European economies in terms of rates of growth in the 1980s and 1990s, and yet this is a country which spends less than 1 per cent of GDP on R&D. It had much less of a historical track record in industry and technology than Italy: it is a '*sistema tecnológico que progresa sin innovar*'. [14] The most spectacularly fast-growing economies in world history have been those of some Asian countries, such as Malaysia, Taiwan, Korea, and most recently and significantly of all, given its size, China. While China has transformed itself and flooded the world with manufactures, the much more innovative Japanese economy has been, by comparison, stagnant. Moreover, while national R&D expenditures have increased in the rich countries in recent decades, economic growth rates have dropped below those found in the long boom.

To add further to these seeming paradoxes, the two countries which both grew very fast and had high and increasing R&D expenditure in the twentieth century, the Soviet Union and Japan, were not especially innovative. The Soviet case is particularly stunning. It spent 2.9 per cent of GNP on R&D in the late 1960s, the same as the USA, and spent more than America in the early 1970s. The number of Soviet scientists and engineers in R&D, in absolute numbers, overtook the US total in the very late 1960s, giving the USSR the largest R&D workforce in the world.[15] Yet it is regarded, perhaps unfairly, as having contributed practically nothing novel to modern industry. Japan did better than the Soviet Union after the Second World War, but its record of innovation is felt, again perhaps unfairly, not to be congruent with huge R&D expenditures.

How can we make sense of this? What general rules are there? Firstly, there is a broad rule that richer countries spend a higher proportion of their output on R&D than poor ones. There are exceptions to this: for example, Italy in recent decades was rich but spent little; the USSR, while very poor, spent as much or more than the richest countries. Secondly, the relationship does not necessarily hold over time: as rich countries got slowly richer in the 1980s and 1990s, the proportion of national income spent on R&D remained broadly static, and in some cases fell. There is a second general rule of thumb, again with important exceptions, that the fastest-growing countries are not the richest. The slowest-growing were already rich. The fastest-growing countries in the twentieth century have been poor countries, which spent very little on innovation. Thus taking these two general rules together we can conclude that rich, slow-growing countries spend a lot more on R&D than fast-growing poor ones.

Why does the techno-nationalist assumption about innovation and growth not hold? The link between innovation and use, and thus economic performance, is far from straightforward. Yet the techno-nationalist assumption implies that the things a nation uses derive from its own invention and innovation, or at the very least that innovating nations have early leads in the technologies they innovate. Yet the site of innovation is not always the major site of even early use of the technology. In the case of the motor car, Germany, where the internal-combustion-powered motor car was invented, was not the main early producer of cars in the first twenty years of the industry. The USA became easily the dominant producer by 1914, and Germany remained less motorised than other rich countries for many decades. The powered aeroplane was innovated in the USA by the Wright brothers in 1903 but Britain, France and Germany had much larger air fleets by 1914. As we shall see, photography and television are other examples.

More significantly, national use of technology is hardly dependent on national innovation. Most technologies are shared across national boundaries; nations acquire more new technology from abroad than they innovate themselves. Italy did not have to invent afresh the technology it used, just as Britain did not either. Both were sharing in a global pool, as was every country in the world. One can make this clearer by looking around one's immediate surroundings and asking about the origins of the things one can see; nowhere in the world would more than a small minority be local. Thus it is unfair to complain that of seventy-five major technologies in use in the Soviet Union through much of its history, five were of Soviet origin and ten of joint Soviet origin.[16] One needs to specify the comparator, and to recognise that for most countries, even the richest and most innovative, the proportions may well have been similar.

The concept of technological sharing is an important one. Yet its importance in the history of the twentieth century is obscured by thinking about the movement of technologies across national boundaries in terms of technology *transfer* from technological leaders to others. The term was first used to describe the export of modern technologies to poor countries. Transfer in this sense is much less significant than the movement of technologies between rich countries. The two-way movements between British and France in the twentieth century have been much more significant than those between Britain and India. This is not to deny the importance of movements across technological boundaries. Indeed one of the most important features of the twentieth-century world economy has been the convergence of certain countries on one technological level. The rich countries of the world are much closer in all economic measures than they were in 1900. These countries have borrowed from each other and perhaps most from a particular technological leader which set the highest level. Italy, Spain, Japan, the USSR and now China have been imitating foreign technologies on a huge scale, and this has been an essential aspect of their rapid economic growth.

There is one very special case in this story of convergence among the richest nations. In the nineteenth century the USA did not catch up with Europe in terms of productivity, it shot ahead. Through the twentieth century it remained ahead, with, in the middle of the century, productivity levels at least twice as great as that of the European industrial giants. This lead did not come from dominance in 'pure science' or even 'industrial research' – in 1900 America was the leader in neither. Where historians have claimed to find US distinctiveness and a particular surge in innovation is in production technology – the sort of thing which led to mass production. Yet, the evidence for the centrality of US invention in this area is not as strong as nationalistic analyses of American technology would have us believe. There were extraordinary flows of technological know-how across the Atlantic in the late nineteenth and early twentieth centuries.[17] By mid-century however, the USA was a clear leader in industrial research and innovation by any standard: it dominated both world production and world innovation. As such it was wholly atypical, and exactly the sort of case where we would expect technologies to derive from national innovation. Only perhaps in the exceptional case of the United States after the Second World War might locally innovated products have registered strongly. Many studies show that US innovation promoted US growth – the mistake was to believe that this applied to other countries too, and that the rate of growth in America was particularly high.

We may conclude, then, that global innovation may be the main determinant of global economic growth, but it does not follow that this is the case for particular nation states. Since national innovation has not been the main source of national technique, it should not be at all surprising that there is no clear positive relationship between national innovation and national rates of growth. Global technological sharing, between rich countries and between rich and poor, has been the norm. Should we, then, discard techno-nationalism, and think techno-globally?

## Techno-globalism

While techno-nationalism has been a core assumption in much thinking about the nation-state and technology in the twentieth century, there has also been a techno-globalism which claimed the globe as the key unit of analysis. It often looked forward to technology eliminating the nation-state, which it regarded as an outmoded organisation. Most techno-globalism has been innovation-centric, and it is this kind of techno-globalism which has been at the heart of any number of histories of the world, the musings of information society gurus, and many a portentous address about science and technology. It has been claimed that the world has been going through a process of globalisation as a result of the latest technologies, for well over a century.

In the late nineteenth century the steam-ship, the railway and the telegraph reached across and into the world which was, with justification, seen as interconnected as never before. Yet that globalisation was ignored when claims for new technologies of globalisation were being made just a little later. Thus in the 1920s Henry Ford in *My Philosophy of Industry* claimed that

Machinery is accomplishing in the world what man has failed to do by preaching, propaganda, or the written word. The aeroplane and wireless know no boundary. They pass over the dotted lines on the map without heed or hindrance. They are binding the world together in a way no other system can. The motion picture with its universal language, the aeroplane with its speed, and the wireless with its coming international programme – these will soon bring the world to a complete understanding. Thus may we vision a United States of the World. Ultimately it will surely come![18]

For Henry Ford, 'The motor-car has done for the United States what the aeroplane and wireless may do for the world.'[19] Twenty years later the Canadian Air Marshal and Great War air ace Billy Bishop claimed that 'The horse and buggy developed purely local geographical cultures. Railway trains and motor cars developed nationalism.' This begs the question, of course, when the age of the train and the motor car was, but in this innovation-centric account, it was passing. With the aeroplane came the necessity, as Bishop saw it, for 'the establishment of *world* culture, a *world* view of the responsibilities of citizenship ... The Air Age must bring us entirely new concepts of citizenship, of national and international relations.' The choice was between 'Winged Peace or Winged Death'.[20]

H. G. Wells was one of the great propagandists for this kind of thinking. In the *Shape of Things to Come: The Ultimate Revolution* (1933) airmen bring peace and civilisation to a war-devastated world.[21] Wells imagined a Conference in 1965 of scientific and technical workers in Basra, Iraq. It was organised by the Transport Union, which brought together surviving aeroplane and sea transport, and used as its language the Basic English of the aviators.[22] As a result there was central control of the airways, with an air force to enforce peace. The unit of currency was the air dollar.[23] The Air and Sea Control and the Police of the Air and Seaways were owned by the Modern State Society, made up of qualified fellows. In 1978 they decided to put down the re-emerging national governments' opposition with a new gas called Pacificin. Wells was not alone in putting forward these ideas. In the early 1930s there were all sorts of suggestions for the creation of an 'international air police' along these lines, and similar thinking continued into the 1940s, usually with the British and Americans as that international police force. In more recent years the atomic bomb, television and above all the internet and the world-wide web have featured in this kind of techno-globalism. As we have seen, it was generally the older technologies which were crucial to global relations – today's globalisation is in part the result of extremely cheap sea and air transport, and radio and wire-based communication.

Historically aware and more knowledgeable commentators could not stomach this kind of stuff. In 1944 George Orwell noted the repetitiveness in the claims:

> Reading recently a batch of rather shallowly optimistic 'progressive' books, I was struck by the automatic way people go on repeating certain phrases which were fashionable before 1914. Two great favourites are the 'abolition of distance' and the 'disappearance of frontiers'. I do not know how often I have met with statements that 'the aeroplane and the radio have abolished distance' and 'all parts of the world are now interdependent'.

But Orwell criticised not only the historical amnesia involved. He claimed there was a quite different relationship between technology and world history. 'Actually,' he claimed, 'the effect of modern inventions has been to increase nationalism, to make travel enormously more difficult, to cut down the means of communication between one country and another, and to make various parts of the world *less*, not more dependent on one another for food and manufactured goods.'[24] He was thinking about what had been happening since 1918, and particularly since the early 1930s. His was a powerful and defensible argument.

The great era of global trade had ended in 1914. In the interwar years trade stagnated and fell, and especially in the 1930s nation-states all over the world became increasingly autarkic. In the middle of the twentieth century the world was much less globalised than it had previously been, and would be at the end of the century. There was a profound nationalisation. There was also a powerful move to turn political empires into trading blocs to a degree unknown before. Innovation-centred political history puts the great age of nationalism in the nineteenth and early twentieth centuries; the age of imperialism is placed between the 1870s and the First World War. Yet empire accounted for a greater proportion of trade in the 1930s, 1940s and 1950s than it did in the pioneering days of the new imperialism. Nationalism was at least as important in the middle of the twentieth century as it had been earlier. And, as Orwell noted, science and technology were key tools of autarky, the policy of national economic self-sufficiency in the 1930s and 1940s. He pointed in particular to the role of the aeroplane and the radio in bolstering this new and dangerous nationalism. In other words, the very technologies that were at the heart of the naïve techno-globalism vision of an interconnected world were the tools of a new national despotism.

One can go much further than Orwell did in ironically inverting the claims of innovation-centric techno-globalist propaganda. For many of the technologies invoked as being somehow essentially internationalising were profoundly national in origin and use. Radio, which had a military origin, was intimately connected to national power. The development of the radio before the Great War was intimately tied to navies – indeed the Royal Navy was the largest single customer for the Marconi Company, which led the world in radio. During and after the Great War, radio and the military remained closely connected; the Radio Corporation of America, for example, was closely tied to the US state.[25]

More stunningly still, the aeroplane was primarily a weapon of war, even in peacetime. Far from threatening to transcend the nation, it was the product of a system of competing nation-states and empires. In peace as in war, the aircraft industry was utterly dependent on the patronage of the military. In peacetime some three-quarters of the output of all the main aircraft industries in the world went to the military. In the interwar years air forces had hundreds of aircraft, airlines tens. Since then, too, the military continue to dominate aircraft industry sales. Yet, to this day histories of technology treat aviation under transportation; histories of aviation are really histories of civil aviation, and technical development is seen as driven by civil transportation needs. Histories of the aircraft-producing industry also overemphasise the significance of the production of civil aircraft; accounts of the industry in peacetime are accounts of the production of civil aircraft.[26]

But radio and the aeroplane were not the only cases. The atomic bomb was also the product of a world of competing states. So too was the internet, born of US military needs and funding. Many other great technologies of the twentieth century were technologies of autarky and militarism. Oil-from-coal, many synthetic fibres and synthetic rubber are just a sample of the technologies which would not have survived in a global liberal free market. They were the product of the particular state system which operated to force nations into certain relations with each other. The very specific role of the state, and the specific nature of its competition with other states, has given *states* particular roles in the promotion of *particular* technologies. Even techno-nationalists have not recognised the centrality of the state system to twentieth-century technology. Techno-national projects were of the greatest importance, though their histories are not to be found in techno-nationalist writings.

## Autarky and things

Political and technological boundaries are different, but states have often acted to bring them into line, by controlling the movement of things across borders and by developing particular national technologies. They have controlled the movement of things by tariffs, quotas and nationalistic procurement policies. They have developed national technologies by insulating the nation from the rest of the world, and by the direct funding of national innovation programmes. This practical technological nationalism has had wonderfully contradictory effects – far from making national technologies different, it has encouraged movement of technologies across political boundaries. It has also helped impoverish nations rather than strengthen them.

In the histories of some nations, autarky became an explicit political economic programme, with the term itself being used by political actors, and historians have had no trouble in using it too. The most obvious and important cases are Italy under fascism, Nazi Germany, and Francoist Spain, where the period of *autarquía* lasted to 1959. Government protected industry, they engaged in import substitution, they promoted strategic industries, linked to the military, and the state often had great control over domestic industry, sometimes through specialist bodies such as Mussolini's IRI (Industrial Reconstruction Institute), and its Spanish variant established in 1941, the Instituto Nacional de Industria.[27] The Soviet and Chinese blocs were also autarkic. Indeed, autarky was to become most extreme in nations which were isolated from the capitalist world and the socialist blocs. In North Korea *Juche* (self-reliance) was pursued from the 1960s when the country was isolated from both China and the USSR. Albania relied on the Soviet Union until 1960 and on China thereafter, but became increasingly autarkic from the early 1970s, and especially from 1978 when China removed all support.

In the middle years of the century many more countries were autarkic. Throughout the world, countries sought to industrialise, to replace imports with domestic goods, produced by local companies. Among the countries that turned to autarky was that previously enthusiastic champion of free trade, Britain. Greece, the great commercial centre of the eastern Mediterranean, hardly known for manufacturing, also turned to autarky, under Metaxas in the 1930s. Often war elsewhere was crucial, forcing autarkic development to replace imports that were no longer available. Virtue was made of these necessities, for example in Argentina under General Perón, where national industrial development became a central policy of the regime. Similarly, India, South Africa and Australia developed new industries in this period.

Autarky was supported by elements of the left, as well as the right. In the 1960s Latin American dependency theorists complained that under free trade nations exported raw materials while even their most basic manufactures were imported; they attacked their own countries as places which made nothing, invented nothing, which were for ever subservient to the metropolis. Breaking away from the world market, and developing national industries was essential to development and to independence. The European left too, at least in part, wanted to promote national industrial development strategies, and thus rejected free trade and indeed the European Common Market.

## Hydrogenation

At the beginning of the twentieth century a French chemist, Henri Sabatier, showed that metal catalysts could be used to make possible the hydrogenation (the chemical addition of hydrogen) of many compounds, organic and inorganic. Three uses of hydrogenation turned out to be particularly important: the manufacture of margarine, ammonia and petrol. All three processes produced substitutes for older products: ammonia was used to make nitrates, replacing nitrate from Chilean guano deposits; petrol made from coal replaced that distilled from petroleum; margarine made from hydrogenated fats and oils substituted for butter and other forms of margarine. All three were to be closely connected to the national question in the twentieth century.

The hydrogenation of nitrogen to make ammonia, pioneered by the German chemical firm BASF before and during the Great War, was of enormous importance to national power, not only because it created locally produced nitrogen fertiliser, but also because nitrate was a major source of explosives. In 1913 BASF began production at Oppau of synthetic ammonia, and a new plant was built at Leuna in 1917. Coke, steam and air were the raw materials. In the war Oppau developed and operated the process for making nitrate from ammonia. No great power, it seemed, could be without 'synthetic ammonia', and governments sought to develop the Haber-Bosch and other processes (for there were a number of alternative ways of making synthetic fertilisers). In Britain, for example, synthetic ammonia, became central to the new enterprise, Imperial Chemical Industries, founded in 1926, taking over an initially state-sponsored project to make synthetic ammonia and nitrates at Billingham. Yet synthetic nitrogen fertiliser (mostly, but not only Haber-Bosch) was to become extraordinarily global, and indeed an industry of profound importance, particularly after the Second World War. Nitrate was poured on to the world's fields after 1945, so much so that, by the end of the century, some one-third of the nitrogen in human food came from human-made nitrate.

Perhaps the most important use of hydrogenation in terms of its national associations was the hydrogenation of coal. In the rich countries of the world, coal was the dominant source of energy of the first half of the twentieth century. Yet, very quickly petroleum became important as a source of power for cars, trucks and aeroplanes (petrol) and ships (diesel and fuel oil). The leading western European nations did not have their own sources of supply – the main producers were the USA, Russia, Romania and Mexico. The German chemist Friedrich Bergius developed processes for making cheap hydrogen from coal; he then hydrogenated heavy oils, and in 1913, coal. Bergius started building a plant in Rheinau in 1915, to produce his oil-from-coal. This massive project was embarked on because Germany was about to become fatally short of petrol for the war effort. But Germany and Austria defeated Romania in 1916, and were thus able to secure access to its huge petroleum production. The lengthy and hugely expensive Rheinau enterprise was not completed before 1924. It was financed by various private firms, including Royal Dutch Shell and then BASF. IG Farben (a merger of the main German chemical firms including BASF) developed a variant of Bergius, with different catalysts and started building a plant at Leuna in 1927 (where it had hydrogen capacity for synthetic ammonia production). This ambitious new project brought together the main German chemical companies in the 1920s. By 1931 300,000 tons of petroleum were being produced (or in oil terminology, 2.5 million barrels) per annum.

For the Nazis, self-sufficiency in fuel was a top priority under the four-year plan of 1936, and the establishment of synthetic-oil production was a key element towards the achievement of that objective.

Hermann Goering was appointed 'fuel commissar'. The process chosen was IG's hydrogenation, and the company built and ran many plants, including one for the new coal-based chemical complex at Auschwitz. As ever there were alternatives, and indeed the Fischer-Tropsch process, involving the hydrogenation of carbon monoxide rather than coal was also used. Other alternatives included generators of gas from wood for powering cars.[28] By 1944 production was up to 3 million tons, or 25.5 million barrels annually. These synthetic oil plants were extremely important to the German fuel economy during the war, and particularly so in the production of aviation fuel.

After it was defeated, Germany was banned from hydrogenating and in 1949 was ordered to dismantle its plants. The Soviet Union took four to Siberia. Later in 1949 the decision was changed and the plants were converted to cracking petroleum. In East Germany, isolated from western oil markets, coal was hydrogenated until the 1960s.[29] The chemical industry remained coal-based until increased shipments of petroleum from the USSR arrived in the 1950s. With the restriction of Soviet oil exports after 1979, there was a shift back to coal during the 1980s, another case of reappearance, with dire ecological consequences as the German brown coal generated a good deal of acid rain.[30]

Coal hydrogenation was taken to many countries, but it never went global. In an autarkic age, technologies of autarchy internationalised. By the early 1920s the key patents were controlled by IG Farben in Germany, but the international rights in the early 1930s were controlled jointly by IG Farben, Standard Oil of the USA, the Anglo-Dutch oil company Royal Dutch Shell and the British chemical combine ICI. In Britain and the United States plants were built. In Britain ICI, taking over a good deal of work done in a government research station, set up a plant in Billingham which produced petrol between 1935 and 1958. As in Germany, the petrol produced had to be subsidised by various means. Spain developed a synthetic-fuel programme at Puertollano (Ciudad Real) following a 1944 deal between the pro-Axis Spanish government and Germany. In 1950 new deals were signed with BASF and others for technology and plant was built.[31] Production started in 1956 and lasted until 1966. Spain had a hugely expensive R&D programme in the late 1940s and early 1950s, reaching 0.5 per cent of GDP, a remarkable proportion for a poor country of the period.[32]

Another case was coal-rich South Africa where in 1955 the Sasol company started producing petrol using the Fischer-Tropsch process. Following the Arab oil embargo of 1973, Sasol II was built; the cutting off of supplies from Iran after that country's 1979 revolution led to Sasol III.[33] Like the German plants, the Sasol complex was bombed, not by the United Nations, but in June 1980 by Umkhonto we Sizwe (Spear of the Nation), the armed wing of the African National Congress. The attack marked a very important point in the development of the guerrilla war against the apartheid regime. Racist South Africa, run by its National Party, produced 150,000 barrels per day, twice the level of synthetic fuel production in Nazi Germany.[34] Oil-from-coal research started up again on a large scale in the 1970s, as the price of oil increased in 1973 and 1979, and looked to stay high. The oil companies and governments were involved once again, and sought out the records of the earlier Nazi effort.

In the history of research and development coal hydrogenation should have a very important place. It was the biggest single project of the world's greatest chemical firm of the 1920s and 1930s, IG Farben, and of Britain's ICI in the late 1920s and early 1930s, as well as post-war Spain, and South Africa. Yet it never produced petrol which could compete in world markets. As a source of petrol it was of minor importance, except in the special cases of Nazi Germany and South Africa. In both places it was significant to history. It kept the Luftwaffe flying and apartheid in business.

### The nation is not everything

Technology, like nationalism, crosses national borders; it does so in times and contexts we might not expect from national histories. For example, in nationalistic, totalitarian, autarkic, fascist Italy of 1935, there were places better connected technologically to the United States than to the rest of Italy. A case in point was the village of Aliano in what is now called Basilicata; there were 1,200 inhabitants, one car, one toilet, and far too many malaria-carrying mosquitoes.[35] Yet the mechanical equipment of the village was American; its weights and measures the pounds and inches of the Anglo-Saxons, rather than the kilogrammes and centimetres of continental Europe. The women wove on ancient looms, but used scissors from Pittsburgh; the axe blades of the peasants came from America.[36] How come? Some 2,000 men from Aliano lived in the US and sent home a 'stream of scissors, knives, razors, farm tools, scythes, hammers, pincers ... all the gadgets of everyday life'. The carpenters of Grassano, a larger and richer town, had American machinery.[37] Connections between peoples did not follow the boundaries of nation-states, and had a consequence for the traffic in things.

More remarkable is the case of military technology after the Second World War. Despite the Cold War and intense national efforts to develop national technology, in the 1950s the USA, Britain and the Soviet Union shared a remarkable amount of technology, aside from captured German technology. The multinational atomic bomb project became more multinational still, not because of scientific or technological internationalism, but because of espionage by *political* internationalists. They helped ensure that the Soviet Union made a near copy of the plutonium bomb in 1949.[38] Britain's bomb, tested in 1952, also replicated the Los Alamos plutonium bomb. The first atomic bomber of these three powers was the same one too: in the early 1950s, all three were using the Boeing B-29. Britain was loaned them by the USA between 1950 and 1954. The USSR had a fleet of Tu 4s, copies of B-29s forced down on Soviet territory during the war. In addition British Nene and Derwent jet engines (and also copies) powered Soviet jet aircraft, notably the MiG15s over the skies of Korea (the transfer was authorised in 1946).[39] Indeed, the Nene engine was everywhere.

After the Second World War a remarkable range of countries decided they needed not only to acquire jet fighters, and to manufacture them, but to design them. Many of the experts came from

*16. One of three passenger, cargo and refrigerated meat liners built in Britain for a newly nationalised Argentine merchant line in the late 1940s. They were named* Eva Perón *(shown here in trials on the Clyde, and the ship on which the author travelled to Britain in 1970),* President Perón *and* 17 de Octubre. *After the fall of Perón they were renamed* Libertad, Argentina *and* Uruguay. *The* Libertad *was in service on the Buenos Aires to Europe route into the early 1970s, before switching to Antarctic cruises.*

Germany, which was banned from having an aircraft industry. Its aeronautical engineers, including the most famous, went not only to the USA or the USSR but to such countries as Spain, Argentina, India and the United Arab Republic. These nations were at different periods and for different reasons 'non-aligned' with the two great power blocs of the post-war era – the Soviet Union and the USA. Argentina, India and Egypt, the main part of the United Arab Republic, had been to different degrees British imperial territories, and in all three German aeronautical expertise was used more than British.

Under the nationalist-populist Perón regime, Argentina built a jet fighter, the *Pulqui*, which first flew in 1947. The name meant 'arrow' in the indigenous language, Mapuche, a sure sign of the nationalist impulse behind it. It was built under the leadership of one of France's great aeronautical engineers, Emile Dewoitine, on the run from France, where he was wanted for collaboration.[40] He had arrived in Argentina in 1946, via Spain where he had gone after the liberation of France, and would stay in Argentina till the late 1960s.[41] He was to be replaced in 1947 by an even more famous designer, Kurt Tank (1898–1983), the key designer at Focke-wulf. Tank had nearly gone to the Soviet Union. He had met with one of the Soviet aeronautical experts, Colonel Grigory Tokaev, who claimed to have put him off from journeying to Moscow to see Stalin. Tokaev would soon defect to the British, partly because he was unhappy with the Russian nationalism that Stalin was imposing.[42] From 1947 Tank designed and built the *Pulqui II* jet, which flew, with Nene engines, in 1950. It was, like the Soviet MiG15, descended from Tank's Ta 183. The *Pulqui II* never went into production and Tank and much of his team moved on to India. There they designed the supersonic Hindustan *Marut* fighter, in service from the 1960s to the 1980s: over 140 were built. This too depended on a British engine. India later collaborated with that failed pan-Arabic nation, the United Arab Republic (UAR), of Egypt, Syria and Yemen to design aero-engines for their national fighters. Again German expertise was central.

The UAR aircraft programme had started in Spain.[43] Spain saw autarkic development in aviation, in the 1940s and 1950s, again with German specialists.[44] Claude Dornier (1884–1969) worked for the CASA company in Madrid, designing light utility aircraft for the military, also later to be built in Germany. Willy Messerschmitt (1898–1978) went to Spain in 1951. First he developed a jet trainer, which could also be used in combat, and a good number were built. Egypt started producing them in the 1950s and some were still in service in the 1980s (they were called *Al-Khahira* (Cairo)).[45] Messerschmitt (with the collaboration of Ernst Heinkel) also built the H300 supersonic fighter which never went into production, and was further developed by the Egyptians through the 1960s, without success. It too depended on British engines. These non-aligned technologies proved not to be very significant. Spain obtained US aircraft from the early 1950s; and Egypt and India turned to the USSR, as well as other suppliers.

### Foreign technology and socialism in one country

The Soviet Union provides a particularly startling case of autarkic development based on foreign technology. Socialism in one country, the central dogma of Stalinism, depended on foreign expertise. The Soviet Union, and thus the rest of the Soviet bloc (including China for a while), relied on processes, and sometimes in effect products, first developed in the capitalist countries, particularly in the USA. Ford was one of many companies that transferred their equipment, skills, personnel and products there. The USSR not only imported but built Fordson tractors, as it did Ford's Model A cars, and Model AA trucks. The tractors were produced in a plant in Kirov reconditioned by Ford, the cars and trucks in a large plant built in Gorky. The result of a deal signed with Ford in 1929, it was easily the largest vehicle plant in the USSR, producing nearly 70 per cent of output by the end of the 1930s, around 450,000 vehicles per annum. The Gorky plant is still the second Russian producer of cars, and the largest maker of trucks and buses.[46] There were two other plants for cars and trucks. The AMO factory in Moscow, rebuilt with US equipment, renamed ZIS and then ZIL, made cars and trucks to US designs. This plant was the parent of the Chinese First Automotive Works, formed in 1953, which made 1.28 million Jiefang (Liberation) trucks between 1956 and 1986, another remarkably long-lived machine which was itself a copy of the ZIL 150 4-ton truck.[47]

Apart from the production of Fordson tractors between 1928 and 1933, the USSR bought two entire new tractor factories from the USA, one for Stalingrad, the other for Kharkov, to make International Harvester 15/30 machines. This was the tractor which had replaced the Fordson on American farms. A third new factory made the tracked Caterpillar 60, called the Stalinets, in Cheliabinsk. Counting the Fordson plant, the USSR had four plants by the mid-1930s, each meant to produce 30–50,000 tractors per annum.[48] The USSR was to be tractorised with American-designed tractors.

The other great symbols of Stalinism also depended on American expertise. Many of the gigantic dams and hydro-electric projects, such as the Dnieper complex, depended on US experts, skilled workers, designs for plants and product, and vast quantities of equipment. The famous steel works at Magnitogorsk, built partly by kulaks thrown off their farms at the time of collectivisation, was a copy of a US Steel Corporation plant. At the peak of construction in 1931 there were 250 Americans, plus other foreigners, directing the work at Magnitogorsk, just as there were in many other places.[49] The US plant was built from 1906 in Indiana on a greenfield site near Chicago named Gary, after Elbert Gary, the then chairman of US Steel. Thus even the naming of factories and cities after important people had roots in the USA.

During the Second World War there was a wave of transfer of technology, though not of production equipment. After the war there was a second wave, covering everything from marine diesels and fishing boats, to the chemical industry. In the 1960s the USSR once more turned to the West for car models and plant. A deal with FIAT led to the supply of (largely American) plant for a huge new complex that would produce versions of the Fiat 124 and 125 at the rate of 600,000 per annum from around 1970. The resulting model, called the Lada in export markets, is still being produced today. The plant remains the largest car maker in Russia, churning out around 700,000 cars a year – at less than half the level of productivity of the main international firms. It was built in a new town on the banks of the Volga named Togliattigrad and was part of a giant scheme involving the building of the Lenin Dam on the Volga. The town was named after the head of the Italian Communist Party, Palmiro Togliatti, who had succeeded the intellectual Antonio Gramsci, as leader. Both had studied and become politically active in Turin, home of FIAT; an essay written in prison by Gramsci was to be the source of the term 'Fordism' for the left at the end of the twentieth century.

The Soviet Union was a poor country. The rate at which it took in foreign technology and industrialised itself was remarkable, as of course was the human cost it was forced to pay by Stalin. Its ambition was not merely to emulate, but to create a new and superior society, more innovative and more capable of using new technologies than crisis ridden, uncoordinated capitalism. The planned economies, with no significant private ownership, and no competition from capitalist enterprises for very long periods, would prove superior, it was claimed. From 1957, following the launch of Sputnik, many non-communists, indeed anti-communists in the West, came to believe that the Soviet Union had indeed cracked the problem of innovation and use of new technology. Khrushchev's famous declaration in the early 1960s that the Soviet Union would overtake capitalism was not a personal exaggeration but an expression of a long-standing and deeply felt interpretation of the likely course of history. Yet despite vast investments in R&D the Soviet Union and its satellites did not lead the world into a new technological era. Generally the Soviet Union lagged, and that lag increased in the 1970s and 1980s. The Soviet historian Roy Medvedev plausibly claimed that Lenin would have been surprised to find that the USSR had not overtaken the capitalist world in technology by the 1980s.

The classical Soviet view was that there was one technology, what mattered was the context in which it operated. It made all the difference in the world, they claimed, that although Soviet workers worked under the same division of labour as capitalist workers and were paid by the piece, they (indirectly) owned the means of production. Yet one finds some suggestions that Soviet technology took a different course from capitalist technology. Notably, it is argued that there was a particular tendency towards gigantism, the most recent expression of which is the Three Gorges dam in China. That seems doubtful as similarly gigantic projects can be found in the USA; indeed the Soviets were inspired by them. However, there may well have been much more pointless gigantism, such as the famous case of the White Sea Canal, extending for over 200km from Leningrad to the White Sea. Though built in the early 1930s, and still open, it has hardly been used. It took more than 100,000 workers to build. Most were convicts, and most of them apparently died during its construction.

After 1945 the most technically advanced part of the Soviet bloc was not the Soviet Union but the German Democratic Republic. And from here came 'group technology', trumpeted as a specifically socialist technology. It involved the grouping of work of particular types of machine in batch production to increase its efficiency. The idea was to analyse components and set up groups of machines (cells) to produce a range of related components. Group technology was not a thing, but a means of organising specific forms of production, and one which turned out to be completely compatible with capitalism. The technological leadership it was hoped would derive from this never materialised.[50] The GDR is also known for a distinctive car, the Trabant, another exceptionally long-lived machine. It had a synthetic body, and a 2-stroke 500cc engine. It was in production in the same factory from 1957 to 1989; around 3 million were built, with maximum output of 100,000 units per annum in 1970s.[51] Yet it was not copied even within the Soviet bloc. It was clearly a particular response to all sorts of shortages of materials, not a brave new venture in car technology. The GDR also provides one of the few cases where it has been shown that a planned system clearly led to rapid diffusion of technology: the GDR's health system pioneered the widespread use of a Swiss technique for dealing with broken bones.[52]

## Nations versus firms

The greatest transnational institutions of the twentieth century were not the Second, Third or Fourth Internationals of the socialists and communists, or bodies such as the League of Nations or the United Nations. They were firms which operated in more than one nation – the so-called 'multinationals' – and among them were most of the world's largest firms. Not only do some of them have larger turnovers than some small states, but many were founded, and operated multinationally, before the majority of modern nation-states were formed.

Even before the First World War, Ford, the Chicago meatpackers, the major electrical firms such as GE, Westinghouse and Siemens, major armourers such as Vickers, and the Singer Sewing Machine company operated around the world.

The technological capacities of firms, national and multinational, need to be distinguished from those of their home nation. The photographic industry exemplifies the need to look at firms and their histories. At the end of the nineteenth century, knowledge about the photographic process was concentrated in Europe, and yet by 1914 a US company, Eastman Kodak, dominated photography in most countries of the world. Kodak was to compete against different kinds of firms. In Britain, specialised photographic firms, merged into Ilford Limited in the 1920s, were a reasonably strong alternative. In Germany and elsewhere, the chemical giant IG Farben, under the trade name Agfa, was the key competitor. Each firm had different technical resources and innovated different kinds of colour photographic processes. IG Farben, the world's leading dye firm, was able to make a film called Agfacolor in which it had embedded most of the complex reagents that were necessary to process the film. The film could thus be processed by amateurs and chemist's shops. Kodak developed expertise in dyes and fine chemicals during the Great War, and it used this to produce Kodachrome, a film that relied on very complex processing, which had to be done by Kodak in its existing network of processing facilities. Kodachrome and Agfacolor, introduced in the 1930s, were 'subtractive' processes. By contrast, the Dufay process, promoted by Ilford, was 'additive' – it essentially created three different photographs, each occupying a third of the image, a process which required no expertise in dye chemistry. By the 1930s Britain had that expertise, Ilford did not.

The early history of television provides another interesting case, though the key connection is not to Germany as in the case of synthetic dyes, but to Russia. Two key technical leaders, Isaac Schoenberg of EMI and Vladimir Zworykin of RCA, were both Russian, and had both studied with the Russian pioneer, Boris Rosing, at the Imperial Institute of Technology in St Petersburg, before the Great War.[53]

Zworykin arrived in the USA in 1919; Schoenberg in Britain in 1914. But the key organisation at the centre of this activity was the Radio Corporation of America, Zworykin's employers. It had investments and technical connections in two key European firms which supplied the modern TV equipment, EMI in Britain (Schoenberg's employers), and Telefunken in Germany. The Marconi–EMI system developed in Britain was directly derived from related RCA work. More intriguingly still, RCA was to transfer a great deal of technology to the USSR before the Second World War, including television, such that RCA technology was used to broadcast TV in the USSR before the USA.[54] Britain, Germany, the USA and the Soviet Union, all developed television in an experimental form at the end of the 1930s, based on RCA technology. It is worth noting that with the exception of what happened in the USA, television, like broadcasting generally, was under the direct control of the state in these countries.

## Nation, empire, race

In thinking about the relations between the global and the national in the history of twentieth-century technology it has been obvious that things, expertise and experts crossed political boundaries all the time. The importance of these boundaries changed, and radically so, over time. The boundaries themselves changed too. Nations were hardly eternal. More than that, multi-national states were hugely important. The USSR was a multi-national state, half its population was non-Russian; its 'national' anthem had been, until 1943, the 'Internationale'. Trans-national political commitments were also important. Italian communist engineers went to the Soviet Union in the 1920s. While post-war Spain had many German and Italian technicians working there, there were many Spanish experts elsewhere. There were Spanish aeronautical engineers working in the French aircraft industry in Toulouse who would not have wanted, or been able, to work in nationalistic and autarkic Spain.[55] Most important in this respect were the close links between the Soviet Union and China between 1949 and 1960. One of the most bizarre was the political link between China and Albania in the 1960s and 1970s following the decisive break in relations between China and the USSR. Albania relied on Chinese technology; the common language was the Russian dominant in the Soviet Union, the source of much of the Chinese technology.

The great empires of the twentieth century were also hugely important trans-national and trans-ethnic political and technological entities. Far from being throwbacks to the past, empires were intimately associated with particular new technologies, for example long-distance radio broadcasting, aviation and tropical medicines. They lasted into the 1950s. But empire not only left a technological mark, post-imperial relations did too. One finds few French cars in India, or British cars in Tunisia.

National and imperial boundaries were often radically less important than racial boundaries within nations and empires. For many European intellectuals a sense of scientific and technological superiority was crucial.[56] Much discussion of inventiveness in particular was associated with racial and cultural analyses which transcended nations. In the United States blacks were deemed by whites to be un-inventive, to the extent that a pioneering sociologist of invention noted that it is 'inadvisable to count in the colored populations of the United States and the British Dominions' in computations of relative national inventiveness 'since these people do not figure in invention'.[57] Another analyst of the 1920s argued that the USA had low per capita inventiveness because 'the United States have a dilution in the negroes in our population.'[58] If women had been distributed unevenly around the world the same argument would have been made about them.

In the USA the armed services were racially segregated, and the black formations were generally of very low status. There were, for example, no black pilots in the US forces in the interwar years. However, from 1941 there was segregated training for black pilots who would go into segregated squadrons; only after the war were US forces officially desegregated. Bell telephone maintained segregation and did not employ black telephone operators pre-war; after the war they did so only because the labour market forced them to.[59] While in the interwar years there were large numbers of black car mechanics and taxi drivers, many whites held blacks to be bad drivers with no mechanical sense.[60] No place in the world is more symbolic of the new technologies of the late twentieth century than 'Silicon Valley' in California. Perhaps 80 per cent of the production workers belong to ethnic minorities; and the great majority were recent immigrants (many of them Spanish-speakers) to the USA, and are women.[61] Many of the technical staff are South and East Asian.

Sometimes, of course, some have celebrated what they see as their lack of invention by their own community. The celebrated Martinican poet of negritude, Aimé Césaire, lauded

> those who invented neither powder nor the compass
> those who have never been able to tame steam or electricity
> those who have explored neither the seas nor the sky
>
> Eia for those who have never invented anything
> for those who have never explored anything
> for those who have never subjugated anything.[62]

But many others, including the *dependencia* theorists, lamented, for example, that '*La diosa tecnología no habla español*', which meant Spanish speakers were not notable in the world of research and invention.[63] '*Que inventen ellos*', said the Spanish essayist and rector of the ancient University of Salamanca, Miguel de Unamuno, before 1911. The phrase has achieved notoriety among those who want to see invention flourish in Spain, and indeed no rector of the University of Salamanca would say it today. A document prepared by a 'western intellectual' around 1960 claimed that Russian and 'Eastern Slavonic nations' were 'much less inventive and imaginative' than the Anglo-Saxon nations. But the Soviet bloc was inventive in many ways and *Homo sovieticus* was not a slav.[64]

These comments reflect very substantial differences in participation in elite inventive activities. Only sixteen non-whites have won Nobel prizes in science and medicine, but not one has been of African descent, despite the fact that the USA, the clear leader in the Nobel prize league table, has a very large African-American population.[65] Very few Spanish speakers have won science or medicine prizes, while Spanish-speaking writers and poets from many nations have been garlanded with the Literature prize. Latin America, Africa and some parts of Asia produce few patents, while most of the Northern Hemisphere, including Japan and Korea, turns them out in prodigious quantities. Uruguay and Brazil give two patents per million population to residents, while Finland gives 187. In the USA there are worthy listings of African-American inventors; the fact that such lists are manageable points to the small numbers involved.

Racial and cultural differentiation was far from confined to invention. In the great empires there was a profoundly racial economy of technology in use. Empire created rich enclaves for European colonisers in colonies and near-colonies, with motor cars, telephones, electricity, running water, cinemas and so on. These were places such as the international settlements in Shanghai, Carthage/Tunis, Casablanca, Ismailia (on the Suez Canal), New Delhi, Singapore, and others. On a smaller scale, enclaves for white engineers and workers from the rich world were dotted around the poor world. Thus American employees of the United Fruit Company lived in special compounds in the company's banana plantations in South and Central America; while American and other engineers had special housing and facilities in the USSR in the late 1920s and early 1930s.

Within imperial territories race was central to social organisation. In all the places where white technology went, white technicians were in control. The pilots who steered ships through the Suez Canal were British and French, not Egyptian. On the vast Indian railway network, the great majority of its senior engineers were white British. In the interwar years whites born in India became more important, as did, at lower levels, mixed-race 'Anglo-Indians' or 'Eurasians', of whom there were over 100,000. Into the 1930s there were still many British-

*17. India's tryst with its modern destiny shown on a postage stamp commemorating India's independence from the British Empire on 15 August 1947. India later designed and built jet fighters rather than the civil transports shown on the stamp.*

born locomotive drivers among the large number of Anglo-Indian train drivers. In the Dutch East Indies (later Indonesia) the railway equipment, down to the rails, was imported from Europe. Until the end of the colonial era, only some parts of carriages and the sleepers (made of teak) were local. At least as late as 1917–18 'not a single clerk, station master or machinist was a non-European'.[66] Motor vehicles were much more open to natives.[67] In 1935 the number of native car owners was just below the number of European owners, and just over the number of 'foreign oriental' owners; however, there were twice as many licensed native drivers as Europeans, who presumably were chauffeurs and taxi drivers.[68]

There was a particular racial order in the vast British merchant marine that served in India and elsewhere. It depended to an extraordinary degree on 'lascars', seamen recruited from the Indian subcontinent. In 1928 there were more than 52,000 lascars aboard British ships; 26 per cent of all crews, and 30 per cent of engine-room crews. Special regulations applied to their employment, for example in voyages through cold seas.[69] There were divisions along geographical, religious and ethnic lines: Catholic Goans served in ships' galleys and acted as waiters and servants; Muslim Punjabis dominated in the engine room; and deckcrews, both Muslim and Hindu, came from many places.[70] Needless to say these British ships were all officered by white British mariners.

The Indian army, officered very largely by white officers, was given older and less powerful equipment than all-white formations of the British army.[71] There was then no Indian Navy or Air Force. In India non-technical higher education was much more widely available to Indians than technical education; British technical education was much more technical than its Indian offshoots.[72] When they took over Malaya from the British, the Japanese boosted technical education for Malays and Indians as well as local industrialisation.[73]

It is little wonder that the end of imperialism was so important to national technological development, and indeed that nations emerging out of empires felt a strong need not only to develop national technologists but national technologies too.

## Asia and techno-nationalism

Japan represents the great twentieth-century exception to white dominance in technology. A strong, imperial state in the early twentieth century – among its colonies were Taiwan, Korea and, for many years, much of China – it was a serious technological power by the interwar years. The so-called Prussia of the East replicated Britain with its great navy and cotton textile industries of the interwar years. Even in defeat after the Second World War, Japan kept control of its economy, and Japanese-owned and -controlled firms not only imported technology, but began to generate technologies of their own. Japan rose to be the second performer of research and development in the world by the 1970s. At the same time its car and consumer electronic industries posed a serious threat to North American and European companies. In this respect the Japanese were much more successful than the

Soviets, another power which had spend a great deal on importing technology and on research and development.

The Chinese case is quite different from the Japanese, or indeed from the Korean and Taiwanese cases. Although nationalism was and remains a very important part of communist politics in China, the opening to the world since the late 1970s has not led to the development of a powerful local technological infrastructure. Most of China's exports, especially in the electronic sector, come from foreign-funded and foreign-owned enterprises, rather than either state-owned or locally privately owned ones. In any case, much of China's exports are low-tech: textiles, toys and all sorts of other cheap goods. If Wal-Mart were a country, it would be China's eighth largest trading partner. There is however one distinctive aspect of foreign enterprise in China – it is mostly eastern rather than western. It comes from Japan, and from the so-called overseas Chinese. The Chinese minorities in Malaysia, Indonesia and the Philippines have been central to industrialisation and technical development in these post-imperial nations. Political structures, and ethnic and linguistic links are interacting in complex ways.

Yet nationalism, and national control, is far from dead in the new globalised China. The internet, supposedly necessarily an agent of internationalisation, is thoroughly controlled in China. Search engines do not recognise words, such as 'democracy', which the government does not like. Sites cease to exist when access is attempted from China. China also pursues some very old-fashioned techno-nationalist enterprises. In 2003, more than forty years after Yuri Gagarin became the first man in space, China put a Shenzhou-5 capsule into orbit carrying a man.

# 6

# War

The First World War was a chemists' war because of the innovation of gas warfare; the Second World War a physicists' war because of radar and atomic weapons. Now we are living through a revolution in military affairs linked to innovations in information processing. Many accounts of the relations of technology and war tell us this simple innovation-based story. But even a cursory look at the military technologies in use will make clear just how misleading a picture that is. Even at the end of the twentieth century, war was a matter of rifles, artillery, tanks and aeroplanes, as it was many decades earlier. These technologies of war are surprisingly invisible as technologies. If we go to the great national science and industry museums of the world, we will not see them. We will find aircraft, radar and atomic bombs, but as applications to war of civilian sciences and technologies.

There is a division, implicit but powerful, between things which belong to the realm of the military and those in the world of science and technology that are taken to be essentially civilian. It suggests that the great innovations in arms in the twentieth century were in essentially *civilian* technologies applied to war, and that they transformed twentieth-century war. They did this by civilianising and totalising it.[1] Put another way the key themes are the industrialisation and civilianisation of war since the late nineteenth century.[2] War becomes a matter of turning over the whole of society to the mass production of weapons, to total, industrial war in which civilians in factories are as much combatants, and thus targets, as soldiers on the front.

The military, and war itself, have often been seen as left-overs from the past. War was not something which modern, democratic, industrial and free-trading nations did. Soldiers, particularly officers, were relics of an older agricultural and warlike society, which like chivalry, would disappear as modernity marched on. Modern war was a tragic clash of old and new.

## The conventional story

The conventional story of the relations of war and technology in the twentieth century uncannily parallels techno-globalist accounts of the place of technology in global history. It is an innovation-centred story invoking some very familiar technologies. It goes like this: in the late nineteenth century, new private arms firms applied the new civil technologies of steel-making and steel-working, and the new chemistry, to armaments, producing new guns, new ships, new explosives and propellants. This led to a new kind of warfare which required the mass mobilisation not only of soldiers but of civilian industry.[3] Later in the twentieth century new technologies developed which further revolutionised and civilianised warfare. The key ones were the aeroplane, not only the product of civil industry but able to make civilians targets. Later came the atomic bomb, the product of civilian (perhaps even pacifist) academic science. More recently, military experts have influentially claimed that there has been what is now widely called a 'Revolution in Military Affairs', driven by information technology.

The civilian, technological way of war was quite different from and superior to older methods.[4] The expert on aviation at London's Science Museum held in the 1940s not only that 'Total war' was 'made possible by the aeroplane', but that it had 'reversed all the traditional concepts of warfare', notably by including many civilians among its casualties.[5] In 1946 H. G. Wells wrote of the First World War: 'First the Zeppelin and then the bombing aeroplane carried war over and past the front to an ever-increasing area of civilian activities beyond. The old distinction maintained in civilised warfare between the civilian

*18. Total, global, civilian war. A terrified baby screams, following the Japanese aerial bombardment of the Shanghai South railway station, 28 August 1937.*

and the combatant population disappeared.'[6] The atomic bomb, the great glory of civilian academic science, went further still – and led to a new kind of war or non-war directed by civilian Dr Strangeloves.

Change in the military, and in war, is seen as driven by civil factors from outside the military. The military, if they are ascribed an ideology at all, are labelled 'militarists' a term which implies backwardness, even in fighting wars. As Ernest Gellner put it, 'civil societies' have vanquished 'militarist romantic' nations.[7] The wimps and cissies, the nerds of history, have overcome the specialists in, and celebrators of, violence. Such oppositions between the military and the civil are deeply ingrained. As George Orwell brilliantly noted, the key oppositions running through H. G. Wells's work were 'On the one side science, order, progress, internationalism, aeroplanes, steel, concrete, hygiene: on the other side war, nationalism, religion, monarchy, peasants, Greek professors, poets, horses.'[8] Again and again, the romanticism of the military is contrasted with enlightened science, technology and industry; militarism and modernity are incompatible, even if they have in practice come together many times in the twentieth century.[9] Like military intelligence, military science (except in the sense of the art of war), and more surprisingly, military technology, are close to oxymoronic. If culture had kept up with science and technology, the argument went, war would have been abolished. The 'cultural lag' was a cause of war.

The military are nearly universally regarded as being particularly prone to the 'cultural lag', not surprisingly since they were themselves seen as a left-over from the past. The military appear in stories about science and technology as resistant to new technology, sometimes for good reasons, usually not. According to one military intellectual, Basil Liddell Hart, writing in 1932, the 'progress of weapons, has out-stripped the progress of the mind – especially in the class who wield weapons. Each successive war of modern times has revealed the lag due to the slow pace of mental adaptation'.[10] Another soldier, in a pio-neering book called *Armament and History*, published in 1946, warned that 'civil progress is so intense that there is not only a danger but a certainty that no army in peacetime can in the full sense be kept up to date.'[11] Lewis Mumford put the point graphically: 'Fortunately for mankind, the army has usually been the refuge of third-rate minds ... Hence the paradox in modern technics: war stimulates invention, but the army resists it!'[12] The histories amplify these stories. Before the First World War, it is claimed, admirals thought submarines ungentle-manly, and generals irrationally defended cold steel and horses against machine guns. Even during the war, it is suggested, the generals failed to understand the logic of the new warfare and kept on fighting old wars, with the result that millions of lives were unnecessarily lost. Histories of interwar armed forces feature sailors who dismissed the power of aviation (despite Billy Mitchell's powerful demonstration of the power of bombs against battleships in the 1920s), and army officers who refused to accept the logic of motorisation and tank warfare. For the years after the Second World War the complaints are more muted. Yet we have soldiers who did not want to give up tanks to helicopters and precision-guided weapons; aviators who do not give up on fighters or bombers, in an age when missiles will obviously take over, and sailors who clung tenaciously to surface ships.

The military, resistant to new technology, needed new technology from the creative, private, civilian sector. For those who believed in this way of thinking about military technology, the results of military conservatives meeting progressive civilian technology were unfortunate. Peacetime military technology had a grotesque, distorted quality. The military corrupted essentially civil technologies. There was then, and this has continued since, a systematic downplaying of the military origins and significance of the aeroplane. Indeed in the 1930s many concerned with writing about aviation saw the military aeroplane as a corrupted and deformed aeroplane. If it had been allowed to develop freely, instead of being frustrated by military needs and nationalistic governments, and the rich, aeroplanes could have developed along more proper or normal lines, and indeed have given the world peace. These ideas have not disappeared. According to one theory, right through the twentieth century the conservative military wanted more powerful versions of existing weapons – battleships, tanks, aeroplanes – not to shift to new ones. The result was a 'baroque arsenal', an over-elaboration of existing technologies of war leading to rapidly diminishing returns, indeed to negative returns. In war, according to this model, crisis conditions result in the overthrow of military conservatism and the adoption of radical new technologies and ways of fighting war, of civilian origin. These new forms themselves become baroque in the ensuing peace.[13]

### Old weapons and killing in war

How plausible is the above account? We have already challenged elements of these stories with accounts of the importance of the horse in the German army, and cost–benefit analyses of strategic and nuclear bombings and the V-2 programme in the Second World War. We have noted the long lives of battleships and some bombers, and have criticised the civilian techno-globalist account of aviation. But there is much more to be said.

One crude but necessary way of approaching the question of technology and war is to ask what technologies killed people in twentieth-century war. Of course, killing is not the key objective in most wars, victory is, but many of the key wars of the twentieth century, against the hopes of the advocates of new technology (who tended to see in them the power to make war short, decisive, humane), killing was the means to victory. The killing of civilians too became a means to victory.

For all the focus on novel weapons, the well-established ones became the great killers. For the Great War of 1914–19, western European images of the Western Front invoke the relatively novel machine gun and poison gas as the main handmaidens of the grim reaper. Yet experts have long known otherwise. Of the 10 million who died in the Great War in Europe, and they were overwhelmingly soldiers, 5 million died from artillery fire and 3 million from small arms in combat. The Western Front saw important developments in artillery practice which hardly enter the popular picture of the war. The last years of the Great War, particularly on the Western Front in 1917–18, saw a revolution which inaugurated, according to a recent account, 'the modern style of warfare'. This involved large forces of heavy artillery, centrally coordinated, firing indirectly (by the map), on to specific targets, obtained by intelligence (including, crucially, that from air observers and aerial photography). This was not the result of any particular technical innovation, but of devising a new system of deploying heavier guns with much more ammunition at their disposal, systematic testing, the development of great accuracy in long-range firing, and the routine use of intelligence and communications. It is a story of the combination of many technologies, with new patterns of organisation.[14] The essentials of 'revolution in military affairs' of the late twentieth century took place more than half a century earlier than is usually claimed.

For all the claims for a new kind of war that emerged in the interwar years, the Second World War was even more artillery-intensive than the Great War. In the Second World War, the Soviet Union alone lost 10 million soldiers; half were killed by big guns, and 2 million were lost to small arms. Of the remainder, 3 million succumbed to starvation and disease in German prisoner of war camps. Taking all the twentieth century wars up to the mid-1950s about 18 million were killed by big guns, 5 million in the Great War, 10 million in the Second World War and 3 million in other wars.[15] This made the big gun the single largest killer of soldiers.

Small arms come second to big guns as a source of combat deaths, reaping the appalling total of 14 million lives, up to mid-century. The rifle in particular has been ubiquitous in twentieth-century armed forces. They are an example of the significance of a relatively simple weapon that was widely used, and indeed of one that was unchanged even in the most powerful armies for very long periods. The British used basically the same Lee-Enfield rifle, the SMLE, from the beginning of the century to the late 1950s. Around 5 million were built worldwide, including for the huge Indian Army which was 2.5 million strong in 1945. In the former British India, British Lee-Enfield 303 rifles are still everywhere. The US army used the M-1 from 1936 to 1957. Four million M-1 Garands were made and nearly 3 million M-1 carbines. A variant of this weapon, the M-14, was in use until the 1960s. The M-16, which replaced it, was a new kind of rifle, lighter, and using a much smaller bullet, (5.56mm), than the .303 inches (7.7mm) of the Lee-Enfield, or the .3006 inches (7.6mm) of the M-1, or the 7.62mm NATO standard. The M-16 and variants (which included the M-4 carbine) were also produced in large number; no fewer than 7 million. It is still in service.

These figures are as nothing compared to those for the Soviet Kalashnikov assault rifles (usually known slightly misleadingly as the AK-47). The Kalashnikov was introduced in 1947 (hence AK-47). It fired 7.62mm ammunition. The 1947 model was replaced in the late 1950s with the AKM which was much lighter (3.2kg). In 1974 the Soviet forces began to adopt the AK-74, a slightly adapted weapon which fired 5.45mm ammunition. Various generations of the Kalashnikov are in service all over the world. It was the weapon not only of the Soviet bloc forces, but of the Chinese too. It was a key weapon of liberation movements. The former Portuguese colony of Mozambique put the Kalashnikov on its flag. But the Kalashnikov was also provided by the US, and other right-wing regimes, to the guerrilla forces they supported, for example the Mujahedeen in Afghanistan. The production history of the Kalashnikov was extraordinary. Estimates range from 70 to 100 million made since 1947, out of an estimated total production of automatic rifles between 1945 and 1995 of 90–122 million. The famously rugged and cheap Kalashnikov may be contrasted with the seemingly more troublesome and 'gold-plated' weapons of the west.

The post-Second World War assault rifles, which could fire powerful bursts of lead, and not just single shots, hugely increased the firepower of small infantry formations. The cost to civilians in war zones has been enormous. With such weapons it was easy to massacre the inhabitants of a village, as US troops did in Vietnam over and over again. Conflicts between people which might have left a few dead were now more likely to kill many more. Not surprisingly the spread of automatic assault rifles to Africa in particular has been a huge cause of concern. It is often suggested that it is new light weapons that have made this trend possible; young boys could not have fired the old heavy ones. Yet the Burmese army trained its boy soldiers, the most numerous in the world, on the heavy, old German G3 which, at four feet in length, was taller than some of the young conscripts.[16] In any case, British schoolboys enrolled in the cadet forces of private schools, long drilled with and fired the heavy .303 Lee-Enfield. It is the cheapness and the power which make the difference.

The rifle was the weapon that civilianised war, much more so than the aeroplane or the gas chamber. In his brilliant book *The Twentieth Century Book of the Dead*, some data from which has been used above, Gil Elliot calculates, for the period before around 1970, that some 6 million civilians were killed in massacres, and 4 million in formal executions.[17] The main rivals to small arms were enforced hunger and disease, and small arms played a critical role here too, by being a key weapon in population control. The Holocaust of Eastern European Jewry was as much a matter of small arms, hunger and disease, as of poison gas. Barbed wire, that simple yet deadly material, played a key role in confining people.[18] Using the most primitive weapons and techniques the German armies in Eastern Europe killed almost 30 million people. In every theatre of war the aeroplane killed, perhaps, 1 million. The cost of small-arms wars in Africa in recent years has been enormous. The second Congo War (1998–) has been responsible for an estimated nearly 4 million lives, mostly civilians lost to disease and starvation. This makes it, some say, the deadliest war since 1945. But they have underestimated the killing in Vietnam.

## Paradoxes of lethality

Measuring the power of military technologies is of course extremely difficult. As in the case of battleships and nuclear weapons we are reduced to some measure of how big a bang they make rather than actual or potential military effectiveness. These problems can be considered by looking at the case of land armaments. Twentieth-century weapons fired more bullets further, they fired more and bigger shells. This is seemingly consistent with the greater number of casualties in twentieth-century wars than in previous ones. However, despite the increase in the raw power of these weapons, the casualty rate in a given period of combat *fell* quite dramatically. In the nineteenth century *daily* casualty (killed, wounded and missing) rates, that is the number fallen in each day of combat, were around 20 per cent for defeated forces and around 15 per cent for the victors. These figures include the American Civil War. There had already been a significant fall: around 1600 the figures had been 30 per cent and 20 per cent respectively. Yet in the twentieth century these daily casualty rates dropped precipitately, to around 10 per cent and 5 per cent for the Great War, the same in the Second World War, and 5 per cent and 2 per

*19. The bomber was a lethal instrument, but bombing could be defended against and lived through under reinforced concrete. The photograph shows the entrance to Hitler's air raid shelter (left) and air shaft (right) in Berlin, after the war. Hitler survived the bombing, to commit suicide as the Red Army approached. The Red Army destroyed the Nazi regime, not the bombers, but had to fight for Berlin street by street.*

cent in the Arab-Israeli wars. This extraordinary paradox is not due to a lower intensity of firepower in a given day of combat. It was due to the way forces responded to greater firepower. They dispersed in space, making themselves much less vulnerable. A Second World War artillery battery could easily destroy an infantry division if it marched into battle in the close order of a Napoleonic division, but dispersed like a twentieth-century infantry division it would be a much harder target.[19] What better illustration is needed of an understanding of the context of use?

Despite the drop in the effectiveness of weapons measured by daily killing rates, the overall level of casualties increased because battles were also dispersed in time. Instead of lasting a few hours, as they did from the classical period into the nineteenth century, they went on for days, weeks, months and even years. Troops could be kept supplied with all the necessities of a fighting army for very long periods, despite the fact that the level of supplies required daily also increased.

### Power and effect – unused and unusable weapons

The aeroplane was not the only great destructive technology of war that did not have the devastating and decisive effect predicted. The great dreadnought battleships of the first half of the twentieth century were among the most powerful weapons of their day. They could deliver, many times over and over huge ranges, the weight of explosive a Second World War bomber could deliver only once every sortie. Battleships of the interwar years could fire many shells of nearly one tonne further than 30km; it could take more than one minute for the shell to reach its target.[20] They could hit moving targets miles away, with the help of computing devices.

Yet, these extraordinary machines, symbols of naval power, were hardly used in their intended role. In the Great War the British and German fleets barely engaged, except in one day-long battle in the North Sea, at Jutland. The Austro-Hungarian dreadnoughts left their Adriatic ports rarely. Overall the losses of battleships and battlecruisers in this otherwise bloody war were low, essentially through lack of combat. At Jutland, Britain lost three and Germany two, but for the whole war only six dreadnoughts and battlecruisers were lost in action (plus twenty pre-dreadnoughts). The great battleship fleets in the Second World War saw more continuous action than they had in the Great War. In many cases the ships were of course the same ones. The result was that the toll of battleships was much greater: Japan lost eleven, Britain five, Germany three, the USA two, Italy one (to

Germany) and the Soviet Union one. The great battleship killers were air power and submarines. British naval air power greatly reduced the Italian battleship threat in 1940; at Pearl Harbor Japanese air power sunk two battleships (and damaged many more), and soon after sank two British battleships; thereafter Japanese battleships faced relentless attack primarily from the air. Only one British battleship was lost to a battleship; two German; and four Japanese. But that total too is greater than Great War losses.

The history of the battleships in the Great War, and to a much lesser extent in the Second World War, points to the significance of the threat of use, rather than actual use. The British battleships stationed in Scapa Flow imposed a punishing blockade on Germany simply by being there. It led to the loss of hundreds of thousands of civilian lives. In the Second World War, the German battleship *Tirpitz* had an extraordinary effect, just by lying in a Norwegian fjord, from where it threatened convoys sailing to the Soviet Union. Indeed twentieth-century military history is full of examples of the significance of non-used technologies of war. In the Second World War *all* the combatants put huge efforts into gas and biological warfare, mostly of Great War types, and defences against them, but they remained unused.[21] Mustard gas was one of the key ones. It would not be used until the Iraq–Iran war of the 1980s, as was a quantity of nerve gases of a type developed in the Second World War. After the Second World War, and especially from 1950, many states had greater peacetime military establishments than ever before. NATO and the Warsaw Pact powers faced each other, particularly in Europe, with military equipment that was in many cases never used in battle conditions. The greatest example was, of course, atomic weapons, whose stock piles were built up relentlessly from trivial numbers even in the early 1950s, decade by decade. Not only were these weapons unused, they were soon unusable. For the power of the H-Bomb introduced in the 1950s was such that firing off a fraction of the arsenals of each side would have destroyed human civilisation. Thus the logic was not of use, but of deterrence.

## Technological and economic determinism in war

One important argument derived from the view that total war was civilian and industrial was that in the final analysis it was the stronger civil economy which would vanquish the weaker one. This view of war has a good deal going for it, at least for the two world wars of the twentieth century. In both of them, the resources Germany and its allies could draw on were significantly smaller than those of its ultimately victorious opponents. And yet, the link between national military capability and national civilian economic and technological strength is not straightforward. Quick victories could be won against economic and technologically superior adversaries. That is what Germany did in 1940: it was not superior to a combination of Denmark, Norway, Holland, Belgium, France and Great Britain, yet it beat them all on the continent of Europe.[22] Germany would lose the war, but primarily to a power that had started economically and technologically weaker than itself, the Soviet Union. It was able to produce vast quantities of weapons despite being desperately poor and technologically backward in many areas. So poor was the USSR that it was very short of paper 'but in this respect the war years were an age of plenty, because with their equipment the British and Americans sent us ton-loads of instructions, printed on one side only and on the reverse of these sheets we planned our Katuishas and aircraft', said one aeronautical engineer.[23]

It is not even obvious that the side with the better machinery of war, other things being equal, will win a battle or a war. What happened in France in May 1940 is an example. Britain's mighty navy and its bomber force could do little to help the French, but more infantry with more rifles and artillery might have made all the difference. Even so, the balance of military equipment on the ground in France did not necessarily favour a German victory: Germany won by using surprise, speed and daring. The conquest of Malaya by the Japanese provides another example. In late 1941 this important and well-developed British colony, centred on Singapore, was held by a large and well-equipped force of British and imperial troops. Yet a *smaller* and technologically *weaker* Japanese force invaded from the north, landing from the sea. Unable to bring horses, they brought a few trucks, and planned to requisition bicycles from the local population. Living off the technological land in this way they were able to equip each infantry division with 6,000 bicycles (along with 500 trucks), and pursued an extraordinary 'bicycle blitzkrieg' along Malaya's good roads, forcing the country to surrender remarkably quickly.[24] Daring generalship, as well as requisitioned bicycles, gave the Japanese an extraordinary victory. For all these brilliant early successes, Japan and Germany saw their forces defeated in the field by overwhelmingly stronger opposition, and their cities and civilians mercilessly attacked. They were comprehensively defeated by powers which did indeed stress the economic and technological factors in war.[25]

After the Second World War the technological way of warfare was central to the armament efforts of the great powers. From nuclear weapons to new anti-personnel weapons, from new communications technology to military psychology and operational research, the military invested huge proportions of their budgets on researching, developing and procuring new weapons and methods of warfare. Strikingly, the technological and industrial intensity of the air and land wars against poor nations from 1950 was much greater than that against richer adversaries in the Second World War. The tonnage of air, land and sea munitions expended per American serviceman, was eight times greater in Korea and twenty-six times greater in Vietnam than in the Second World War.[26] Not surprisingly the disparity in casualties was stupendous. In Korea in 1950–53, the US-led forces used 43 per cent of the munitions used by America in the Second World War, expending perhaps ten to twenty times the amount spent by the North Koreans and Chinese. They suffered 94,000 dead; on the other side military casualties were three times greater. Civilian casualties on both Korean sides came to 2 million.[27] In Indochina, from the 1960s and into early 1970s, the USA used twice the quantity of munitions it used in the Second World War, blasting an unseen enemy with indirect artillery fire and aerial bombardment. American dead were just under

60,000. The South Vietnamese army suffered much heavier losses, some 270,000, while the North Vietnamese army and the Vietcong lost 1,100,000 dead. Vietnamese civilian deaths were atrocious: some 200–400,000 civilians in *South* Vietnam alone. The North Vietnamese estimate is of 4 million dead civilians, North and South.[28]

Disparities in killing power did not determine victory, however. In Korea the US was fought to a standstill by North Korean and Chinese forces, with Soviet assistance. Most spectacularly and significantly of all, Vietnamese peasants, enrolled in the Vietcong and the regular army of North Vietnam, defeated a superpower. The bicycles of the Ho Chi Minh trail defeated the B-52s. That such a weak power could even stand up to the USA and its modern weapons had a profound political effect around the world. Military and economic might, it seemed, could be defeated by political commitment. For some soldiers it revealed the need to return to older military thinking rather than what was seen as an engineers' quantitative approach to war, a position reflected in the film *Apocalypse Now*.[29]

This US reverse had a major consequence for thinking about technology on the Left. The socialist and communist movements had been deeply committed to some kind of economic or technological determinism – this was a standard official interpretation of Marxism in the first two-thirds of the twentieth century. It suggested that military might followed from technological might. Thus, for Stalin, economic and technological development was a matter of military necessity. Yet even within this tradition the view emerged that morale and political commitment could overcome technologically superior forces. Chinese Maoists, in particular, focused as they were on the peasantry, saw both reactionaries and nuclear weapons as 'paper tigers'. But in the 1960s, the Western Marxists too turned decisively away from 'economism' and indeed technological determinism, to emphasise political action, culture, ideology. Peasants and students would form the new revolutionary vanguard, not the industrial working class of the rich countries.

Guerrilla rebellions took place in many parts of the world. In Africa and South America a wave of military activity was stimulated by the possibility of victory. A particularly striking example is the still-continuing rebellion against India by Maoist guerrillas known as the Naxalites, who since the 1960s have had extraordinary success in the tribal areas of eastern India, relying in part on bows and arrows and 'country made guns', including flint-locks.[30] But by the late 1970s the great powers, as well as non-socialist movements, were using guerrillas against stronger forces. The United States, too, had learned about the power of the guerrilla. It funded guerrilla armies attacking the legitimate government of Nicaragua, and most importantly the Islamicist peasant war against the Soviet Union in Afghanistan in the 1980s. The weak have developed new military techniques, among the most notable being the suicide bomber, a tactic employed by the Tamil Tigers in Sri Lanka, the Palestinians in the occupied territories, and, on a much larger scale, by insurgents in Iraq following the US-led invasion of 2003.

## Iraq and the past

The history of war in Iraq over the last two decades provides many examples of the complex interaction of the old and new in warfare, and of the dangers of naïve futurism. Here old wars were fought, and the wars of the future were supposedly pioneered by applying the Revolution in Military Affairs.

The story starts in 1979. Contrary to all the models of modernity, a brutal, modernising monarchy – the apple of America's eye – had been toppled by conservative forces led by an ayatollah. In 1980 Iraq attacked the newly established Islamic state in Iran. Over the next eight years of conflict, some 1 million would lose their lives on both sides. It was a war of mass attacks, artillery and tanks used as artillery. It was also one which saw more sinister old weapons used. The Iraqis resorted to mustard gas on a much larger scale than any use since the First World War (it had been used by the Italians in Abyssinia, and the Japanese in China). The war brought the first-ever combat use of the first nerve gas discovered in the 1930s, Tabun, used for killing Iranians between 1984 and 1988.

20. *Unknowingly preparing to fight the next war but one: a fifteen-inch naval gun being made by Vickers before the Great War. More than 180 were produced for British battleships. Most were still in service in the Second World War, where they found more use than in the Great War.*

The war also saw the first large-scale use of ballistic missiles since the Second World War. The rockets were derived from the V-2 of that conflict. In 1955 the Soviet Union deployed a V-2 based missile later called the Scud A. In 1962 it put into service a derivative Scud B, which was to become AK-47 of the missile world. Iraq got its supplies from the Soviet Union in the 1970s, while Iran obtained them from Syria, Libya and North Korea. Each side bombarded the other's cities with these weapons. Iraq had to modify its Scud Bs very considerably to hit Tehran, which it did for some weeks in 1988, a period of the conflict known as the 'war of the cities'. Hundreds of Scud Bs were fired. On the eve of, and following, the Soviet withdrawal in 1989, Afghanistan was supplied with many Scuds which were fired against Mujahedeen positions.

The year 1991 saw the US engage in major warfare directly for the first time since Vietnam. It launched a massive attack to force Iraq out of Kuwait. In mid-January an extraordinary air offensive began which would see some 6,000 tons of 'smart' bombs, and some 80,000 tons of 'dumb' bombs, dropped. The result was the destruction of Iraq's infrastructure, including its electricity supply, oil supply and communications. For all the talk of 'smart bombs' decapitating command and control this was Second World War economic warfare at particularly high intensity and precision. Thirty-one per cent of US bombs were dropped by the ancient B-52s. Recall too that the USS *Wisconsin* was present, bombarding the land with 16-inch shells. As ever, despite rampant propaganda that strategic bombing was finally effective, this verdict has been powerfully contested.

While the destruction was overwhelming the effect on the capacity of the Iraqi army to operate and fight was nowhere as significant as implied. The army was bulldozed into the ground by superior US land forces, which would easily have won without the strategic bombardment. The land war was extraordinarily one-sided, as was shown by the minimal US casualties compared with the undisclosed level of Iraqi losses. As some American analysts put it afterwards, this was a first-world army confronting a third-world force, but in circumstances where might would win.[31] Yet we should recall that these land forces were composed, on both sides, of formations deploying weapons familiar from the Second World War: many tanks, field artillery, rocket launchers, and large numbers of infantry carrying rifles.

Apart from smart bombs, the most public new technology of the first Gulf War (1991) was the Patriot anti-missile system deployed by the USA. A key part of the Star Wars programme, anti-missile systems were themselves controversial. During and after the war US officials claimed the Patriot was a stunning success, destroying more than 96 per cent of Scud-type missiles fired against Saudi Arabia and Israel.

That claim for their accuracy was reduced in the face of criticism to 61 per cent, representing, it was claimed, twenty-seven successes against forty-four Scuds. Using the army's methods, a 61 per cent success rate is fully consistent with the known conclusion that 'Patriot did not destroy a single Scud warhead.'[32] What they had done was to claim success for the Patriot if 1) a Patriot missile got to where it was told to go by its targeting computer, which was most of the time; and 2) if the Scud caused no significant damage or casualties on the ground. Simply by missing a target – hitting the sea, or the desert, or failing to explode – the Scud became a victim of the Patriot. The army was assuming, implicitly, that the Scud was a 100 per cent effective weapon, when it was a very poor one indeed.

In the second Gulf War of 2003, strategic bombing was repeated, and this time also an army was immediately victorious, conquering the whole of Iraq very quickly. But controlling the country proved much more difficult, and continuing operations against US forces have kept this Gulliver pinned down in central Iraq. The disproportion in casualties between the imperialist forces and the locals becomes ever greater, but victory is no more assured.

## Torture

The United States responded with counter-insurgency operations linked with systematic interrogation and torture. This became known to the world through photographs of what had been done at an Iraqi prison, Abu Ghraib. Torture was, as ever, explained away as the unauthorised work of low-ranking soldiers, the result of indiscipline. There is a much bigger story to be told. Before the Second World War torture was seen as a feature of more bestial past times, and a few foreign despotisms. What was certain was that it was disappearing, and had no place in civilised society. In a history of torture published in 1940 there is not much on the twentieth century, and little if anything that is seen as new.[33] Of course the Nazis were associated with torture, but they were generally seen as a throwback. Yet the years after the Second World War, far from seeing the retreat of torture, saw its extension and its technological refinement. New forms of torture were devised and used on a widespread scale, becoming routine in their application, and in many cases brutally effective.

One of the most distinctively modern forms of torture was the use of electric shocks. It has been claimed that the *picana eléctrica* was invented in Argentina, where it was introduced in 1934.[34] This little machine was, apparently in a different version, used by the French in Indochina and above all in Algeria. The French exported their techniques directly to Argentina and to the United States, whence they went to the rest of Latin America and to Vietnam.[35] It is known that officers of the United States government trained the police and military of friendly governments, such as Iran, in the use and methods of torture from at least the late 1960s. One such instructor, Dan Mitrione, under the cover of being an official of the Agency for International Development (AID), set up a torture school in a house in Montevideo in the late 1960s. According to a fictionalised account, he started by lecturing army and police officers on the nervous system, but 'at no point … does he hint that these nerve centres and sinews will later be used to guide the electrical prod: he goes over everything as though this were a medical faculty lecture room, employing only the most aseptic, neutral, scientific terminology'.[36] Later in the week four beachcombers are brought in to be used as 'case studies' for the class – all are tortured with the electric prod, and then killed. The electric prod, the infamous *picana*, became the instrument of choice of South America's torturers in the 'dirty wars' of the 1970s.[37] Torture was a key instruments of an unbridled state terrorism which flourished particularly in that decade: it was applied to tens of thousands of mostly young people.

## War, technology and the history of the twentieth century

Most military technologies of the twentieth century have had military origins and limited applications outside war. That is obviously the case for small arms, artillery, explosives and tanks. To this list other technologies should be added, despite the impression that is often given that they are civilian technologies merely temporarily applied to war. The aeroplane, as we have seen was primarily a military technology. The radio, too, was first a military technology and was long connected to state power. Radar, an important new application of radio, developed in many countries in the interwar years, mostly in military-related contexts. The British radar system, which was far from being the only one installed in the late 1930s, drew on long military experience of air defence going back to the Great War.[38]

Even the atomic bomb project, so often seen as the work of scientists, and thus primarily academic and civilian, was directed by the military and related agencies. The military engineer Brigadier-General Leslie Groves, not the academic physicist Robert Oppenheimer, ran the project. Among the many great industrial enterprises involved was DuPont, which was not just a chemical company, but long the major military explosives supplier in the USA.[39] In any case much of the theoretical work on the bomb was not a matter of nuclear physics, but of fluid mechanics, the science at the core of aerodynamics. The bomb was the product of old institutions and old sciences, as well as new ones. The military have been much more important in the development of technology than the civilian innovation-centric picture has allowed.

As a consequence we have underestimated not only the contribution of military institutions to military technology, but to civil technology as well. The civil aircraft industry was just a branch of the core military industry; nuclear power was a spin-off from nuclear bombs and submarine reactors; much of radio and radar likewise is a spin-off. Early control theory and computing were a spin-off from problems relating to the control of heavy naval guns.[40] And one could add other names and other technologies, notably computers and the internet, to the Japanese camera firm Nikon.[41] Sometimes examples have been used to help justify military expenditures. At other times the military origin of civilian technology is used to show the negative influence of militarism on modernity.[42] An example is the computer-numerically-controlled machine tool, introduced through US air force funding in the 1960s for the manufacture of aircraft, and then very widely diffused. Military funding has pushed technologies towards being more authoritarian than they would otherwise have been. Far from liberating us, modern technology has been the tool of conservative not revolutionary forces. Old power relations are transmitted through new technology.

The aeroplane, the radio, radar, the atomic bomb should be in military museums, alongside guns, tanks, uniforms and regimental colours. The military are not usefully thought of as remnants from the past who were reluctant adopters of the new. Rather, they were among the key shapers of the new. They should thus also have a place in museums of science and technology, along with the seemingly old weapons that did so much to shape twentieth-century war. But neither sort of museum is likely ever to have a section on killing technologies, to which we now turn.

# 7

# Killing

The history of the non-military technology of killing is confined to the chambers of horrors, black museums, the private collections of ghouls. It has no place in more respectable museums except in the special case of genocide memorials. A museum of killing technology would confront us with uncomfortable questions. Killing, like war and the military, has been seen as something barbaric which the civilising process had left behind. But the rate of killing – of all sorts of living things – increased in the twentieth century, and did so drastically. For plants, bacteria, insects, cattle, whales, fish and human beings, the twentieth century was murderous. The civilising process did not reduce killing. What it did was to remove killing from the public arena – whether the execution of the criminal or the despatch of a chicken.

Putting killing into the history of the twentieth century is a particularly powerful way of exploring the interaction of old and new. It is a story which includes, in unexpected ways, nationalism, globalisation, war, production and maintenance. It will particularly disturb our sense of technological time, and of what is significant.

## Innovation in killing
An innovation-centric history of twentieth-century killing would be focused on the killing of insects, plants and micro-organisms, principally but not only in relation to farming. Around 1900, there were few killing techniques available to the farmer: a few insecticides and fun-

*21. In the supposedly transparent twentieth century even the killing of animals has been put beyond reach, not only of the public but also of photographers. In the late nineteenth century one could find stereographs of the great butchers of the New World, including this rare image of an animal being killed. The original caption read: 'Sticking Hogs, Armour's Great Packing House, Union Stockyards, Chicago, USA.'*

gicides, and the hoe. The twentieth century saw many new chemicals designed to kill small living things. The 1930s and 1940s were a particularly innovative period. In the 1930s an IG Farben chemist discovered organophosphate insecticides. The organophosphates were one key set of post-war organic insecticides, the others were chlorinated organic

*22. Demonstrating the use of DDT to kill lice in order to control typhus, probably during World War Two. DDT prevented mass break outs of typhus in North Africa and southern Italy.*

compounds. The first and most famous of these was DDT. First used for the killing of lice and mosquitoes, it became a general-purpose and very widely used insecticide. Many others would follow, and continue to be used after DDT was increasingly restricted from the 1970s. Chemical herbicides also changed radically in 1940s. The main new one was 2,4-D, an amazing example of simultaneous discovery – four separate groups, two in the UK and two in the US, came up with it.[1]

DDT, organophosphates as well as 2,4-D and other herbicides were a crucial part of the green revolution in the rich countries. Their use transformed production and the landscape. As a result of these herbicides unwanted weeds perished in vast quantities leaving fields of uniform crops. Insects suffered from this, as well as from insecticides. These powerful chemicals introduced new and invisible dangers to the countryside. This was exposed in one of the great books of scientific activism of the century, the naturalist and science writer Rachel Carson's *Silent Spring*, in 1962.

Insecticides and pesticides also found applications in warfare. DDT was widely used, as we have seen, to clear areas of malarial mosquitoes in the Second World War, as well as to control the typhus-carrying louse. The USA's chemical warfare service looked at possible military applications of 2,4-D. In South East Asia throughout the 1960s a programme called, of all things, 'Operation Ranch Hand', used up to twenty-five aeroplanes to drop 19 million gallons of herbicide to destroy the economic basis of the Vietcong and to remove cover. The infamous 'agent orange' was nothing more than a particular mixture of standard commercial herbicides including 2,4-D.[2]

The killing of micro-organisms also saw a great deal of innovation in the twentieth century. Best known were the new compounds used to kill bacteria in humans, such as Salvarsan, the sulphonamides of the 1930s and the most important, penicillin, developed in the 1940s. Such compounds were used not just in humans, but also in animals, where they were essential to control disease in the tightly packed animal populations of the new industrialised husbandry. There were other applications: in the 1940s it was discovered that penicillin made chickens grow faster, for reasons still unclear. As a result, in the mid-1950s one-quarter of all US antibiotic production was put into animal feed; by the 1990s, with production much higher, it was about one half, mostly for growth promotion.[3]

The twentieth century brought innovation in anti-virals: treatments for herpes, polio and smallpox were developed in the 1950s, though they were in the latter cases overtaken by immunisation; Acyclovir in the 1970s; and in response to HIV/AIDS, AZT in the 1980s. Antifungal treatments received an enormous boost with the 1957 launch of Nystatin. This was an unusual substance since it was patented by two female scientists who worked in the public sector, in this case the New York state department of health (hence the name). The 1960s brought Daktarin. New anti-malarials, such as paludrine and chloroquine, came out of a massive targeted research effort in the USA and Britain during the Second World War. No one has ever estimated the toll taken of the world's viruses, bacteria, mould, amoebae, insects and plants by these new poisons.

In terms of the killing of higher animals, the innovation-centric museum would have relatively little to show. The key killing technology has remained the knife blade applied to the throat, though this was in some cases, as in chicken-killing, mechanised. Fish were generally still suffocated after being caught in a net, and whales harpooned. Such significant innovations as there were came in stunning technology.

The history of innovation in killing humans is better known. Chemical warfare arose in the First World War with such agents as mustard gas and phosgene; atomic and bacteriological warfare followed in the Second. There were subsequent innovations in all these areas. In the 1930s organophosphate insecticides were recognised as exceedingly toxic to humans, and this led to effective 'nerve gases'. Tabun and Sarin were manufactured by the Germans during the Second World War, and in the 1950s Sarin became a standard nerve gas, produced in, among other places, Britain. In the 1950s the company ICI introduced a new organophosphate insecticide that proved too toxic to use. Transferred to the USA, it formed the basis for a new class of chemical weapons, the 'V-agents'.[4] VX, one such agent, was central to the US and Soviet arsenals. Uranium and plutonium bombs led to a variety of more powerful fusion weapons, and such things as neutron bombs, which were designed to kill people without destroying things. All sorts of gruesome biological agents were developed too. Again the years of the long boom proved very productive.

Outside warfare, the innovation-centric story had few reference points. First was the gas chamber in the 1920s in the USA (the electric chair was a late nineteenth-century innovation), and the lethal injection in the 1980s, also in the United States. Only one other country figured in this story: Germany. For the central innovation in the killing of humans, and by far the most problematic for our understanding of modernity, is the killing with Zyklon B in the Holocaust. Innovation-centredness leads to looking at Auschwitz as the great modern factory of human death.

An innovation-centric history of killing would be a great advance over the current neglect of killing. Yet in the case of killing in particular the deficiencies of an innovation-centric approach are particularly obvious. For we all know of the continuing use of long-established means of killing, particularly human beings and higher animals, things such as ritual slaughter knives, gallows, the garrotte, the guillotine or the electric chair. Just as in the case of war, killing technologies provide, as we shall see, many examples of long-lived, disappearing, reappearing and expanding 'old' technologies. Without recognising this the history of killing makes little sense.

## Whaling and fishing

Whaling, often thought of as a nineteenth-century industry supplying oil for lamps and whale-bone for corsets, went through a revolution in the 1920s. The new whaling relied on hunting the difficult-to-catch rorqual whales (a family of baleen whales including the Blue, Minke and Humpback) in Antarctic waters. The killing was carried out with a nineteenth-century invention: the deck-mounted harpoon. It was hoped that new methods of killing would replace it, but nets, poisons, gas injections and rifles did not produce better results. In 1929 a German engineer called Albert Weber started working in Norway on means of electrocuting whales, which was further experimented on in the 1930s and 1940s; however the expected result that modern electricity would replace the barbarous harpoon did not materialise. The nineteenth-century killing technology would have to do. [5]

It came to be used more than ever, as whaling expanded enormously, driven by the demand for margarine and by economic nationalism.

Already before 1914 whale oil was being hydrogenated for margarine, but by the 1930s this was its main use. It was used to make some 30–50 per cent of all European margarine.[6] In 1930–31 Atlantic whale oil production was the same as French, Italian and Spanish combined olive oil production. Whale oil margarine was mainly consumed in Germany, Britain and Holland, and supply was dominated by the Anglo-Dutch firm Unilever. In 1933 the Nazis began promoting German butter against margarine and Unilever, making a point of stressing the use of whale oil. Yet Unilever was forced to finance the building of a German-flagged whaling fleet, making Germany a whaling nation for the first time. Fats were important for national security.

The new whaling involved processing whales in floating factories that hauled dead whales into their bellies through a ramp at their sterns. The first floating factory built in Germany, the *Walter Rau,* named for the owner of the main German margarine firm, went to the southern oceans in the mid-1930s. In its first season it processed 1,700 whales, from which it produced 18,264 tons of whale oil, 240 tons of sperm oil, 1,024 tons of meat meal, 104 tons of canned meat, 114 tons of frozen meat, 10 tons of meat extract, 5 tons of liver meal, 21.5 tons of blubber fibre and 11 tons of glands for medical experiments.[7] By 1938–9 the Germans were deploying five owned and two chartered factory ships. The Japanese also went into large-scale whaling at this time. After the Second World War Germany was prevented from whaling for some years but its factory ships were used by other powers.[8] Whaling boomed, and up to twenty floating factories were operating in the Antarctic, more than ever before, but the catch never reached the peaks of the 1930s, and collapsed in the early 1960s.[9] Whales are one of the most significant cases of disappearing animals of the twentieth century, more extreme than the case of elephants.

Whaling is closely related to the development of industrialised fishing, which is in turn intimately connected with refrigeration. Fishing ports had long had large refrigeration plants to make ice to chill fish at sea, but freezing fish itself at sea was not successfully accomplished until decades after the freezing of meat. The driving force was Commander Sir Charles Dennistoun Burney, inventor of the mine-sweeping paravane in the Great War, a key figure in British airships in the 1920s and a Conservative MP. He developed new freezing equipment, and adapted his mine-sweeping paravane for trawling. Burney converted a wartime minesweeper into the 1,500 ton *Fairfree,* the first stern trawler, one which hauled in its nets just as a whale factory ship hauled in dead whales. In 1949 *Fairfree* was bought by the Scottish shipping and whaling firm Christian Salvesen, which then built the first fully designed factory stern trawler, the *Fairtry.*[10]

As with so many cases of innovation, it was not the innovating nation which would most use the new technology. Copies of the *Fairtry* were built for the Soviet Union, first in Germany and then in the USSR.[11] The first Soviet freezer trawler, the *Pushkin,* went into service in 1955, and the Soviet fleet would soon dominate world factory fishing, especially with a class of ship called the BMRT, introduced in the 1960s. The Soviet fleet became many times larger than its nearest rivals, and led the way in strip-mining the fish colonies. Catches went up so much that they reduced fish populations. The great Newfoundland Grand Banks fishery peaked in 1968; thereafter its yield plummeted.[12] Yet for all the destruction of stocks in particular areas, factory fishing continued to expand. The most modern ships, for example the *American Monarch,* of 6,000 tons GRT, can process 1,200 tons of fish a day. Since the total global catch is now 100 million tons per annum, this suggests that, say, 300 of these ships could catch all the fish now caught worldwide.[13] Just one new ship accounts for 15 per cent of Ireland's entire catch.

Of course, the factory trawlers are not the only means of catching and killing fish – the world still has an enormous variety of fishing vessels. Around the world boat-building yards still construct fishing-boats out of wood, even though they will be equipped with engines, radar and synthetic nets. These new hybrid technologies are as new a part of the fishing fleets of the world as the factory trawlers. Other types of fishing technology are themselves expanding. For example, around the coast of Borneo bamboo fish-traps have made an appearance in recent years.

## Slaughterhouses

Just over one hundred years ago, at the very end of the nineteenth century, the British writer George Gissing visited poverty-stricken southern Italy looking for remains of Greek and Roman civilisations. In the city of Reggio di Calabria he found one of the few new things he thought worthy of praise: a 'handsome' building, which he thought was a 'museum or gallery of art'. To his surprise he found this 'fine structure, so agreeably situated, was nothing else but the town slaughterhouse'. He saw it as a 'singular bit of advanced civilisation', surprised that such a building which reminded him of 'the pole-axe and the butchers' knife' should so advertise itself. He had the odd sense of 'having strayed into the world of those romancers who forecast the future; a slaughterhouse of tasteful architecture set in a grove of lemon trees and date palms, suggested the dreamy ideal of some reformer whose palate shrinks from vegetarianism'.[14] Advanced thinkers of the time, such as Gissing's friend, H. G. Wells, were attracted to vegetarianism and a vegetarian future.

On the other side of the Atlantic, another writer was to picture a very different kind of slaughterhouse. Upton Sinclair, in his great socialist novel of 1906, *The Jungle,* described the booming, corrupt, business-dominated city of Chicago. Among the giant enterprises he discussed were the great meatpackers, a world away from Europe's most modern municipal abattoirs (another, mentioned with approval, was the International Harvester factory). Here was a new kind of mass industry, with astonishing methods of production and unprecedented control over workers and government. Around the Union Stockyards was 'a square mile of abominations', where 'tens of thousands of cattle crowded into pens whose wooden floors stank and steamed contagion'. Here too were the 'dingy meat factories' with their 'rivers of hot blood, and carloads of moist flesh, and rendering vats, and soap cauldrons, glue factories and fertilizer tanks, that smelt like the craters of hell'.[15] Here was 'pork-making by machinery, pork-making by applied mathematics'. The 'slaughtering machine ran on ... like some horrible crime committed in a dungeon, all unseen and unheeded, buried out of sight and out of memory'.[16]

The central character in the novel, a Lithuanian immigrant, becomes a socialist. He learns that the Beef Trust was 'the incarnation of blind and insensate Greed. It was a monster devouring with a thousand mouths, trampling with a thousand hoofs; it was the Great Butcher – it was the spirit of Capitalism made flesh.' Bribery and corruption were its methods, it stole water from the city, dictated sentences for strikers; it lowered the price of cattle, ruined butchers, controlled the price of meat, controlled all refrigerated food transport.[17]

To understand the uniqueness and significance of these reeking factories of death, it is illuminating to cross not the Atlantic with the thousands of Calabrians who went to North America and the River Plate, but instead the Mediterranean a century later, against a new tide of migration *into* Europe. In late twentieth-century Tunisia, on several main roads through the desert there were concentrations of nearly identical small buildings lining each side of the road. Tethered next to many were a few sheep; hanging from the buildings were the still fleece-covered carcasses of their cousins. For these were butchers' shops and restaurants. As the heavy traffic roared by one could dine, on plastic tables, without plates or cutlery, on delicious pieces of lamb taken straight from the displayed cadaver and cooked on a barbecue crudely fashioned from sheet metal. Clearly this spectacle was not a left-over from the past, or the sort of thing which attracted tourists. It was something new: a drive-in barby for the Tunisian motorist and lorry-driver in a hurry.

Along the road one could see the upmarket version – a skinned sheep's carcass in a refrigerated glass case placed outside a roadside restaurant with more elaborate facilities and no live animals to be seen. The fridge was a mark of affluence here, as it had been only a few decades earlier to southern Italians, who in the post-war boom were introduced to the delights of northern dairy produce, and many other products of the new food industry.

Refrigeration was crucial to the new globalised food industries of the twentieth century. It was used to preserve fish, meat, fruit, butter, cheese and eggs.[18] But in the case of meat it had particular importance, making possible a new kind of global meat supply system. The 1911 *Encyclopaedia Britannica* claimed that refrigeration on a 'commercial scale has more powerfully affected the economic conditions of England and, to a less degree, of the United States than any other scientific advance since the establishment of railways and steamboats'. It is a big claim, both because refrigeration does not seem to be that important, and because few remember just how important the importation of refrigerated food into Britain was even before the Great War, or how important this was for the global economy. For the late twentieth-century world the claim would be stronger still, and applied not just to Britain and the USA, but to the whole world, crisscrossed as it was by refrigerated lorries carrying every kind of material in what came to be called 'cold-chains'.[19] Many carried equipment made by a company called Thermo-King which, from 1940, manufactured the refrigeration gear patented by an inventor, Frederick Jones (1893–1961). He was the first black (as he is universally labelled, despite having a white father) to be awarded the National Medal of Technology of the United States. The other major company, the Carrier Corporation, pioneered air-conditioning at the beginning of the century. Its founder, Dr Willis H. Carrier, was named one of the hundred most influential people of the century by *Time* magazine in 1998.

There were alternatives to refrigeration, even in the case of meat. For example, the River Plate had been at the centre of a global meat system decades before the introduction of refrigeration. Up to 1910 Uruguay's exports were still dominated by *tasajo*, or *carne seca* (salted dried beef). Previously given to slaves in the Americas, it now fed their descendants, particularly in Cuba and Brazil, and still features in the cuisine of both countries. *Criollo* (creole) cattle were slaughtered and processed at '*saladeros*', salting plants (which also produced hides

23. *The Frigorífico Anglo, Fray Bentos, Uruguay, in the interwar years, showing the chilled meat warehouse (cold store) on the water's edge. A plant had existed here since the 1860s, first making Liebig's Extract of Beef. The plant remained in operation until the 1970s and is now preserved as a Museum of the Industrial Revolution.*

and much else). Uruguay was also the centre of mass export of a new preserved meat product at Fray Bentos, the site of a specially built plant of the Liebig Extract of Meat Company. The extract, invented by the celebrated chemist Justus von Liebig, was from 1899 named OXO in the British market. The Fray Bentos brand remains famous for *canned* meat products in the British market.

Refrigeration greatly increased the long-distance trade in meat. In Chicago – a city which had grown in the late nineteenth century as a producer of *salted* pig-meat which went in barrels to markets far away – meat was chilled by ice and sent to eastern cities in railroad cars. Later, meat was also frozen and chilled mechanically. Drawing on vast supplies of cattle, the Chicago meatpackers turned into massive concerns such as Swift, Armour, Wilson & Co, Morris, and Cudahy, the Beef Trust. The giant US meatpackers had been important exporters of meat – salted, canned and chilled beef – but by 1900 they could not supply much to the world market from the

USA. That market was largely Britain, which imported half its meat and accounted for 70–80 per cent of all meat traded internationally. In some places in Britain, the proportion was higher still. For example, over 80 per cent of all the beef consumed in London in the 1920s was imported, mostly from Argentina. Indeed much of Britain's meat came from a trans-equatorial trade: from the River Plate, Australia and New Zealand. Already by 1912 there were four Southern hemisphere plants capable of freezing or chilling more than 500 beef carcasses a day, all in Argentina.[20] In this trade the Chicago meatpackers were to be crucial, along with British firms.

Uruguay's first *frigorífico* was not opened till 1904. Swift set up the second meatpacker (Frigorífico Montevideo) and Armour the third (Frigorífico Artigas). The fourth was set up in the early 1920s when the British Vestey family took over and remodelled the Liebig plant, now named Anglo del Uruguay as a *frigorífico*. The Vestey companies – centred on Union Cold Storage – formed one of the largest food enterprises in the world in the interwar years, rivalling the giant American firms. It owned not only slaughterhouses, but a shipping line (the Blue Star Line, created in 1911), cold-storage facilities and an enormous chain of butchers' shops (till 1995) in Britain.[21] The Vestey firm was an early case of one of the least recognised features of twentieth-century international trade, that much of it took place not between nations, but *within* firms.

The oldest plant was taken over by the government and supplied the local market, while the Swift, Armour and Fray Bentos plants exported their products. How was the killing done? We have a description by a refrigeration engineer of the workings of the Fray Bentos plant in the interwar years. The killing was carried out in an approximately square, three-storey building, 30m long on each side. The cattle walked up a ramp to the third floor, where they were stunned with pole-axes, and then hung on a conveyor, had their throats cut and were bled. They were then taken off the conveyor and skinned, after which they were hauled up on to the rail once more for further processing. The hides and offal went down chutes, the offal to the first floor, and the hides to the ground. The carcass was cut in half, and the sides of beef then travelled down a 100m inclined and enclosed ramp to the four-storey chilling plant on the water's edge. From the chilling plant, the sides went by covered way into the holds of the refrigerated ship.[22] But there was much else going on, for every bit of the animal was used, and some 40 per cent in weight was removed to make what is called a 'dressed' carcass; this was turned into a wide range of products, from brushes to pharmaceuticals.

The killing rate in the *frigorífico* was extraordinary, especially if we remember it was done by stunning with a pole-axe and then cutting the throat with a knife. Through much of the twentieth century Uruguay slaughtered 1 million head of cattle per annum, mostly in the four plants. In the 1930s the Anglo in Fray Bentos dispatched 200 an hour.[23] According to Upton Sinclair, one Chicago plant was already killing twice that thirty years earlier. Fifteen to twenty beef cattle were stunned with a pole-axe every minute, and then killed: 400 to 500 an hour, around 4,000 a day.[24]

These giant meatpackers were unknown in the Old World; they were found only in the River Plate, the USA and Oceania. European slaughterhouses, often municipally owned, as in the case of La Villette in Paris, were spaces where many butchers could work, killing their own cattle on a small scale, for local consumption.[25] British slaughterhouses were tiny, supplied local markets and were not known for humane treatment of animals.[26] Even the new interwar municipal abattoir in Sheffield, which had a monopoly of killing in its area, dealt with only 600 cattle a week.[27] The point was not that Britain was resistant to new killing technology, or did not have access to it. Far from it, for Britain owned and used such plant on a huge scale, but it was in Fray Bentos rather than Sheffield. The British worker lived in a global village – fed with beef from the River Plate and margarine derived from South Atlantic whales.

## Killing animals in the long boom and after
In 1906 Sinclair described 'a line of dangling hogs a hundred yards

in length; and for every yard there was a man, working as if a demon was after him'.[28] Here was a disassembly line that would within a few years inspire the assembly lines of another American town, Detroit. Henry Ford himself recalled that 'The idea came in a general way from the overhead trolley that the Chicago packers use in dressing beef.'[29] Just as importantly, the Chicago meatpackers suggested the mechanical handling of things, and the use of gravity to pull things down through buildings, which Henry Ford also used on a large scale.[30] The new world did indeed pioneer both mass killing and mass production. But both would spread and grow particularly strongly in the long boom.

The second half of the twentieth century saw huge increases in world production of meat, and the generalisation of mass killing. Annual global production increased from 71 million tonnes in 1960, rising to nearly 240 million at the end of the century. Per head of population meat consumption nearly doubled over the period. It could easily increase a good deal further as the global average consumption is only about a third of the meat consumption of the richest countries. Much of the change in meat eating in the twentieth century has come from increasing consumption of chicken and pork; they provide two-thirds of all the meat consumed today compared to one half in 1970.

Killing for meat takes place on a scale difficult to comprehend. Britain alone killed 883 *million* animals for food per annum at the end of the century, made up of 792 million chickens, 35 million turkeys, 18 million ducks, 18.7 million sheep, 16.3 million pigs, around 3 million cattle, 1 million geese, 10,000 deer and 9,000 goats. The United States kills 8 *billion* chickens a year. In some cases the sheer scale of killing demanded new technologies of killing, including electric stunning and killing (with tongs for pigs and sheep), and gassing with carbon dioxide for pigs. In the case of chickens the change has been extraordinary. Chickens were killed on automated lines from the 1970s. They were strung up by the legs on a conveyor, and their heads dipped into a conducting solution. A current passing through their bodies stunned them before their necks were cut. Those not despatched by the machine are killed by a human being. They are then plucked and gutted by machine, and chilled. The whole process takes two hours. The largest chicken slaughterhouses now process 1 million birds per week.[31] This scale of chicken-killing is unimaginable by other means. It is difficult to envisage British local butchers and householders handling and killing 2 million chickens every day of the year.

In the case of beef, the technologies of killing would hardly change at all from one end of the century to the next – the big changes were the introduction of the captive-bolt pistol to replace the pole-axe and the chain-saw to replace the axe.[32] In the years after the Second World War, however, the vast New World slaughterhouses of the early part of the century went out of fashion, and much smaller and more dispersed operations took over. The great plants of the River Plate and Chicago closed. The old Anglo plant in Fray Bentos struggled into the 1970s, long enough to be preserved as a museum, the appropriately named Museum of the Industrial Revolution, a place which figures in tourist guides to the Southern Cone. European self-sufficiency in meat, particularly in the British case, and the rise of the Common Market, which de-globalised the trade in meat, put paid to it. In the USA the great meatpackers of Chicago lost markets to new rural, non-unionised, low-skill, single-storey meatpackers, which sent out boxed meat to supermarkets instead of sides of beef to butchers (and of course to the new giant mass producers of beefburgers and the like).

Since the 1970s, and especially the 1980s, new plants and new meat-packers, more concentrated even than those of Chicago's prime, appeared. Four new meatpackers killed more than 80 per cent of US meat at the end of the century.[33] In 2001 the world's largest chicken producer, Tyson Foods, took over the biggest meat producer, IBP. IBP is, it claims, 'the largest provider of protein products on the planet'. It employs 114,000 workers and has sales of $26 billion. Although the methods of slaughtering and processing cattle remains essentially the same, the rate of killing has been pushed up: plants in the 1980s slaughtered 175 an hour, rising to 400 an hour, down a single line.[34] These large plants, located in such states as Nebraska, Kansas, Texas and Colorado (in that order) were also everywhere once again staffed by immigrants, now Latino and Asian.[35] The end of the unionised workforce meant not only a radical speeding up in production, but decreasing real wages. And, just as had also been the case when Sinclair wrote, the new meat industry had enormous political power.

## Executions and other killings

In judicial killing respect for tradition is felt to be appropriate. Until they abolished capital punishment well after the Second World War, the British relied on the gallows, the Spanish on the garrotte, the French on the guillotine. Many continued using the firing squad, and the twentieth century saw plenty of beheadings and stonings too.

The United States showed a remarkable appetite for developing new means of execution. In the 1880s, when the state of New York looked for new ways of executing its errant citizens, they came up with thirty-four possible methods, and four real contenders – gallows, garrotte, guillotine and firing squad. They liked none, for they mutilated the body of the deceased, and in some cases had unfortunate political associations. Two new methods were suggested – electrocution and lethal injection. The first was chosen, with the assistance of Thomas Edison, who ensured that alternating current, and not his own direct current, was used. In 1889 the first victim was killed in New York. By 1915, twenty-five American states had the technology. But innovation did not stop there. In 1924 the gas chamber was introduced in Nevada, and its use too spread quickly. Hydrogen cyanide was the killing gas, produced by the simple means of dropping a bag of sodium cyanide into dilute sulphuric acid. The lethal injection was innovated in Texas in 1982.[36]

Once introduced, a given killing machine lasted for a very long time. Thus the gas chambers, mostly installed in the 1920s and 1930s, were still in use in the 1980s and 1990s, and very old electric chairs remained in use for decades too, until – like many gas chambers – they became too troublesome to maintain. The last gassing was in 1999.[37] Gas chambers were replaced by lethal-injection machines, which were much cheaper than designing and building a new gas chamber or electric chair. Another factor was that in some US states those to be executed were given a choice and most seem to have gone for lethal injection.

Lethal injection has spread around the world, just as earlier, colonial powers took their execution technologies to their colonies.[38] At the end of the twentieth century the Philippines introduced lethal injection; it had wanted gas chambers, but none could be bought. China began to use lethal injection in the 1990s, Taiwan allowed its use but continued shooting, and Guatemala adopted it. In Thailand the machine gun replaced beheading in the 1930s; it has recently been replaced by lethal injection.

Despite the progressive change towards lethal injection, the twentieth century saw expansion in the use of older techniques. The guillotine, perhaps the first killing technique devised to minimise pain to the executed, came into use in the French Revolution. Associated with the beheading of nobles and the Terror, it was to have a particularly gruesome future. In the nineteenth century a number of European nations adopted it, including many German states. The new German Reich beheaded all its capital offenders from 1870, though not all by guillotine; some states retained the axe, until it was abolished in 1936. But the execution rate was, as elsewhere, but a handful a year. The great age of the guillotine was about to begin. Under the Nazis the execution rate increased drastically – in the Nazi era some 10,000 people were executed after a judicial process, peaking at many thousands per year during the war. Hitler is reported to have ordered twenty guillotines. He introduced hanging as an alternative in 1942, using very crude gallows.

In most places judicial execution was a rare occurrence, and from the 1940s would become rarer still. It was regarded in most of the rich world as a barbarous practice which should be abolished. In the United States, some 120 people were executed ever year in the interwar years. By the 1960s there were few executions, and between 1972 and 1976 there were none for technical legal reasons. Elsewhere too the number of executions generally fell, and many countries abolished the death penalty altogether.

The United States in particular deviated from this trend. Executions resumed in 1977, with the killing by firing squad of Gary Gilmore in Utah. But far from continuing on a downward path the number of executions surged in the 1980s and 1990s. Texas, using lethal injection, executed forty in the year 2000, leading the way back to capital punishment levels in the USA not seen since the 1950s. Although lethal injection dominated, the gas chamber and the electric chair returned to use.

The application of capital punishment has never been merely a judicial matter. The noose, electric chair and lethal injection were not neutral. Politics and race have mattered a very great deal. In Britain around twelve people a year were hanged in the twentieth century, yet the British judicially hanged over 1,000 Kenyans between 1952 and 1959 (and killed tens of thousands by other means) during the Mau Mau rebellion. Between 1608 and 1972 only 41 per cent of those executed in the USA were white, despite it being an overwhelmingly white nation; since 1930 more than half of all those executed have been black.[39] In some southern states the fall in lynchings of blacks in the early part of the century merely led to a rise in state executions of blacks.[40] Only since the reintroduction of capital punishment has the number of executed whites slightly exceeded the number of blacks.

## Technologies of genocide

At certain times, in certain places, governments have sought to eliminate particular populations, or simply kill large numbers of people. In doing so they were sometimes forced to think about methods of killing, and sometimes to innovate in killing techniques. For example, in the Great War the Ottoman Empire decided to deport its very large Armenian Christian population from its central Anatolian territories. It was at war with Christian Russia and Armenia was on the Ottoman–Russian border. The deportations were themselves brutal forced marches with much death and killing on the way. The process did not stop until the creation in 1923 of a Turkish state in Anatolia, now free not only of Armenians but of Greek Orthodox peoples too. It is estimated that around 1.5 million Armenians died. Other massacres were small by comparison. In the Soviet Union, during the Great Terror of the mid-1930s, hundreds of thousands were executed by shooting. In a few weeks after their capture of Nanking in December 1937, the Japanese killed, it is roughly estimated, some 100–300,000 Chinese soldiers and civilians, mostly by shooting.

It was the Germans who innovated, under cover of secrecy and war. Using conventional means – shooting, hanging, starving – the horse-drawn German forces killed many millions in Eastern Europe between 1941 and 1945, including millions of civilians. The first large-scale killing of Jews, in what had been eastern Poland and the Soviet Union, used conventional means. Four specially created and remarkably small killing squads, *Einsatzgruppen*, together with local accomplices, killed around 1.3 million Jews with small arms.[41] Soon the *Einsatzgruppen* began to use gas vans on a small scale, but even the small number of these (around thirty is the largest estimate) could kill many thousands a day. Indeed the first mass-killing operation, using just three gas lorries, started in Chelmno in late 1941, taking roughly 1,000 lives a day. From December 1941 until early 1943 around 300,000 were killed. In 1942 three more extermination centres were established – Sobibor, Belzec and Treblinka. With Chelmno, they were responsible for the deaths of around 2 million people. Treblinka was the largest, killing around three-quarters of a million people. All these were small places, deep in the forest, and all were destroyed by the Germans, mostly by 1943. They killed using carbon monoxide from engine exhausts. Its advantage was not that it killed faster – it was that it spared dedicated squads of killers the grisly task of killing directly.[42] This carbon-monoxide killing technology had already been used to kill tens of thousands of mentally and physically handicapped Aryans by 1941.

It is telling that our central image of the Holocaust is not one of small arms and engine exhausts, though these and hunger were the great killers. It involves a large industrial site, a specialised killing gas, Zyklon B (hydrogen cyanide), and industrial-scale crematoria to dispose of bodies. The one major killing site using these means, Auschwitz-Birkenau, killed more than any other single place, around 1 million. There were survivors, and indeed much of the camp itself remained. For these and other reasons it was not typical. Auschwitz-Birkenau, the last extermination centre to come on line, and the last to operate, was not a pure extermination camp. It was an enormous labour camp, supplying manpower, with other camps in the area, for a vast new Upper Silesian industrial complex in territory incorporated into the Reich. Auschwitz-Birkenau was intended at one point to be a camp for the extraordinary number of 200,000 inmates.

Zyklon B was used in Auschwitz, as elsewhere in the Nazi camp system, to disinfect clothes to keep lice-born disease under control. There it was found that it could kill people effectively too. Two houses were turned into gas chambers, and the designs of projected large morgues attached to crematoria, intended for the disposal of the bodies of the many who died from hunger and disease, were changed to convert them into gas chambers.[43] By this twisted road was Auschwitz-Birkenau created as an extermination camp with a novel killing technology.

One of the great industrial enterprises the camps supplied with labour were new plants belonging to IG Farben. The company was building, for the first time contiguously, plant for synthetic oil and rubber, and for many other intermediate and final products, exploiting the inter-relatedness of the processes. This major undertaking never produced oil or rubber but it did manufacture other materials of importance for the war effort. The conjunction tempts us to see connections with the Holocaust; both were linked to a resurgent German nationalism. Treating Auschwitz as if it was a killing factory, in the same way that Leuna or Leverkusen were chemical factories or Krupps in Essen an armament maker, is to miss other crucial aspects. The Auschwitz-Birkenau killing facilities were neither very large, automated nor smooth running, nor especially capital-intensive.

The crematoria often broke down, and many bodies were buried or burned in pits. They worked intermittently as the supply of victims was variable. The greatest killing spree of all, that of Hungary's Jews, which took around two months, was too much for the existing capacity, and needed extra killing, and especially incineration, facilities. Great sloping pits were built, with firewood as fuel. Furthermore the path that led to adapting lice-killing technology to humans and the steps that led to the processes for the manufacture of synthetic oil and rubber were very different.

The image of Auschwitz as a radically modern factory of death nevertheless remains powerful. It has served as a strong critique of modernity in general, as a stark reminder of where modern science and industry could lead. It has helped fuel a retrospective debate as to whether Auschwitz should have been bombed, as if it were a great machine susceptible to destruction, such as a synthetic-oil plant or a V-2 factory.

Simple though horrifying calculations make clear that although killing 2 million people in a year seems to be a stupefying task, it was well within the capabilities of much older killing technology. The four large slaughterhouses of small Uruguay could dispatch 1 million cattle a year with nothing more elaborate than a pole-axe; Chicago's largest were doing this even before the Great War. And, as we have seen, small arms and car exhaust took a terrible toll. Large-scale killing was not as new, nor as difficult, as the technological meditations on the Holocaust suggested.

The nature and power of the killing machines at Auschwitz in particular have been at the centre of the claims of Holocaust deniers. Much of the denier case is that it is inconceivable that so many people could be killed in gas chambers, a few gas vans and with rifles. In this sordid story a genuine expert on killing technology, Fred A. Leuchter Jr, a maintenance and repair man for execution equipment, became a central figure.[44] *Mr Death*, as Errol Morris called his brilliant film on Leuchter, made a modest career in the United States reconditioning and remodelling execution equipment after executions resumed there in 1977. Leuchter renovated gallows for Delaware, and improved a gas chamber for Missouri.[45] He also invented an automatic lethal injection machine for New Jersey. As perhaps the only living expert on gas chambers, Leuchter was hired in 1988 to testify on behalf of a Holocaust denier – a nice illustration of the role of maintenance man as expert. He visited Auschwitz, and convinced himself that there were no gas chambers there. His report became a key document in the Holocaust denier's armoury. Holocaust denial, more accurately gas chamber denial, has led to research that shows in surprising detail how the SS built and used the gas chambers, weakening even further the denier case.[46]

If in innovation-centric history too much is made of Auschwitz, the Holocaust was nevertheless novel. Following the Holocaust genocides cannot be considered a throwback to earlier barbarity, however tempting that line of argument remains. There have been modern motivations, and planning, and in an already established pattern, the use of existing tools in new ways. This is clear in two later, smaller genocides.

In Cambodia, between 1975 and 1979 some 1.7 million people were killed by the Pol Pot regime before it was defeated by the Vietnamese. Some 20 per cent of the population died, with the urban and rural Chinese, Vietnamese and Thai minorities being especially affected.[47] Enforced starvation was the main cause of death, but some 200,000 were executed, according to one estimate. They were killed in many places and by a variety of methods: shooting, skulls bashed in with shovels, hoes and iron bars, and – an innovation – suffocation with a plastic bag.[48]

In 1994 central Africa was the scene of a spectacularly fast genocide. At least 500,000 Rwandan Tutsis (some estimates put the figure as high as 1 million), the minority population, were killed, 99 per cent between April and December.[49] Most victims were killed by machete (38 per cent), clubs (17 per cent) with firearms accounting for only 15 per cent of deaths.[50] The Hutu government had even acquired machetes in advance. In 1993 alone around 1 million machetes, weighing around 500 tons and costing less than a US dollar each, were imported, around one machete for every three males in the country.[51] This was something new – never before had so many been killed so quickly by machete, which appeared as a major killing machine for the first time in history. Invention happens at unexpected times and places.

# 8

# Invention

Since the Second World War, in the Anglophone world, technology has come to be closely identified with invention. This conflation has been unhelpful to the understanding of technology and has also had negative effects on our understanding of invention. We do not have a history of invention, but instead histories of the invention of only *some* of the technologies which were later *successful*. That in itself biases our understanding. But the history of inventions we have is itself innovation-centric. It focuses on (some) aspects of what is new in invention, and it highlights changes in invention, not what does not change.

The innovation-centric picture comes in a number of different versions. One focuses on inventions in academic scientific research; another on what are taken to be the crucial technologies; yet another looks at what are taken to be the most novel inventing organisations. Very often an overall argument is made that as time has passed novelty has itself become ever more novel. Each of these images, while it has some points in its favour, deserves to be challenged. One of the most important and interesting things about invention is that it exhibits important continuities which are insufficiently recognised, and indeed that it has changed in ways we do not sufficiently appreciate. Prolific invention has been with us for a long time – novelty is not new, but there are new things to say about it.

## Academic science and invention

The academic research picture focuses on what it takes to be the most important and innovative aspects of science, and claims that crucial inventions which then shape our world derive from them. Implicit in this view is the argument that something called 'science' has become, since the late nineteenth century, the main source of technologies. What is meant by 'science' is something very particular. Just as technology and invention are conflated, so are science and research. The twentieth-century belief that 'Science implies the breaking of new ground' has made science research.[1] But just as most engineers are not inventors, and most scientists are not researchers, so most science is not research.

Even the research that is referred to when 'science' is used, is usually only a small part of all scientific research – that done in universities or similar bodies. There is a very particular innovation-centred view of academic research, which privileges organic chemistry and electricity in the nineteenth century, nuclear physics in the first half of the twentieth century, and molecular biology since the 1950s. From these particular academic researches, come, implicitly and explicitly, world-changing technologies – synthetic chemistry, electricity, the atomic bomb and biotechnology. The list will by now be familiar. Indeed, our standard picture of what is important in the history of invention in academic research has been profoundly affected by what are taken to be the most important technologies of the century.

Only a tiny proportion of twentieth-century academic research was in particle physics and molecular biology. These branches of physics and biology did not even dominate those fields, let alone academic research as a whole. One of the most striking omissions is chemistry, the largest academic science for most of the century; others are academic engineering and medicine. In these sectors too, the constant generation of novelty became the rule in rapidly expanding universities. Most novel university research has been in what are wrongly taken to be 'old' subjects.

In any case new subjects of research in universities derived from older practices. The university was keeping up with a changing technological world rather than creating it: there was flight before there was aeronautical engineering; there was photography long before any theory of the photographic process; there was any amount of highly specialised metal manufacture before metallurgy; and solid-state devices existed before solid-state physics. Industrial firms, not universities, pioneered the scientific study of photography, metallurgy and the semi-conductor; the academy followed.

The relations between the world of practice and invention in the academy have long been close. For all the talk of ivory towers, academic science, engineering and medicine have been closely connected to industry, as well as the state, since at least the late nineteenth century. The great German organic chemistry centres in the universities had close links with German industry before and after the Great War. Fritz Haber, of the Haber-Bosch process, was an academic. Academic experts on coal and in chemistry were involved in coal hydrogenation. The University of Goettingen was an important centre of aeronautical research before the Great War. Penicillin was spun-off from St Mary's Medical School and the University of Oxford in the 1940s. MIT set up a spin-off arm before the Second World War. Stanford was also spinning out in the 1930s – its Klystron microwave generator became the first great product of what much later would be Silicon Valley.

Yet historically-ignorant analysts insist that only in the last two decades have the barriers between the academy and industry been broken down with the creation of great entrepreneurial universities. These are only now, it is claimed, driving the creation of new industries. Not only is the novelty of this greatly exaggerated, so is its significance. At the beginning of the twenty-first century US universities and hospitals were receiving around $1 billion worth of licence (largely royalty) income from their intellectual property per annum. That is a huge sum, but needs to be kept in proportion. The largest recipients got no more than tens of millions of dollars, with most of the money coming from a very few patents in the medical field, a notable case being Florida State University's patent related to the cancer drug Taxol.

It was far from self-financing. Most university patents were the result of huge *public* investments in academic research. The Bayh–Dole Act of 1980 was critical in that it gave universities intellectual property rights on the results of federally funded research. The universities and hospitals were spending some $30–40bn on research per annum, some $20–25bn funded by the federal government, with the balance coming from industry, local and state governments and the institutions themselves. The big story in US academic research continues to be what it has been since the Second World War: federal research funds, military and civil. For all the emphasis on private health care in the USA, the federal government has played a massive role in funding academic medical research, one which has increased very significantly in the past decade.

Academics have wanted funding to be provided by government, and to be independent of funding directly concerned with invention and development, which was largely a matter for industry.[2] That there is a particularly widespread belief in the significance of academic science as a source of invention is testimony to the great influence of academic research scientists. There are indeed cases where academic research has led to new technologies. Many examples are given, but not all are convincing. Good ones would be X-rays and atomic weapons; poor ones, the cavity magnetron and the laser. The cavity magnetron, which generates high-power high-frequency radio waves, was used before academics studied it. The laser was the product of academic research guided and stimulated by the US military.

The great bulk of invention – let alone the development of inventions – takes place, and always has done – a long way from university research laboratories, and no serious analyst of invention ever believed otherwise. Most invention has taken place in the world of use (including many radical inventions) and furthermore has been under the direct control of users. It has been the realm of the individual inventor, the laboratories, workshops and design centres of industrial firms, and the laboratories, workshops and design centres of governments, and especially their armed forces.[3]

## Stage models of invention

One important myth is that invention is highly concentrated in particular areas where the most radical inventions happen. These are taken to be the technologies which are thought to shape particular historical eras. In the case of industrial technology, invention is thought to be concentrated in electricals and chemicals in the first half of the century, giving way to electronics and rockets, and then to computers and biotechnology. In recent years one could be forgiven for believing that there was no invention going on outside information and biotechnology. There is evidence of shifts in inventive effort between areas over time, and to a lesser extent of changes in inventive output over time, but it does not correspond to the stages suggested. Inventive effort in electricity and chemicals not only persisted, but radically expanded in the twentieth century. So did invention in mechanical engineering. However, the proportion devoted to rockets and electronics undoubtedly grew in the 1950s and 1960s and it undoubtedly shrunk in the last decades of the century. It is the case that within industry life-sciences research, whether in pharmaceuticals or agriculture, has increased while heavy-chemicals research has fallen. That has happened even within particular firms.

Perhaps the most powerful proof of the importance of the old is that the largest private spenders on research and development at the end of the twentieth century were not computer giants, or even pharmaceutical firms, but motor-car producers – General Motors and the Ford Motor Company top the list, not Microsoft or Novartis (see Table 8.1, p. 204). The cost of design of a new car at the end of the twentieth century was around £100–500 million and about the same for a new car engine. It is in the same range as a new drug. Of course, it may be that research and development in these areas is expensive because to produce anything worthwhile, one needs to put a lot in. In other areas the returns may be much larger, and technical change much swifter. Micro-electronics may be the key case.

There is no doubt that there has been a belief that technical progress has concentrated in particular areas, but it is hard to untangle whether

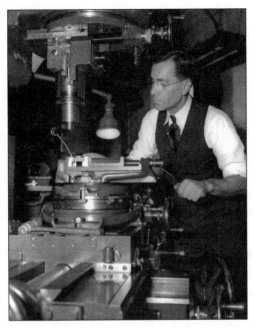

24. *John Garand, employee of the US Federal Armoury at Springfield, and inventor of the US Army's semi-automatic rifle, the M-1, at work in his model shop. The M-1 was the standard US infantry rifle of the Second World War. Mechanical inventions by employees of corporations and governments, and by private individuals, remain a significant proportion of all patents in the twenty-first century.*

this is because a lot of effort is devoted to it, or because it is productive. There is an old Soviet joke which goes to the heart of the issue: an inventor goes to the ministry and says: 'I have invented a new button-holing machine for our clothing industry.' 'Comrade,' says the minister, 'we have no use for your machine: don't you realise this is the age of the Sputnik?'[4] Such sentiments shaped policy, not only in rockets, and not only in the Soviet Union. Planners hope to focus invention and development on what they take to be the 'cutting edge', or some other similar cliché, of technological advance. Much more has been invested by governments in invention in aviation than in shipping, or in nuclear power than other energy technologies. Of course military imperatives to build rockets and nuclear stations, subsequently justified by claims about their general technological fecundity, for example in the notion of spin-off, were important. Yet behind the spin-off argument was a key hidden assumption that spin-off happens only in what are considered advanced technologies. We believe that spin-off from rockets is more likely and more significant than from button-holing machines.

So powerful is the idea that important invention is confined to new technologies, that a special concept was used to explain innovation in old industries. It was the 'sailing ship effect'. This is the argument that firms in old industries innovated only in response to new technology that threatened their survival. The examples given, all nineteenth-century ones, are: the sailing ship improving after the introduction of steam; the development of the Welsbach mantle for gas lights, which followed the introduction of electricity; and improvements in the Leblanc process for making alkali, following the introduction of the Solvay process. However, in all these cases there is no evidence that invention was not happening anyway in the 'old' industry.[5] In some instances there may indeed be a sailing ship effect. The speed up in invention in condoms and other forms of contraception after the introduction of the Pill is a case. But it may be explained by the special circumstances of the industry.

Invention and innovation have been happening everywhere. Agriculture has been an important site of invention and development activity, with the devising of new agricultural practices as well as many new plant varieties, such as IR8, the new dwarf rice introduced in 1966 by the International Rice Research Institute in the Philippines. Intensive development led to new animal hybrids (for example, in the case of chickens) and husbandry practices such as the use of growth-promoting antibiotics. The declining British cotton industry and government supported research and development in the growing of cotton, and the manufacture of cotton goods, on a large and increasing scale from the 1920s. In the early decades of the twentieth century the largest single corporate research project in the USA may well have been the American Tobacco Company's development of a cigar-making machine.[6] Armed forces paid for research and invention in small arms and artillery, as well as in aviation and radio. Inventive activity in shipping has not only led to much larger ships but to such now widespread twentieth-century things as the bulbous bow. Even though it was very unfashionable and badly under-resourced, work was done for decades after the Second World War on improving the performance of steam locomotives.

By the 1960s it was felt by some that whole areas of technology were not receiving the inventive attention they deserved. At its most basic there was an argument that too much was spent on aircraft, rockets and nuclear power, often labelled 'prestige' projects. More should be spent, it was argued, on bread and butter research and development, on improving electronics, and chemicals, even trains and buses. A particularly strong and interesting version of the argument came from the economist E. F. Schumacher. He argued for the development of 'intermediate technologies' which would stand between the traditional technologies of the poor world, and the capital-intensive large-scale ones of the rich world, an idea developed in a famous book called *Small is Beautiful* (1973). These ideas were very influential, leading to the development, on a small scale and funded by charities, of a very wide range of new and improved things. For example, an academic engineer at the University of Oxford, Stuart Wilson (1923–2003) developed an improved cycle-rickshaw, called the 'Oxtrike'. It was designed to be more efficient than the standard rickshaw, and also to be easily manufactured in small workshops in the poor world. Yet it, like many such technologies, did not diffuse around the poor world to any great extent. There was suspicion of such technologies as second-rate technologies. Why should not poor countries have the best, they asked?

There is a great difference between invention *for* the poor world and invention *in* the poor world. The invention and development taking place outside the world of western NGOs was surely much more significant than these efforts. Although not recorded in patents or copyrights, it too is important, changing the material structure of the world, for example in the case of the poor mega-city, the work of millions of untutored architects, engineers and builders.

## New inventive institutions

The third kind of account focuses on telling the story of successive kinds of inventive organisation. In essence, it goes like this. In the heroic period of the industrial revolution invention was the work of individual inventors. From the late nineteenth century science and technology came together, and invention became the province of the corporate research laboratory, particularly in electricity and chemicals. By the 1970s and 1980s the key inventive institution had become the biotechnology and information technology start-up, the science park and the entrepreneurial university. Again, there is something in the story, but the timings and the substance are very misleading.

Take the timing. Around 1900 there is little doubt that a majority of patents were still granted to individual inventors. Only as the century progressed did significant proportions of patents go to large firms. Corporate research laboratories and state organisations, while active around 1900, really came into their own only after 1945. Since then, the individual inventor has not disappeared – he (for invention has been a very masculine activity) has operated in a new context. Nor indeed has the large corporate inventor. One of the most striking features of the history of invention is the long lives of inventing organisations.

Around 1900 one could see an important change within some industries and some firms as to how they organised some of their inventive activity. 'Research' was established in firms for the first time, to supplement the existing scientific and engineering work.[7] A majority of scientists and engineers continued to be employed in routine jobs, in production, in analytical labs and in development labs.

The first research revolution in industry was not, as used to be thought, derivative of a research-centred academy, a kind of application in industry of an academic model. It was the result of a revolution that was taking place slowly but simultaneously in industry, government and the academy. In each a new research-focused science and engineering emerged. Universities went from being teaching institutions to teaching and research institutions (as did medical schools); government scientists and engineers became concerned not just with building roads, or enforcing, say, food standards, but also creating new knowledge and new things.[8]

Research organisations were typically created in firms which were already large and technologically progressive, indeed often dominant in their field. The German synthetic dye firms, such as BASF, Hoechst, Bayer and AGFA, were well-established world leaders in synthetic dyes when they introduced research laboratories. Bayer did so in 1891, and only 20 per cent of its chemists were in research by the early part of the new century. In the United States the research revolution was led by even larger firms. The first case usually cited is the 1900 establishment of the General Electric Laboratory. Other significant research laboratories were established by the explosives firm Du Pont (1902 and 1903), telephone company AT&T (around 1911, when a research branch was added to the engineering department of its manufacturing arm, Western Electric), and the photographic giant Eastman Kodak (c. 1912). All these firms were already very large, innovative in 'science-based' technologies, and employed an abundance of scientists and engineers. Kodak and General Electric were already powerful multinational enterprises, leading the world photographic and electrical industries. AT&T dominated American telephony and telegraphy.

One of the main factors leading to the establishment of research in these firms was potential threats to their dominance from *European* innovations. These innovations were not themselves the product of industrial research. Eastman Kodak felt threatened by the Lumière brothers' Autochrome process, which produced beautiful colour images. GE was concerned about a radically different kind of electric light invented by the German academic chemist Walter Nernst. His lamp was made of a material which conducted electricity and glowed when hot. It could be lit with a match. The rights had been acquired by the German electrical firm AEG, and they made Nernst a rich man. The lamp was to have only modest success, mostly in micro markets. One such was in the first successful photoelectric fax machines, which were designed by Arthur Korn and in use before the First World War.

*25. One of the world's great centres of invention, the Bayer works at Leverkusen, c. 1947.*
*It was a great centre for the production of dyestuffs, pharmaceuticals, and much else*
*besides, from the late nineteenth century to the present. Like many great researching*
*corporations it is older than most nation-states.*

AT&T feared radio would undercut its telephone business; radio was the work of individual European inventors, among them Guglielmo Marconi.

Industrial research would prove to be one of the factors that kept these firms dominant for decades, hence the familiarity of their names. The main research laboratories of General Electric and Du Pont are still where they were established more than one hundred years ago. At least fifteen out of the twenty-three firms listed as the top R&D spenders in 1997 (and 2003) were formed before 1914, and of these at least five were important in industrial research. Of course there were new entrants to the top ranks, and they include Japanese car and electrical firms in particular.

The great industrial research centres founded around 1900 had a history of expansion. Before the Great War Du Pont spent around 1 per cent of its turnover on R&D, going up to 3 per cent in the interwar years. Between the 1950s and 1970s it was at 7 per cent of a much larger company. At the end of the 1960s Du Pont declared its programme of development of new products from its own research an expensive failure. In the 1970s it cut back on its R&D expenditures, and short-range work on existing products was emphasised. By 1975 the research intensity fell to 4.7 per cent, and to 3.6 per cent by 1980. The 1980s saw a return of interest in R&D, but largely in the life sciences. Yet Du Pont remains among the great spenders. It is still in the list in 1997, but because of cuts in research it dropped way down by 2003.

Another example of long-term dominance is AT&T. Its research branch was incorporated into its subsidiary Bell Labs in the 1920s, a company which saw quite extraordinary growth and output through the twentieth century. It was a world leader in information technology from the 1920s and expanded enormously through the 1930s and up to the late 1970s. Among its products are the transistor, invented in 1947, the UNIX operating system of the 1960s, and the Digital Signal Processing chip in 1979, now ubiquitous in mobile phones and much else. Much reduced since by the breakup of AT&T's telephone monopolies and its transfer to Lucent Technologies, it was nevertheless still in the top twenty in 1997, well ahead of, for example, Intel. Since then it has shrunk enormously, but it is still bigger than it was in the mid-1920s.

The development of the transistor and the integrated circuit in the 1950s, 1960s and 1970s was in part the work of entrepreneurial small firms. Transistor development and production were quickly taken by Bell staff to smaller and newer enterprises. Texas Instruments, with a former Bell employee, made the first silicon transistor in 1955. William Schockley, one of the inventors of the transistor, set up a semiconductor firm in California. Experts left to form Fairchild Semiconductor in 1957, the company that introduced the key planar process for the making of integrated circuits. Fairchild and Texas Instruments were granted key patents in 1959. Fairchild employees set up most of the new semiconductor enterprises of the 1960s, largely in the area that became known as Silicon Valley, which had since the 1930s welcomed new industries and had strong connections to new universities and, critically, the expanding US military. Among the new semiconductor enterprises was Intel (1968), which introduced the microprocessor, the computer on the chip, in 1971.

The great firms in information-technology invention today are a mixture of ancient firms, and start-ups of decades ago: Siemens, IBM, Microsoft, Nokia, Hitachi and Intel (see Table 8.1, p. 204). They have R&D budgets only ever exceeded by those above them in the list today. In semiconductors and software the age when the small entre-preneurial university-linked start-up was crucial was the 1950s, 1960s and 1970s, not the later period when they were supposedly dominant. Hitachi and Siemens were both formed before the Great War, as of course was Bell Labs. But perhaps the most telling case is International Business Machines (IBM), for decades synonymous with the computer, from the mainframe to the PC. Even before the Great War it was a huge force in calculating machines around the world. In the 1940s and 1950s it still led, now in electro-mechanical machines. In the 1950s an MIT engineer designed a vast computerised system for US air defence, project SAGE. The contract to build these machines was given to IBM, despite it not having any experience of electronic computers. From this IBM would become, unexpectedly, the leading force in electronic computing, especially with the launch of System 360 in the early 1960s. It remains a major R&D spender.

In the case of biotechnology too, the boom in pharmaceutical research has been led by gigantic spenders, not by start-ups. And they have also been around for a very long time. All the largest spenders on R&D in pharmaceuticals/biotechnology are very old firms. Pfizer, Johnson and Johnson, Roche, each of the Swiss companies that merged to form Novartis (Ciba, Geigy, Sandoz) and those that merged to form Aventis (Hoechst and Rhone Poulenc) were all founded in the nineteenth century, as were all the parts of Glaxosmithkline (Glaxo, Wellcome, Smith, Kline French, Beechams, Allen & Hanbury). Not all, but many, were important in pharmaceutical research and production before 1914. The start-ups of the 1970s and 1980s are well behind.

Although the big car companies which head the list of R&D spenders today existed well before the First World War, they were not known for R&D until well after the Second, with the partial exception of General Motors. They did little research, yet they were very inventive. The Model T launched in 1908 was a new kind of car: it was a sturdy, light, cheap vehicle, well adapted for use in the countryside. It did not come out of a laboratory, but from a small firm. By January 1910 Ford moved into a vast new concrete and glass factory at Highland Park, with its own palatial power station. It employed 3,000 production employees in 1910, expanding to over 14,000 by 1913.[9] Few of today's fastest-growing companies could match that rate of growth.

In the car industry, and many others, there were few if any laboratories, but plenty of development workshops and testing facilities such as tracks, wind tunnels and hydrodynamic tanks. Such facilities were important in generating much-needed knowledge of things such as propellers, hull shapes, aeroplanes and materials. In these places the designers and the engineers long held sway. They were trying to achieve particular levels of performance, often through incremental change, and much design work involved a great deal of calculation and modelling.

The Second World War brought a radical change in scale in this inventive and development activity. Aircraft and aero-engines alone were huge elements of post-war R&D, largely funded by the state. Alongside this and organised in a similar way were the rocket programmes and the development of new computing machines. Decisions were made to devote huge resources to particular projects, resulting not only in an increase in spending, but in a progressive reduction in the number of projects. The DC3 airliner cost around $300,000 to develop in the late 1930s, while the larger DC4 in the mid-1930s took $3.3m; in the 1950s the DC8 cost $112m.[10] The cost of aircraft development continued to increase, as did that of car development.

Missiles, short-range and intercontinental, as well as space launchers also consumed vast sums in development expenditure.

The phrase 'research and development' became a term of art especially around the Second World War in both government and industry. It is an unfortunate term, as 'development and research' would more accurately reflect the fact that development expenditure was much larger than research expenditure.

## How does the bomb project fit in?

In the history of twentieth-century science, technology and invention, no project has so central a place as the US atomic bomb project of the Second World War (though not the later work). It has profoundly affected what we take to be significant in the history of twentieth-century science, especially before 1939, and figures as one of the great technologies of the middle of the century. It also marks what is regarded as a hugely important organisational innovation in the history of science and technology – the rise of 'big science'. It is made unprecedented in world history through the discounting of the many precedents that existed. Once we put the old into the story, it will look very different.

Let us start with the name. The use of the term 'Manhattan Project' obscures an important word in its full name, which was 'Manhattan Engineer District'. It was so-called because it was run by the US Army's Corps of Engineers, a prestigious old institution that had long taken the best graduates from the West Point military academy. The Corps was organised into districts, and they created one for this new project, which was a production, development and research project. In the usual stories about big science, its phenomenal cost of $2bn is referred to as if this was the cost of the research and development effort, when, in fact, most of the $2bn went on the building of two nuclear factories at Oak Ridge and Hanford. General Leslie Groves, the head of the project and senior member of the US Army Corps of Engineers, had previously supervised the building of munitions plants, issuing contracts worth much more than the entire cost of the Manhattan Project.[11]

Through the war the research and development cost was $70m

26. *The military engineer Brigadier General Leslie Groves was the director of the Manhattan Engineer District project, running everything from its research to the construction of the factories. Yet it is often implied that one of his subordinates, the director of the Los Alamos laboratory, Robert Oppenheimer, was in charge. The academic-research-centred view of invention systematically downplays the crucial non-academic and non-physics elements of such projects as the bomb.*

($800m in 1996 dollars). This was a very large sum for the time, but within an order of magnitude of other projects. Assuming each type of bomb cost $35m to develop, that was around ten times the development cost of the pre-war DC4 aircraft, and about the same as that of a new car today. There were many other very large projects, even in the USA. Among them were radar development, a huge effort to make new synthetic rubbers following the fall of the world's main rubber plantations to the Japanese, and indeed large projects in medicine, among them penicillin and anti-malarial compounds. These all built on decades of experience in large-scale research and development, from nylon to coal hydrogenation, from motor cars to large airships.

## Is the rate of invention ever increasing?

Given the paucity of and poor quality of the data, constructing a historical story of the changing patterns of invention is problematic. We should thus be sceptical of any claim for an increase or a decrease in the rate or significance of inventions in any particular historical period. The measures by which any such conclusion could be arrived at simply do not exist, and such measures as do exist suggest caution should be exercised. The main statistical information we have on invention is numbers of patents. Patents are legal documents granted to inventors giving them exclusive rights to the invention for fixed periods. Yet only some inventions are patented, and many developments cannot be patented. The existence of a patent gives no indication of its significance, nor that of the underlying technology. Furthermore different nations adopted different patent systems, and all changed over time. Inventors have differed in their desire to get patents too. Only a small proportion of patents are ever worked; indeed only 10 per cent or less have been kept in force for their permitted time. Unlike most property, most patents turn out to have no value at all. Patents are a particular kind of legal claim on a certain invention, not necessarily one anywhere near being exploited successfully.[12]

Yet we can get some useful hints from this statistical history. Firstly, and perhaps most surprisingly, the rate of patenting has not changed much over time. US patents granted to US residents varied between around 30,000 per annum to 50,000 per annum between 1910 and 1990, despite population growth, and even more significant economic growth. In some periods, notably the early 1930s, there were significant falls in patenting activity. This led to the belief among many that large US monopolies were retarding technological progress.[13] Since the early 1980s there was a steady increase, such that resident patent grants reached around 80,000 at the beginning of the twenty-first century. In the European Union growth has been slower. To reinforce the earlier caution about drawing too many conclusions we should note that by these measures Japan was, at the end of the twentieth century, three times more inventive than the United States, and Korea more than twice as inventive. Is this plausible?

Another way of getting at these issues is to look at research and development expenditure. This is an input into some, but certainly not all invention. Most has gone on the development not invention as such. R&D expenditure was tiny in comparison to the economy in 1900, then these expenditures, by both government and industry, grew rapidly through the decades to the 1960s, much faster than the growing economy, especially in the long boom, and reached around 3 per cent of GDP for the richest countries. From the late 1960s R&D grew about as fast as the economies of rich countries, meaning that the proportion of GDP accounted for by R&D has hardly changed. Given that the rate of growth of the main R&D performers was low by historic standards, it follows that the rate of increase of R&D expenditures slowed down in the last decades of the twentieth century. Although the rate of growth of R&D has slipped very considerably, the actual amounts spent were greater year on year, with falls in some years.

Increases in R&D expenditure suggest that inputs into invention and development have grown very significantly with time. Yet, these increases did not lead to any comparable rise in the number of patents. This suggests, again, that patents may be a very poor indicator of invention, and certainly of development. It could also suggest that over the century the costs of invention and development have been rising. Some have felt that innovations became increasingly trivial and expensive.[14] One area where there has been a clear decline in R&D productivity is in pharmaceuticals. The number of new chemical entities (NCEs) approved by the US Food and Drug Administration doubled between 1963 to the end of the century: they averaged about fourteen per annum in the 1960s and 1970s, rising from the 1980s to reach around twenty-seven in the 1990s. Yet over the same period the R&D expenditure of the pharmaceutical industry grew nearly twenty-fold.[15] The common explanation is that the development costs of drugs have increased, especially as clinical testing becomes more expensive and time-consuming. A recent estimate of the total cost of

R&D to achieve an approved new chemical entity in the pharmaceutical industry is about $400m, though it needs to be recognised that this includes costs of projects which were stopped before they reached the end; thus the costs of *successful* projects are lower.[16]

Another factor needs to be taken into account. The NCE measure tells us nothing about the efficacy of new approved drugs, nor how different they are from each other. It could be that new drugs are radically better than old ones, yet there have been few if any drugs of the significance of those produced decades earlier. Pharmaceutical companies make huge investments in the development, testing and marketing of 'me-too' drugs, minor variants of existing treatments. They are inventing and developing better mousetraps.

The pharmaceutical firms now account for around one-third of all development and research expenditure. Pharmaceuticals plus the motor-car industry perform around half the world R&D total. Yet it is hardly the case that the *new* products of either industry have been making anything like the radical difference made when these industries spent much less on R&D. There is nothing as novel or as significant as penicillin or the Model T.

What then of biotechnology, a central case for the argument that invention has shifted from corporate laboratories? The record here has been very disappointing if one looks behind the hype. Even in the face of low invention in traditional pharmaceuticals, only about a quarter of new pharmaceuticals are of biotechnological origin, though on a stricter definition it is considerably lower. Even on the widest possible definition, biotechnology-originated pharmaceuticals account for only 7 per cent of drug sales. In 2004 the leading biotech firm (Amgen, founded in 1980) had sales only one-fifth of each of the leading three or four firms in the pharmaceutical industry. The pioneering company, Genentech, founded in 1976, had sales of $4bn in 2004. There have been twelve significant new biotechnological drugs in terms of sales since the 1980s, three of them synthetic replacements for existing ones. Only sixteen new biotechnological drugs offering more than minimal improvement over previous treatments have been launched since 1986. More interestingly, biotech innovations are already declining in additional clinical efficiency, and there has been a lot of me-too innovation in this field too. The impact on overall health will be minimal, despite enormous private and public investment in invention, partly because the drugs are for rare conditions.[17]

It is little wonder that in the pharmaceutical industry and biotech the investment in public relations and marketing is so huge. Pharma companies spend more on marketing than R&D – which tells us that they are not selling products that are obviously superior to those of their competitors. Penicillin did not need marketing; particular variants did.

It is against that background that we should consider easily the most cited piece of evidence for a rapidly increasing rate of change in technology in recent years – the power of computing. It has proceeded at an astonishingly fast rate. In 1965 Gordon Moore, the research and development director of Fairchild Semiconductor, and soon to be one of the founders of Intel, suggested that the number of transistors on an integrated circuit that could be economically made would continue to grow at the same rate as in the early 1960s. In 1975 he thought growth would continue, but at *half* the rate he was measuring in 1965. Indeed the rate did fall, but there was a steady increase at roughly the rate predicted in 1975. But that rate of change was enormous. Between the 1970s and the early 1990s Intel's own processors increased the number of components at the constant rate of 100 times per decade. In the late 1990s that rate increased, though not to 1960s' levels.

That one-hundred-fold-a-decade rate of change sustained for forty-five years is unprecedented. We do not find it in motor cars at the beginning of the century or since. We do not find it anywhere else today either. It cannot stand for technical change in general.

By the standards of the past, the present does not seem radically innovative. Indeed judging from the present, the past looks extraordinarily inventive. We need only think of the twenty years 1890–1910 which gave us, among the more visible new products, X-rays, the motor car, flight, the cinema and radio, most of them expanding technologies to this day.

## Table 8.1  R&D expenditures of the largest R&D-funding firms in the world 1997 and 2003, £m at 1997 and 2003 exchange rates

| Company | 1997 R&D spend £m | Company | 2003 R&D spend £m |
|---|---|---|---|
| General Motors | 4983.591 | Ford Motor | 4189.71 |
| Ford Motor | 3845.266 | Pfizer | 3983.58 |
| Siemens | 2748.690 | DaimlerChrysler | 3925.45 |
| IBM | 2617.601 | Siemens | 3883.17 |
| Hitachi | 2353.534 | Toyota Motor | 3483.99 |
| Toyota Motor | 2106.695 | General Motors | 3184.18 |
| Matsushita Electric | 2032.720 | Matsushita Electric | 3019.18 |
| Daimler-Benz | 1914.146 | Volkswagen | 2917.14 |
| Hewlett-Packard | 1870.670 | IBM | 2826.1 |
| Ericsson Telefon | 1856.885 | Nokia | 2802.99 |
| Lucent Technologies | 1837.243 | Glaxosmithkline | 2791.00 |
| Motorola | 1670.111 | Johnson & Johnson | 2616.61 |
| Fujitsu | 1649.168 | Microsoft | 2602.65 |
| NEC | 1629.157 | Intel | 2435.62 |
| Asea Brown Boveri | 1614.805 | Sony | 2309.76 |
| El du Pont de Nemours | 1576.516 | Ericsson | 2275.52 |
| Toshiba | 1554.453 | Roche | 2152.67 |
| Novartis | 1538.814 | Motorola | 2106.59 |
| Intel | 1426.401 | Novartis | 2098.21 |
| Volkswagen | 1487.240 | NTT | 2063.94 |
| NTT | 1535.634 | Aventis | 2060.32 |
| Hoechst | 1348.656 | Hewlett-Packard | 2040.11 |
| Bayer | 1339.868 | Hitachi | 1938.1 |
|  |  | AstraZeneca, UK | 1927.83 |

Italics – company founded before 1914. In the case of NTT, the crucial date is the foundation of the telephone and telegraph system in Japan, both nineteenth century.
Source: 2004 and 1998 R&D Scoreboards.
http://www.innovation.gov.uk/projects/rd_scoreboard/downloads.asp

## Table 8.2 **Industrial Nobel prizes**

### Physics

1909  Guglielmo Marconi – Marconi Co.

1912  Nils Gustaf Dalén – Swedish Gas Accumulator Co. (AGA)

1937  Clinton Davisson – Bell Labs

1956  William Schockley, John Bardeen and Walter Brattain – Bell Labs

1971  Dennis Gabor – British Thomson-Houston (AEI)

1977  Philip W. Anderson – Bell Labs

1978  Arno Penzias – Bell Labs

1986  Gerd Binnig and Heinrich Rohrer – IBM Switzerland

1987  Georg Bednorz and Alex Mueller – IBM Switzerland

1997  Steven Chu – Bell Labs

1998  Horst Stormer – Bell Labs

2000  Jack Kilby –Texas Instruments

### Chemistry

1931  Friedrich Bergius – various and Carl Bosch – BASF/IG Farben

1932  Irving Langmuir – General Electric

1950  Kurt Alder – academia/IG Farben

1952  Archer Martin and Richard Synge – Wool Industries Research Association, Leeds

### Medicine

1936  Henry Dale – academia/Burroughs Wellcome

1948  Hermann Mueller – Geigy

1979  Godfrey Hounsfield – EMI

1982  John Vane – academia/Wellcome

1988  James Black – ICI/SKF/Wellcome, Gertrude Elion – Wellcome USA and George Hitchins – Wellcome USA

In some of these years the prizes were awarded to more scientists and engineers than those named here. The firms given are those associated with the Nobel prize work – the Laureates were sometimes elsewhere when they were awarded the prize.

*Source*: my analysis of the extensive online information available for Nobel Laureates provided by the Nobel Foundation (*www.nobel.se* or *www.nobelprize.org*).

# Conclusion

We have long been told that we live with an 'ever-increasing rate of change', yet there is good evidence that it is not always increasing. Measuring change is extremely difficult, but let us start with economic growth in the rich countries as a crude measure. While there was rapid growth before the Great War, there was slower growth overall between 1913 and 1950. There was spectacular growth in the long boom, followed by less strong growth since. In other words, growth rates were lower in the interwar years than before 1914, and average rates of economic growth after 1973 were considerably lower than in the period 1950–1973. In the 1970s there was a 'productivity slowdown' and since then the rich world has continued to grow, but not at historically unprecedented rates.

Since the 1980s one could be forgiven for believing that high growth rates had returned, not least because of the constant evocations of the notion of 'ever increasing change', and all the talk of fundamental transitions to new economies and new times. But in the USA, Japan, the EU and Britain, growth rates were lower in the 1990s than in the 1980s, lower in the 1980s than in the 1970s and lower in the 1970s than in the 1960s.[1] In the USA it appears that productivity growth increased in the late 1990s, but there is still a dispute as to whether this was general, or concentrated in the computer-manufacturing sector.[2] Growth is not the same as change but there is no evidence that structural change in the rich countries was any faster in recent decades than in the long boom. Once again, our future-oriented rhetoric has underestimated the past, and overestimated the power of the present.

Not all parts of the world grew at these same rhythms. For example the USSR grew very fast in the 1930s, while the rest of the world did not.

Especially since the 1970s many economies in the Far East have grown very fast, but from a low base. The increasing scale of the Chinese economy in particular has meant that its growth has been enough to alter the global statistics materially. For example, global steel production is growing at long boom rates again thanks to China.

Another important feature of change in the last three decades is that there has been a decline of economies, as well as growth. In some places the last years of the twentieth century saw retrogression. The income per head of the 700 million sub-Saharan Africans fell from $700 per head in 1980 to the even more miserable $500 at the end of the century; to make matters worse for the majority, 45 per cent of this output was produced in South Africa so the real fall elsewhere was even worse.[3] Malaria has become more common, and new diseases such a HIV/AIDS have swept through the continent as no other. Yet this is not a reversion to an old world, for this is a continent with cars and new kinds of shanty towns, a rapidly urbanising world without what is taken to be modern industry.

From 1989 there was a remarkably rapid collapse in the economies of the Soviet Union and its former satellites, of 20, 30 and 40 per cent, far outstripping the capitalist recession of the early 1980s. Although this dramatic fall in output cannot be characterised generally as a technological retrogression such a phenomenon was evident in some places. Now independent Moldova, formerly part of the USSR, lost 60 per cent of its output. Machines virtually phased out as the economy had developed since the Second World War, things such as 'spinning wheels, weaving looms, butter churns, wooden grape presses and stone bread ovens – are now back in use', it was reported in 2001. The 'only way to survive is to be totally self-sufficient,' claimed the curator of the ethnological museum in Belsama, 'and that means turning the clock back.'[4] Cuba, as we have seen, expanded the number of its oxen as it lost its supply of tractors.

In some industries, such as shipbreaking, there has been a move towards a new kind of low-tech future. By the 1980s Taiwan had become by far the largest shipbreaker, demolishing more than a third

*27. The Brazilian aircraft carrier* Minas Gerais, *broken up with a novel lack of modern technology on Alang Beach, Gujarat, India, in 2004. Alang Beach became the single largest centre of the shipbreaking industry, and a startling example of the new technological retrogression. The ship, originally HMS* Vengeance, *launched in 1945, was built at a time when shipbreaking was more capital intensive.*

of the world's ships. By the early 1990s it was out of this industry, now dominated by India, Pakistan and Bangladesh, which between them had more than 80 per cent of the world market by 1995.[5] Taiwan used specialised dock facilities, but the new shipbreaking was on beaches, with the most minimal equipment, carried out by thousands of barefoot workers. The reason shipbreaking was done in these places was that scrap steel was in demand locally. But it is used in a markedly different way from other places and times: it is re-rolled, re-worked, rather than used to make fresh steel.

What seems at first technological retrogression was perhaps not unknown in earlier years of the century. No one had ever attempted to build such a large canal with what were then such primitive means as were used on the White Sea canal or in the erection of the great steel works of Magnitogorsk. Collective farming itself involved technological retrogression, for all the emphasis on the tractor. However, not for many centuries has a global industry retrogressed like shipbreaking has.

This book has argued for the importance of the seemingly old. It is also a plea for a novel way of looking at the technological world, one which will change our minds about what that world has been like. And implicit in it is a plea for novel ways of thinking about the technological present.

We should be aware, for example, that most change is taking place by the transfer of techniques from place to place. The scope for such change is enormous given the level of inequalities that exist with respect to technology. Even among rich countries there are very important differences in, for example, carbon intensity. If the USA were to reduce its energy-use levels to those of Japan, the impact on total energy use would be very significant. But for poor countries, as well as for rich ones, such a message is often unwelcome. For *imitating* is seen as a much less worthy activity than innovating. To imitate, to replicate, is to deny one's creativity, to impose upon oneself what was designed for others by others. '*Que inventen ellos*' ('Let *them* invent') is seen not as sensible policy advice, but a recipe for national humiliation. To have technology or science is, it is often deeply felt, to create something new. The answer to such concerns that is implicit in this book is that all countries, firms, individuals, with rare and unusual exceptions, have relied on others to invent, and have imitated more than they have invented.

Arguments about imitating policies and practices for innovation might seem to fall in the same category. That is to say, that it might seem like a good thing that they should be the same or similar around the world. Indeed there is a remarkable lack of originality in innovation policies globally, and many explicit calls for copying those perceived as the most successful models. Yet while copying existing technology is very sensible, imitating innovation policies may be a mistake. For if all nations, areas and firms are agreed about what the research should be, by definition it will no longer be innovative; and it might not be a good thing that all nations pursue the same policies for research, because they are likely to come up with similar inventions only a few of which will be used even if technologically successful. 'If I knew the future of jazz I'd be there already,' said one wise musician.

Calling for innovation is, paradoxically, a common way of avoiding change when change is not wanted. The argument that future science and technology will deal with global warming is an instance. It is implicitly arguing that in today's world only what we have is possible. Yet we have the technological capacity to do things very differently: we are not technologically determined.

Getting away, as this book has, from the conflation of use and invention/innovation will in itself have a major impact on our thinking about novelty generation. The twentieth century was awash with inventions and innovations, so that most had to fail. Recognising this will have a liberating effect. We need no longer worry about being resistant to innovation, or being behind the times, when we chose not to take up an invention. Living in an inventive age requires us to reject the majority that are on offer. We are free to oppose technologies we do not like, however much interested pundits and governments tell us it is essential to accept, say, GM crops. There are alternative technologies, alternative paths of invention. The history of invention is not the history of a necessary future to which we must adapt or die, but rather of failed futures, and of futures firmly fixed in the past.

We should feel free to research, develop, innovate, even in areas which are considered out of date by those stuck in passé futuristic ways of thinking. Most inventions will continue to fail, the future will remain uncertain. Indeed the key problem in research policy should be ensuring that there are many more good ideas, and thus many more failed ideas. Stopping projects at the right time is the key to a successful invention and innovation policy, but doing this means being critical of the hype that surrounds, and often justifies and promotes funding for invention.

Although we can stop projects, it is often said that we cannot un-invent technologies, usually meaning that we cannot get rid of them. The idea is itself an example of the conflation of invention and technology. For most inventions are effectively un-invented, in being forgotten and often lost. A few things are going out of use as the world economy grows – among them are asbestos, declining since the 1970s, and refrigerants like CFC gases. And one of the new tasks faced by scientists and engineers is actively making old technologies disappear, some of which, like nuclear power stations, are extremely difficult to dispose of.

Thinking about the technological past can give us insights into 'the question of technology' – what is it, where does it come from, what does it do? But this book has attempted to do much more than take historical examples to address this perennially interesting question. It has been concerned primarily with asking questions not about technology, but about technology in history – asking questions about the place of technology within wider historical processes. This important distinction is not obvious, but it is central to a proper historical understanding of technology. It will help wean us off the idea that invention, 'technological change' and the 'shaping of technology' need to be the central questions for the history of technology. Instead the history of technology can be much more; and it can help us rethink history.

If we are interested in the historical relations between technology and society we need a new account not only of the technology we have used but also of the society we have lived in. For existing histories of twentieth-century technology were embedded in particular assumptions about world history, while world histories had embedded in them particular assumptions about the nature of technological change and its impact – each was already defined, usually implicitly, in relation to the other. Hence the history of the society into which this new account is placed is very different from the one usually found: for example, it takes as central the expansion of a new kind of poor world, a world which has been almost continuously at war, and in which millions have been killed and tortured. This necessitates an account of the global technological landscape that is very different from those found implicitly and explicitly in existing global histories and histories of technology – and an account that might help revise our views about world history.

It is a measure of the importance of technology to the twentieth century, and to our understanding of it, that to rethink the history of technology is necessarily to rethink the history of the world. For example, we should no longer assume that there was ineluctable globalisation thanks to new technology; on the contrary the world went through a process of de-globalisation in which technologies of self-sufficiency and empire had a powerful role. Culture has not lagged behind technology, rather the reverse; the idea that culture has lagged behind technology is itself very old and has existed under many different technological regimes. Technology has not generally been a revolutionary force; it has been responsible for keeping things the same as much as changing them. The place of technology in the undoubted increase in productivity in the twentieth century remains mysterious; but we are not entering a weightless, dematerialised information world. War changed in the twentieth century, but not according to the rhythms of conventional technological timelines.

History is changed when we put into it the technology that counts: not only the famous spectacular technologies but the low and ubiquitous ones. The historical study of things in use, and the uses of things, matters.

# Notes

## Introduction

1. Michael McCarthy, 'Second Century of Powered Flight is heralded by jet's 5,000mph record', *Independent*, 29 March 2004, pp. 14–15.
2. Milton O. Thompson, *At the Edge of Space: the X-15 Flight Program* (Washington: Smithsonian Institution Press, 1992).
3. *http://www.nasa.gov/missions/research/X-43_overview.html* (opened 29 March 2004).
4. See David Edgerton, 'De l'innovation aux usages. Dix thèses éclectiques sur l'histoire des techniques', *Annales HSS*, July–October 1998, Nos. 4–5, pp. 815–37 ; Svante Lindqvist, 'Changes in the Technological Landscape: the temporal dimension in the growth and decline of large technological systems', in Ove Granstrand (ed.), *Economics of Technology* (Amsterdam: North Holland, 1994), pp. 271–88. This approach needs to be distinguished from the long-standing interest in the influence of users on invention and innovation, as seen in, for example, Ruth Schwartz Cowan, 'The consumption junction: a proposal for research strategies in the sociology of technology', in W. Bijker et al., *The Social Construction of Technological Systems* (Cambridge, MA: MIT Press, 1987), Ruth Oldenzeil, 'Man the Maker, Woman the Consumer: The Consumption Junction Revisited' in Londa Schiebinger et al., *Feminism in the Twentieth Century. Science, Technology and Medicine* (Chicago: Chicago University Press, 2001); and Nelly Oudshoorn and Trevor Pinch (eds.), *How Users Matter: the Co-construction of Users and Technology* (Cambridge, MA: MIT Press, 2003).
5. Bruno Latour, *We Have Never Been Modern* (New York: Harvester Wheatsheaf, 1993), pp. 72–6.
6. Lester Brown et al., *Vital Signs* (London: Earthscan, 1993), pp. 86–9.

## 1. Significance

1. This is my reading of Thomas Parke Hughes's *American Genesis: a Century of Invention andTechnological Enthusiasm* (New York: Viking, 1989) and recent textbooks, namely Ruth Schwartz Cowan, *A Social History of American*

*Technology* (New York: Oxford University Press, 1997), Carroll Pursell, *The Machine in America: a Social History of Technology* (Baltimore: Johns Hopkins University Press, 1995) and Thomas J. Misa, *Leonardo to the Internet: Technology and Culture from the Renaissance to the Present* (Baltimore: Johns Hopkins University Press, 2004). In the latter, 1900–1950 is also dealt with in terms of modern architecture. See also Bertrand Gille, *Histoire des Techniques* (Paris: Gallimard La Pléiade, 1978) trans as *The History of Techniques* (New York: Gordon and Breach Science Publishers, 1986), 2 vols., Robert Adams, *Paths of Fire: an Anthropologist's Enquiry into Western Technology* (Princeton: Princeton University Press, 1996), Donald Cardwell, *The Fontana History of Technology* (London: Fontana, 1994) and R. A. Buchanan, *The Power of the Machine: Impact of Technology from 1700 to the Present* (London: Penguin, 1992), as well as the long-wave literature associated with Christopher Freeman discussed below.

2. Schwartz Cowan, *Social History,* p. 221.

3. Christopher Freeman and Francisco Louçã, *As Time Goes By: from the Industrial Revolutions to the Information Revolution* (Oxford: Oxford University Press, 2002) passim, but see summary table p. 141.

4. Harry Elmer Barnes, *Historical Sociology: Its Origins and Development. Theories of Social Evolution from Cave Life to Atomic Bombing* (New York: Philosophical Library, 1948), p. 145.

5. Ernest Mandel, *Marxist Economic Theory* (London: Merlin Press, 1968), p. 605.

6. For the Marxist Harry Braverman, *Labor and Monopoly Capital* (New York: Monthly Review Press, 1974), the scientific-technical revolution was much more broadly based, and was evident from the late nineteenth century.

7. *You and Yours* survey, April 2005, BBC Radio 4, *http://www.bbc.co.uk/radio4/ youandyours/technology_launch.shtml*

8. R. W. Fogel, 'The new economic history: its findings and methods', *Economic History Review*, Vol. 19 (1966), pp. 642–56.

9. Henry Porter, 'Life BC (Before the Age of the Computer)', *The Guardian*, 14 February 1996.

10. *The Net*, BBC2, 14 January 1997.

11. Charles W. Wootton and Carel M. Wolk, 'The Evolution and Acceptance of the Loose-leaf Accounting System, 1885–1935', *Technology and Culture*, Vol. 41 (2000), pp. 80–98.

12. See Martin Bauer (ed.), *Resistance to New Technology: Nuclear Power, Information Technology and Biotechnology* (Cambridge: Cambridge University Press, 1995).

13. Gijs Mom, *The Electric Vehicle: Technology and Expectations in the Automobile Age* (Baltimore: Johns Hopkins University Press, 2004), p. 144.

14. Ibid., pp. 31–2.

15. Gijs Mom, 'Inter-artifactual technology transfer: road building technology in the Netherlands and competition between brick, macadam, asphalt and concrete', *History and Technology*, Vol. 20 (2004), pp. 75–96.

16. Mark Harrison, 'The Political Economy of a Soviet Military R&D Failure: Steam Power for Aviation, 1932 to 1939', *Journal of Economic History*, Vol. 63 (2003), pp. 178–212.

17. Eric Schatzberg, 'Ideology and Technical Choice: the decline of the wooden airplane in the United States, 1920–1945', *Technology and Culture*, Vol. 35 (1994), pp. 34–69, and *Wings of Wood, Wings of Metal: Culture and Technical Choice in American Airplane Materials, 1914–1945* (Princeton: Princeton University Press, 1998).

18. G. M. G. McClure, 'Changes in suicide in England and Wales, 1960–1997', *The British Journal of Psychiatry* vol. 176 (2000), pp. 64–7.

19. See Ted Porter, *Trust in Numbers: the Pursuit of Objectivity in Science and Public Life* (Princeton: Princeton University Press, 1995).

20. The figures are from the St Mary's surgeon Dickson-Wright, the calculations in James Foreman-Peck, *Smith and Nephew in the Health Care Industry* (Aldershot: Edward Elgar, 1995).

21. Tami Davis Biddle, *Rhetoric and Reality in Air Warfare: the Evolution of British and American Ideas about Strategic Bombing, 1914–1945* (Princeton: Princeton University Press, 2002) and Walt Rostow, *Pre-invasion Bombing Strategy: General Eisenhower's Decision of March 25, 1944* (Austin: University of Texas Press, 1981), pp. 20–21.

22. Sir Arthur Harris, *Despatch on War Operations 23 February to 8 May 1945* (October 1945) (London: Frank Cass, 1995), p. 40.

23. Ibid., p. 30.

24. Ibid., p. 39, para. 205.

25. Speer interrogation, Sir Charles Webster and N. Frankland, *The Strategic Air Offensive against Germany, 1939–1945*, Vol. IV, *Annexes and Appendices* (London: HMSO, 1961), p. 383.

26. Among the experts were Paul Nitze and John Kenneth Galbraith. Biddle, *Rhetoric and Reality in Air Warfare*, p. 271.

27. Noble Frankland, *History at War: the Campaigns of an Historian* (London: Giles de la Mare, 1998).

28. Webster and Frankland, *Strategic Air Offensive*, Appendix 49 (iii).

29. United States Strategic Bombing Survey: Summary Report (Pacific War), 1 July 1946 (Washington: United States Government Printing Office, 1946). Available online.

30. Ibid.

31. Ibid., p. 25.

32. Ibid.

33. Notes of the Interim Committee Meeting, 31 May 1945, *http://www.trumanlibrary.org/whistlestop/study_collections/bomb/large/interim_committee/text/bmi4tx.htm*.

34. Memorandum for Major General L. R. Groves regarding the Summary of Target Committee Meetings on 10 and 11 May 1945 at Los Alamos, 12 May 1945. *http://www.trumanlibrary.org/whistlestop/study_collections/bomb/large/groves_project/text/bma13tx.htm*. Kyoto was later removed by the US government.

35. Jacob Vander Meulen, *Building the B-29* (Washington: Smithsonian Institution Press, 1995), p. 100.

36. These figures come from the remarkable Brookings Institution study on Stephen I. Schwartz, *Atomic Audit: The Costs and Consequences of U.S. Nuclear Weapons since 1940* (Washington: Brookings Institution Press, 1998).

37. Barton J. Bernstein, 'Seizing the Contested Terrain of Early Nuclear History: Stimson, Conant, and their Allies Explain the Decision to Use the Atomic Bomb', *Diplomatic History*, Vol. 17 (1993), pp. 35–72 and 'Understanding the Atomic Bomb and the Japanese Surrender: Missed Opportunities, Little-known Near Disasters, and Modern Memory', *Diplomatic History*, Vol. 19 (1995), pp. 227–73.

38. R. V. Jones, *Most Secret War: British Scientific Intelligence 1939–1945* (London: Hamish Hamilton, 1978) and *Reflections on Intelligence* (London: Heinemann, 1989).

39. Michael J. Neufeld, *The Rocket and the Reich: Peenemunde and the Coming of the Ballistic Missile Era* (Washington: Smithsonian Institution Press, 1995), p. 264.

40. Figures from Brookings Institution study on Schwartz, *Atomic Audit*.

41. *http://www.teflon.com*.

42. *http://www.tefal.com*.

43. The Americans had already generated electricity from nuclear power at a nuclear facility, and the Soviets had already put power into a grid.

44. For a devastating cost–benefit analysis of the British nuclear programme, with some important general comments about politics, culture and high technology after the Second World War, see P. D. Henderson, 'Two British

Errors: their probable size and some possible lessons', *Oxford Economic Papers* (July 1977), pp. 159–94.

45. An exception is the marvellous Andrea Tone, *Devices and Desires: a History of Contraceptives in America* (New York: Hill and Wang, 2001).

46. Figures for LRC, which had a practical monopoly, Monopoly and Mergers Commission, *Contraceptive Sheaths* (London: HMSO, 1975), Appendix 8.

47. Hera Cook, *The Long Sexual Revolution: English Women, Sex, and Contraception, 1800–1975* (Oxford: Oxford University Press, 2004), pp. 271–4, 319–37.

48. Tone, *Devices and Desires*, p. 268.

49. Mark Harrison, *Disease and the Modern World* (Cambridge: Polity Press, 2004).

50. I am indebted to Claire Scott for this information.

51. Quoted in Edmund Russell, *War and Nature: Fighting Humans and Insects with Chemicals from World War I to Silent Spring* (Cambridge: Cambridge University Press, 2001), p. 117.

52. Socrates Litsios, 'Malaria Control, the Cold War, and the Postwar Reorganization of International Assistance', *Medical Anthropology*, Vol. 17, No. 3 (1997), and Paul Weindling, 'The Uses and Abuses of Biological Technologies: Zyklon B and Gas Disinfestation between the First World War and the Holocaust', *History and Technology*, Vol. 11 (1994), pp. 291–8.

53. Gordon Harrison, *Mosquitoes, Malaria and Man* (London: John Murray, 1978), p. 258.

## 2. Time

1. George Kubler, *The Shape of Time: Remarks on the History of Things* (New Haven: Yale University Press, 1962), p. 80.

2. Rudolf Mrázek, *Engineers of Happy Land: Technology and Nationalism in a colony* (Princeton: Princeton University Press, 2002), p. 239, n. 93.

3. Anthony Smith (ed.), *Television: an International History* (Oxford: Oxford University Press, 1995).

4. It is true that television came late to some African countries: the notable laggards are South Africa, a special case, Niger, Lesotho, Cameroon, Chad, Central African Republic, Angola, Mozambique, Djibouti and Zanzibar which did not have television until the 1970s and 1980s.

5. Sixty per cent of Britain's capital stock in railways as it stood in 1961 was constructed before 1920, and 54 per cent of harbours, docks and canals. See Geoffrey Dean, 'The Stock of Fixed Capital in the United Kingdom in 1961', *Journal of the Royal Statistical Society*, A, Vol. 127 (1964), pp. 327–51.

6. E. J. Larkin and J. G. Larkin, *The Railway Workshops of Britain 1823–1986* (London: Macmillan, 1988), pp. 230–33.

7. *Historical Statistics of the United States: Colonial Times to 1957* (Washington: US Bureau of the Census, 1960), pp. 289–90.

8. Colin Tudge, *So Shall We Reap* (London: Allen Lane, 2003), p. 69.

9. John Singleton, 'Britain's Military Use of Horses 1914–1918', *Past and Present* 139 (1993).

10. R. L. DiNardo and A. Bay, 'Horse-Drawn Transport in the German Army', *Journal of Contemporary History*, Vol. 23 (1988), pp. 129–41.

11. This compares with 300 draught-horses in a Saxon division in the Napoleonic Wars (a 1:20 draught-horse:man ratio) *http://www.napoleon-series.org/ military/organization/c_saxon11.html*. I have seen estimates for the *Grand Armée* of around 50,000 draught-horses for an invading army of around 400,000.

12. M. Henriksson and E. Lindholm, 'The use and role of animal draught power in Cuban Agriculture: a field study in Havana Province', *Minor Field Studies*, 100 (Swedish University of Agricultural Sciences, Uppsala, 2000), citing Arcadio Ríos, *Improving Animal Traction Technology in Cuba* (Instituto de Investigación Agropecuaria (IIMA), Havana, 1998).

13. Timothy Leunig, 'A British industrial success: productivity in the Lancashire and New England cotton spinning industries a century ago', *Economic History Review*, Vol. 56 (2003), pp. 90–117.

14. John Singleton, *Lancashire on the Scrapheap: the Cotton Industry, 1945–1970* (Oxford: Oxford University Press, 1991), pp. 93–4.

15. Ibid., pp. 93–4, 167.

16. Tanis Day, 'Capital-Labor substitution in the home', *Technology and Culture*, Vol. 33 (1992), p. 322.

17. For some white European intellectuals in the interwar years, a critique of western industrial civilisation was built on celebration, often with noble savage overtones, of the ancient less corrupted cultures of Africa and Asia. A very few non-white intellectuals, and fewer African and Asians, were themselves putting this forward, among them Rabindranath Tagore and Mahatma Gandhi. See Michael Adas, *Machines as the Measure of Men: Science, Technology and Ideologies of Western Dominance* (Ithaca: Cornell University Press, 1989), pp. 380–401.

18. Gustavo Riofrio and Jean-Claude Driant, *¿Que Vivienda han construido? Nuevos Problemas en viejas barriadas* (Lima: CIDAP/IFEA/TAREA, 1987).

19. *Slums of the World*, p. 25 – quoted in Mike Davis, 'Planet of Slums', *New Left Review*, second series, No. 26 (2004), pp. 5–34.

20. http://www.ucl.ac.uk/dpu-projects/Global_Report/pdfs/Durban.pdf
    *Understanding Slums: Case Studies for the Global Report on Human Settlements*
    (Development and Planning Unit, University College London). See http://
    www.ucl.ac.uk/dpu-projects/Global_Report/.
21. Julian Huxley, *Memories* (London: Allen & Unwin, 1970), Vol. 1, p. 269.
22. Davis, 'Planet of Slums', p. 15.
23. Jean Hatzfield, *A Time for Machetes. The Rwandan Genocides: the Killers
    Speak*, trans. Linda Coverdale (London: Serpent's Tail, 2005), pp. 71–5. (First
    published in French, 2003.)
24. The ten largest consumers of asbestos in 2000 were: Russia 446,000 tons;
    China 410,000 tons; Brazil, 182,000 tons; India 125,000 tons; Thailand 120,000
    tons; Japan 99,000 tons; Indonesia 55,000 tons, Korea 29,000 tons; Mexico
    27,000 tons; Belarus 25,000 tons. These countries accounted for 94 per cent of
    the world total 'Worldwide Asbestos Supply and Consumption Trends from
    1900 to 2000', by Robert L. Virta, US Geological Survey, Reston, VA, http://
    pubs.usgs.gov/of/2003/of03-083/of03-083-tagged.pdf.
25. Appendix 8 of 'The socio-economic impact of the phasing out of asbestos in
    South Africa', a study undertaken for the Fund for Research into Industrial
    Development, Growth and Equity (FRIDGE), Final Report, http://www.
    nedlac.org.za/research/fridge/asbestos/.
26. Patrick Chamoiseau, *Texaco* (London: Granta, 1997).
27. It is also used for languages – the languages of the ex-slaves of the colonies,
    principally in the Caribbean that went from 'pidgin' simplified versions of
    English, French, Portuguese, Spanish etc. to become separate 'creoles'. On
    language, see Ronald Segal, *The Black Diaspora* (London: Faber, 1995), chapter
    34.
28. Carl Riskin, 'Intermediate Technology in China's rural industries', in Austin
    Robinson (ed.), *Appropriate Technologies for Third World Development*
    (London: Macmillan, 1979), pp. 52–74.
29. See the statistics in World Watch Institute, *Vital Signs 2003–2004* (London:
    Earthscan, 2003) and earlier editions.
30. I am indebted to a marvellous book: Rob Gallagher, *The Rickshaws of
    Bangladesh* (Dhaka: The University Press, 1992).
31. See Tony Wheeler and Richard l'Anson, *Chasing Rickshaws* (London: Lonely
    Planet, 1998).
32. Erik E. Jansen, et al., *The Country Boats of Bangladesh: Social and Economic
    Development Decision-making in Inland Water Transport* (Dhaka: The
    University Press, 1989).
33. *http://www.sewusa.com/Pic_Pages/singerpicpage.htm.*

34. Robert C. Post, '"The last steam railroad in America": Shaffers Crossing, Roanake, Virginia, 1958', *Technology and Culture*, 44 (2003), p. 565.
35. Tim Mondavi, quoted in *Independent*, 8 January 2002.

## 3. Production

1. See Paul Hirst and Jonathan Zeitlin, 'Flexible specialisation versus Post-Fordism: theory, evidence and policy implications', *Economy and Society*, Vol. 20 (1991), pp. 1–56.
2. In the Scandinavian countries, estimates of national income from the interwar years included household production. Duncan Ironmonger, 'Household Production', in the *International Encyclopedia of the Social & Behavioral Sciences* (Oxford: Elsevier Science, 2001), pp. 9–10.
3. Sandra Short, 'Time Use accounts in the household satellite account', *Economic Trends* (October 2000).
4. Siegfried Giedion, *Mechanization Takes Command: a Contribution to Anonymous History* (New York: Oxford University Press, 1948; W. W. Norton edition, 1969).
5. As the insightful work of Bowden and Offer, and of Ralph Schroeder, shows. Sue Bowden and Avner Offer, 'Household appliances and the use of time: the United States and Britain since the 1920s', *Economic History Review*, Vol. 67 (1994), pp. 725–48; Ralph Schroeder, 'The Consumption of Technology in Everyday Life: Car, Telephone, and Television in Sweden and America in Comparative-Historical Perspective', *Sociological Research Online*, Vol. 7, No. 4.
6. Claude S. Fischer, *America Calling: a Social History of the Telephone to 1940* (Berkeley: University of California Press, 1992).
7. Ronald R. Kline, *Consumers in the Country: Technology and Social Change in Rural America* (Baltimore: Johns Hopkins University Press, 2000), pp. 78–9.
8. *Historical Statistics of the United States: Colonial Times to 1957* (Washington: US Bureau of the Census, 1960), pp. 284–5.
9. US census data in Katherine Jellison, *Entitled to Power: Farm Women and Technology 1913–1963* (Chapel Hill: University of North Carolina Press, 1993), pp. 54–5.
10. Ibid., p. 61.
11. Giedion, *Mechanization Takes Command*, pp. 614–6.
12. See Ben Fine et al., *Consumption in the Age of Affluence: the World of Food* (London: Routledge, 1996), p. 40.
13. For details, see the Nobel Foundation website *www.nobel.se*.

14. *http://www.aga.com/web/web2000/com/WPPcom.nsf/pages/History_ GustafDalen.* AGA history site homepage: *http://www.aga.com/web/web2000/ com/WPPcom.nsf/pages/History_Home?OpenDocument.*

15. Jordan Goodman and Katrina Honeyman, *Gainful Pursuits: the Making of Industrial Europe, 1600–1914* (London: Edward Arnold, 1988).

16. R. B. Davies, *Peacefully Working to Conquer the World: Singer Sewing Machines in Foreign Markets, 1854–1920* (London: Arno Press, 1976), p. 140, quoted in Sarah Ross, 'Dual Purpose: the working life of the domestic sewing machine', MSc dissertation, Imperial College, London, 2003.

17. Frank P. Godfrey, *An International History of the Sewing Machine* (London: Robert Hale, 1982), p. 157.

18. Ibid., p. 281.

19. *http://www.ibpcosaka.or.jp/network/e_trade_japanesemarket/machinery_ industry_goods/sewing96.html.*

20. Richard Smith, 'Creative Destruction: capitalist development and China's environment', *New Left Review*, No. 222 (1997), p. 4.

21. *http://reference.allrefer.com/country-guide-study/china/china171.html.*

22. I owe this insight to Sarah Ross, 'Dual Purpose'.

23. Arnold Bauer, *Goods, Power, History: Latin America's Material Culture* (Cambridge: Cambridge University Press, 2001), pp. 170–71, f, Paul Doughty, *Huaylas: an Andean District in Search of Progress* (Ithaca: Cornell University Press, 1968) and *Young India*, 13 November, 1924 in M. K. Gandhi, *Man Vs. Machine* (edited by Anand T. Hingorani) (New Delhi and Mumbai: Bharatiya Vidya Bhavan, 1998). Available online at *http://web.mahatma.org.in/books/s.*

24. Observed by author, August 2003.

25. *Young India*, Gandhi, *Man Vs. Machine.*

26. M. K. Gandhi, *Harijan*, 13 April 1940; see *http://web.mahatma.org.in.* See also M. K. Gandhi, *An Autobiography, Or the Story of My Experiments with Truth*, trans by Mahadev Desai (Ahmedabad: Navajivan Publishing House, n.d.), pp. 407–14; facsimile online on *http://web.mahatma.org.in.*

27. Joel Mokyr, *The Gifts of Athena: Historical Origins of the Knowledge Economy* (Princeton: Princeton University Press, 2002), pp. 150–51.

28. John Ardagh, *France*, third edition (Harmondsworth: Penguin, 1977), p. 419.

29. Paul Ginsborg, *A History of Contemporary Italy, 1943–1980* (London: Penguin, 1990), p. 29.

30. 'Epameinondas', proclamation cited in an archival source by Mark Mazower in his *Inside Hitler's Greece: the Experience of Occupation, 1941–1944* (London: Yale University Press, 1993), pp. 312–3.

31. Eirik E. Jansen, et al., *The Country Boats of Bangladesh. Social and Economic Development and Decision-making in Inland Water Transport* (Dhaka: The University Press, 1989), pp. 103–5.
32. *http://www.livinghistoryfarm.org/farminginthe20s/machines_08.htm*.
33. Jellison, *Entitled to Power*, p. 110.
34. Ibid., p. 36.
35. Ibid., chapter 6.
36. By Jakob Mohrland, *The History of Brunnental – 1918–1941*, interview of 16 January 1986; *http://www.brunnental.us/brunnental/mohrland.txt*.
37. Sheila Fitzpatrick, *Stalin's Peasants: Resistance and Survival in the Russian Village after Collectivisation* (New York: Oxford University Press, 1994), p. 136.
38. Ibid., p. 138.
39. Angus Maddison, *Dynamic Forces in Capitalist Development: a Long-run Comparative View* (Oxford: Oxford University Press, 1991), p. 150.
40. Deborah Fitzgerald, 'Farmers de-skilled: hybrid corn and farmers' work', *Technology and Culture*, Vol. 34 (1993), pp. 324–43.
41. Simon Partner, 'Brightening Country Lives: selling electrical goods in the Japanese countryside, 1950–1970', *Enterprise & Society*, Vol. 1 (2000), pp. 762–84.
42. A. J. H. Latham, *Rice: the Primary Commodity* (London: Routledge, 1998), pp. 6–7.
43. John McNeill, *Something New under the Sun: an Environmental History of the Twentieth Century* (London: Penguin, 2000), pp. 225–6.
44. Dana G. Dalrymple, *Development and Spread of High-yielding Rice Varieties in Developing Countries* (Washington DC: Agency for International Development, 1986), and the companion for Wheat.
45. Something similar, but much less dramatic was happening in beef production: in 1960 there were around 1 billion cattle in the world, at the end of the twentieth century around 1.3 billion. Yet in that period beef and veal production doubled by weight.
46. William Boyd, 'Making Meat: Science, Technology, and American Poultry Production', *Technology and Culture*, Vol. 42 (2001), Table 1, p. 637.
47. Julian Wiseman, *The Pig: a British History* (London: Duckworth, 2000), pp. 155–6.
48. Richard Barras, 'Building investment is a diminishing source of economic growth', *Journal of Property Research* (2001), 18(4) 279–308, which gives data for Britain.

49. Craig Littler, 'A history of "new" technology', in Graham Winch (ed.) *Information Technology in Manufacturing Processes: Case Studies in Technological Change* (London: Rossendale, 1983), p. 142.

50. Ginsborg, *Italy*, p. 239.

51. Stefano Musso, 'Production Methods and Industrial Relations at FIAT (1930–1990), in Haruhito Shiomi and Kazuo Wada (eds.), *Fordism Transformed: the Development of Production Methods in the Automobile Industry* (Oxford: Oxford University Press, 1995), p. 258.

52. Ginsborg, *Italy*, p. 240.

53. *Oxford Economic Atlas of the World*, fourth edition (Oxford: Oxford University Press, 1972), p. 55.

54. Paul R. Josephson, ' "Projects of the Century" in Soviet History: Large-scale Technologies from Lenin to Gorbachev', *Technology and Culture*, Vol. 36 (1995), pp. 519–59.

55. Philip Scranton, *Endless Novelty: Specialty Production and American Industrialization, 1865–1925* (Princeton: Princeton University Press, 1997, paperback, 2000).

56. As is clear in the work of one of the advocates of the notion, See Danny T. Quah, 'Increasingly weightless economies', *Bank of England Quarterly Bulletin*, February 1997.

57. *Independent*, 15 September 2003.

58. Martin Lockett, 'Bridging the division of labour? The case of China', *Economic and Industrial Democracy*, Vol. 1 (1980), pp. 447–86.

59. See the special issue of the *Journal of Peasant Studies*, Vol. 30, Nos. 3 and 4 (2003).

## 4. Maintenance

1. Langdon Winner, *Autonomous Technology: Technics-out-of-Control as a Theme in Political Thought* (Cambridge, MA: MIT Press, 1977), p. 183.

2. Ibid., p. 173.

3. Karl Wittfogel, *Oriental Despotism: A Comparative Study of Total Power* (New Haven: Yale University Press, 1957).

4. Lewis Mumford, 'Authoritarian and Democratic Technics', *Technology and Culture*, Vol. 5 (1964), pp. 1–8.

5. Ivor H. Seeley, *Building Maintenance*, second edition (London: Macmillan, 1987).

6. United Nations, *Maintenance and Repair in Developing Countries: Report of a Symposium …* (New York: United Nations, 1971).

7. Arnold Pacey, *The Culture of Technology* (Oxford: Blackwell, 1983), p. 38.

8. Maintenance and repair expenditures as a proportion of investment varied a great deal across industrial sectors. For the period 1961–93 it was more than 100 per cent in forestry, 75 per cent in construction, and 50 per cent in manufacturing to just above 10 per cent in services. Ellen R. McGrattan and James A. Schmitz, Jr, 'Maintenance and Repair: Too Big to Ignore', *Federal Reserve Bank of Minneapolis Quarterly Review*, Vol. 23, No. 4, Fall 1999, Table 3.

9. Ibid., pp. 2–13.

10. Michael J. Duekerz and Andreas M. Fischer, ' Fixing Swiss Potholes: the Importance and Cyclical Nature of Improvements', November 2002, *http:// www.sgvs.ch/documents/Congres_2003/papers_jahrestagung_2003/B5-fixing per cent20Swiss per cent20Potholes.pdf.*

11. Commonwealth Bureau of Census and Statistics, *Capital and Maintenance Expenditure by Private Business in Australia, 1953–1959*, Canberra, 1959.

12. The figure of £3bn is from the Ministry of Technology, *Report on the Working Party on Maintenance Engineering* (London: HMSO, 1970), a skimpy and insubstantial paper.

13. S. Brand, *How Buildings Learn: What Happens after They're Built* (London: Penguin, 1994), p.5.

14. Roger Bridgman, 'Instructions for use as a source for the history of technology', MSc dissertation, University of London, 1997.

15. Gijs Mom, *The Electric Vehicle: Technology and Expectations in the Automobile Age* (Baltimore: Johns Hopkins University Press, 2004).

16. Henry Ford, *My Life and Work* (Garden City, NY: Doubleday, Page & Co., 1922). Available online at *www.gutenberg.org.*

17. E. B. White, *Farewell to Model T* (first published 1936) (New York: The Little Bookroom, 2003), p. 13.

18. Stephen L. McIntyre, 'The Failure of Fordism: reform of the automobile repair industry, 1913–1940', *Technology and Culture*, Vol. 41 (2000), p. 299.

19. Admiral of the Fleet Lord Chatfield, *It Might Happen Again*, Vol. II, *The Navy and Defence* (London: Heinemann, 1948), p. 15.

20. John Powell, *The Survival of the Fitter: Lives of Some African Engineers* (London: Intermediate Technology, 1995), p. 12.

21. Ibid., p. 3.

22. Ibid., pp. 13–14.

23. Ibid.

24. Birgit Meyer and Jojada Verrips, 'Kwaku's Car. The Struggles and Stories of a Ghanaian Long-Distance Taxi Driver', in Daniel Miller (ed.), *Car Cultures* (Oxford: Berg Publishers, 2001), p. 171.

25. David A. Hounshell, 'Automation, Transfer Machinery, and Mass Production in the U.S. Automobile Industry in the Post–World War II Era', *Enterprise & Society* 1 (March 2000), pp. 100–138. See also his 'Planning and Executing "Automation" at the Ford Motor Company, 1945–1965: the Cleveland Engine Plant and its Consequences', in Haruhito Shiomi and Kazuo Wada (eds.), *Fordism Transformed: the Development of Production Methods in the Automobile Industry* (Oxford: Oxford University Press, 1995), pp. 49–86.

26. E. J. Larkin and J. G. Larkin, *The Railway Workshops of Britain 1823–1986* (London: Macmillan 1988), p. 103.

27. Ibid., p. 107.

28. Ibid., p. 110.

29. Derived from data in Ronald Miller and David Sawers, *The Technical Development of Modern Aviation* (London: Routledge and Kegan Paul, 1968), pp. 151, 209.

30. Ibid., p. 226.

31. Derived from ibid., p. 207.

32. Specific fuel consumption fell by only 20 per cent and made a much smaller contribution to cost reduction. Ibid., p. 89.

33. Ibid., esp. pp. 86–9, 147, 150, 186, 197.

34. Nathan Rosenberg, 'Learning by Using', in Nathan Rosenberg, *Inside the Black Box* (Cambridge: Cambridge University Press, 1982), pp. 120–40.

35. *Report of the Committee of Enquiry into the Aircraft Industry*, Cmnd 2853 (London: HMSO, 1965), pp. 8–9.

36. Lord Chatfield, *It Might Happen Again*, Vol. II, pp. 17–18.

37. Ibid., Vol. I (London: Heinemann, 1942), p. 233.

38. Ibid., Vol. II pp. 30–31.

39. James Watson, 'On Mature Technology', Humanities Dissertation, Imperial College, London, May 2001.

40. *http://www.fleetairarmarchive.net/*. One source gives an extraordinary list of Second World War warships still in service in 1980: many were in Latin America, often transferred in the 1970s. *http://usuarios.lycos.es/christianlr/01d51a93a111e350c/01d51a93ef125ce07.html*.

41. BBC online, 26 November 2004.

42. J. Watson, 'On Mature Technology'.

43. Brian Christley, ex-chief Concorde instructor, letter 20 October 2003, *The Guardian*.

44. Livio Dante Porta, obituary in *The Guardian*, 8 January 2003.

45. White, *Farewell to Model T* , p. 13.

46. '"Take a Little Trip with Me": Lowriding and the Poetics of Scale', in Alondra Nelson and Thuy Linh N. Tu (eds.), *Technicolor: Race, Technology, and Everyday Life* (New York and London: New York University Press, 2002), pp. 100–120.

47. Shigeru Ishikawa, 'Appropriate technologies: some aspects of Japanese experience', in Austin Robinson (ed.), *Appropriate Technologies for Third World Development* (London: Macmillan, 1979), pp. 101–103.

48. Yuzo Takahashi, 'A Network of Tinkerers: the advent of the radio and television receiver industry in Japan', *Technology and Culture*, Vol. 41 (2000), pp. 460–84.

49. Ibid.

50. Christopher Bayly and Tim Harper, *Forgotten Armies: the Fall of British Asia, 1941–1945* (London: Penguin, 2004), pp. 301–2.

51. Powell, *Survival of the Fitter*.

52. Valdeir Rejinaldo Vidrik, 'Invios caminhos: a CESP/Bauru e a inovação tecnológica nos anos 80 e 90', PhD thesis, University of São Paulo, 2003.

53. Lindqvist, 'Changes in the Technological Landscape', in Granstrand (ed.), *Economics of Technology*, p. 277.

## 5. Nations

1. John Ardagh, *France*, third edition (Harmondsworth: Penguin, 1977), p. 82.

2. 'Es, sin lugar a dudas, el inventor argentino más importante de toda nuestra historia, y el paradigma del "inventor profesional" comprometido con su rol social a favor del progreso de la humanidad' (Asociación argentina de inventores). *http://puertobaires.com/aai/diadelinventor.asp*.

3. Robert Wohl, 'Par la voie des airs: l'entrée de l'aviation dans le monde des lettres françaises, 1909–1939', *Le Mouvement Social*, No. 145 (1988), pp. 60–61.

4. Modris Eksteins, *Rites of Spring: The Great War and the Birth of the Modern Age* (London: Bantam, 1989), p. 427.

5. Sir Walter Raleigh, *The War in the Air*, Vol. 1 (Oxford: Oxford University Press, 1922), p. 111.

6. Kendall Bailes, 'Technology and Legitimacy: Society, Aviation and Stalinism in the 1930s', *Technology and Culture*, Vol. 17 (1976), pp. 55–81.

7. Alexander de Seversky, *Victory through Air Power* (New York: Hutchinson & Co., 1942), pp. 350, 352.

8. Eksteins, *Rites of Spring*, p. 359.

9. Valentine Cunningham, *British Writers of the Thirties* (Oxford: Oxford University Press, 1988), pp. 176–81.

10. In the case of much of the work of Chris Freeman, the USA is missing – for he holds to a Listian national techno-economic perspective in which in the recent past Germany and the Prussia of the East, Japan, are the central nations. For the Listianism in Freeman, I am indebted to Simon Lee.

11. John A. Hall (ed.), *The State of the Nation: Ernest Gellner and the Theory of Nationalism* (Cambridge: Cambridge University Press, 1998).

12. Francisco Javier Ayala-Carcedo, 'Historia y presente de la ciencia y de la tecnología en España', in Francisco Javier Ayala-Carcedo (ed.), *Historia de la Tecnología en España*, Vol. II (Barcelona: Valatenea, 2001), pp. 729–52.

13. Ben Steil, David G. Victor and Richard R. Nelson (eds.), *Technological Innovation and economic performance*, a Council for Foreign Relations Book (Princeton: Princeton University Press, 2002).

14. Santiago López, 'Por el fracaso hacia el éxito: difusión tecnológica y competencia en España', in Emilio Muñoz et al. (eds.), *El espacio común de conocimiento en la Unión Europea: Un enfoque al problema desde España* (Madrid: Acadenua Europea de Ciencias y Artes, 2005), pp. 229–51. Academias Europeas de las Ciencias, discussion document.

15. Charles Feinstein, 'Technical Progress and technology transfer in a centrally planned economy: the experience of the USSR, 1917–1987', in Charles Feinstein and Christopher Howe (eds.) *Chinese Technology Transfer in the 1990s: Current Experience, Historical Problems and International Perspectives* (Cheltenham: Edward Elgar, 1997), pp. 62–81.

16. A. C. Sutton, *Western Technology and Soviet Economic Development 1945 to 1965* (Stanford: Hoover Institution, 1973), Vol. 3, p. 371.

17. David A. Hounshell, 'Rethinking the History of "American Technology"', in Stephen Cutcliffe and Robert Post (eds.), *In Context: History and the History of Technology* (Bethlehem: Lehigh University Press, 1989), pp. 216–29.

18. Henry Ford, *My Philosophy of Industry* (London: Harrap, 1929), pp. 44–5.

19. Ibid., pp. 25-6.

20. Air Marshal William A. Bishop (RCAF), *Winged Peace* (New York: Macmillan, 1944), pp. 11, 175.

21. H. G. Wells, *The Shape of Things to Come* (London: Hutchinson, 1933; J. M. Dent/Everyman edition, 1993). See E. M. Earle, 'H. G. Wells, British patriot in search of a world state', in E. M. Earle (ed.) *Nations and Nationalism* (New York: Columbia University Press, 1950), pp. 79–121.

22. Wells, *The Shape of Things to Come*, p. 271.

23. Ibid., p. 279.

24. George Orwell, 'As I Please', *Tribune*, 12 May 1944, reprinted in *CEJL*, Vol. 3, p. 173.

25. R. F. Pocock, *The Early British Radio Industry* (Manchester: Manchester University Press, 1988); Daniel Headrick, *The Invisible Weapon: Telecommunications and International Politics, 1851–1945* (New York: Oxford University Press, 1991).

26. See *A History of Technology*, Vol. 7, *The Twentieth Century, c. 1900 – c. 1950,* Parts I and II (Oxford: Oxford University Press, 1978), where the only chapter with an explicitly military connection is one on atomic weapons. Aviation is alongside transport technologies, and there is treatment of the military aspect within the chapter. The condensed version by T. I. Williams, *A Short History of Twentieth-Century Technology, c. 1900–1950* (Oxford: Oxford University Press, 1982) has a chapter, not in the original on military technology, which is taken essentially as guns, tanks and suchlike. Charles Gibbs-Smith, *The Aeroplane: an Historical Survey of its Origins and Development* (London: HMSO/Science Museum, 1960) and developed into *Aviation: an Historical Survey from its Origins to the End of World War II* (London: HMSO/Science Museum, 1970) and second edition (London: HMSO/Science Museum, 1985). Gibbs-Smith worked not at the Science Museum but at the Victoria and Albert. R. Miller and David Sawers, *The Technical Development of Modern Aviation* (London: Routledge and Kegan Paul, 1968), pp. 58, 257. Peter King, *Knights of the Air* (London: Constable, 1989) and Keith Hayward, *The British Aircraft Industry* (Manchester: Manchester University Press, 1989). Much the same has happened in the case of the US aircraft industry. See, as an example, Roger Bilstein, *Flight in America 1900–1983: from the Wrights to the Astronauts* (Baltimore: Johns Hopkins University Press, 1984).

27. Santiago López García and Luis Sanz Menéndez , 'Política tecnológica versus política científica durante el franquismo', *Quadernos d'Historia de l'Ingeniería,* Vol. II (1997), pp. 77–118.

28. Arnold Krammer, 'Fueling the Third Reich', *Technology and Culture*, Vol. 19 (1978), pp. 394–422; Anthony Stranges, 'From Birmingham to Billingham: high-pressure coal hydrogenation in Great Britain', *Technology and Culture*, Vol. 26 (1985), pp. 726–57.

29. Anthony Stranges, 'Friedrich Bergius and the Rise of the German Synthetic Fuel Industry', *ISIS*, Vol. 75 (1984), pp. 643–67.

30. Rainer Karlsch, 'Capacity Losses, reconstruction and unfinished modernisation: the chemical industry in the Soviet Zone of Occupation (SBZ)/GDR, 1945–1965', in J. E. Lesch (ed.), *The German Chemical Industry in the Twentieth Century* (Dordrecht: Kluwer Academic, 2000).

31. Elena San Román and Carles Sudrià, 'Synthetic Fuels in Spain, 1942–1966: the failure of Franco's Autarkic Dream', *Business History*, Vol. 45 (2003), pp. 73–88.

32. At first, during the Second World War, there were attempts to bring over Nazi technology (for example the oil-from-coal case discussed below); after the war German and Italian scientists and engineers were given places in Spanish industries and research institutes. In Spain, the state promotes the creation of SEAT in 1950, but this has participation from FIAT, and makes FIAT cars, including the famous FIAT 600. Manuel Lage Marco, 'La industria del automóvil' in Ayala-Carcedo (ed.), *Tecnología en España*, pp. 499–518.

33. *http://www.fischertropsch.org/DOE/DOE_reports/13837_6/13837_6_toc.htm.*

34. *http://www.sasol.com/sasol* gives the history.

35. Carlo Levi, *Christ Stopped at Eboli* (London: Penguin Classics, edition 2000; first published in English 1947, in Italian 1944), pp. 82, 96. The gentry did not know what to make of a woman doctor, the peasants, many of whom had been to America, did (p. 89).

36. Ibid., pp. 128–9.

37. Ibid., p. 160.

38. David Holloway, *Stalin and the Bomb: the Soviet Union and Atomic Energy, 1939–1956* (London: Yale University Press, 1994).

39. The politics of these transfers is nicely explored in Jeffrey A. Engel, '"We are not concerned who the buyer is": Engine Sales and Anglo-American Security at the Dawn of the Jet Age', *History and Technology*, Vol. 17 (2000), pp. 43–68.

40. Ignacio Klich, 'Introducción' to the CEANA final report, *http://www.ceana. org.ar/final/final.htm.* CEANA was set up by the Argentine foreign minister Guido Di Tella to study the role of the Peronist government in bringing Nazis to Argentina. The report named 180 war criminals who went to Argentina, including many French and Belgian. See Robert A. Potash y Celso Rodríguez, 'El empleo en el ejército argentino de nazis y otros técnicos extranjeros, 1943–1955', in the CEANA final report. French sources are vague and embarrassed; see Raymond Danel, *Emile Dewoitine: créateur des usines de Toulouse de l'Aerospatiale* (Paris: Larivière, 1982).

41. Diana Quattrocchi-Woisson, 'Relaciones con la Argentina de funcionarios de Vichy y de colaboradores franceses y belgas, 1940–1960', CEANA final report, *http://www.ceana.org.ar/final/final.htm.*

42. G. A. Tokaev, *Comrade X* trans. Alec Brown (London: Harvill Press, 1956). A work to be treated with caution.

43. Hans Ebert, Johann Kaiser and Klaus Peters, *The History of German Aviation: Willy Messerschmidt – Pioneer of Aviation Design* (Forlag: Schiffer Publishing Ltd, 1999).

44. Jose Antonio Martínez Cabeza, 'La ingeniería aeronáutica', in Ayala-Carcedo (ed.), *Tecnología en España*, pp. 519–35.

45. One was given to the Smithsonian in the 1980s, from where this data comes.

46. But productivity turned out to be about 50 per cent lower than that of Ford's US factory. Cf. John P. Hardt and George D. Holliday, 'Technology Transfer and Change in the Soviet Economic System', in Frederic J. Fleron, Jr, *Technology and Communist Culture: the Socio-cultural Impact of Technology under Socialism* (New York and London: Praeger, 1977), pp. 183–223.

47. Chunli Lee, 'Adoption of the Ford System and Evolution of the Production System in the Chinese Automobile Industry, 1953–1993', in Haruhito Shiomi and Kazuo Wada (eds.), *Fordism Transformed: the Development of Production Methods in the Automobile Industry* (Oxford: Oxford University Press, 1995), p. 302.

48. A. C. Sutton, *Western Technology and Soviet Economic Development 1930 to 1945* (Stanford: Hoover Institution, 1971), pp. 185–191.

49. Ibid., pp. 62–3, 74–7.

50. Raymond G. Stokes, *Constructing Socialism: Technology and Change in East Germany 1945–1990* (Baltimore: Johns Hopkins University Press, 2000).

51. Werner Abelhauser, 'Two kinds of Fordism: on the differing roles of industry in the development of the two German states', in Shiomi and Wada (eds.), *Fordism Transformed*, p. 290.

52. Thomas Schlich, 'Degrees of control: the spread of operative fracture treatment with metal implants: a comparative perspective on Switzerland, East Germany and the USA, 1950s–1960s', in Jennifer Stanton (ed.), *Innovation in Health and Medicine: Diffusion and Resistance in the Twentieth Century* (London: Routledge, 2002), pp. 106–25.

53. Brian Winston, *Media, Technology and Society* (London: Routledge, 1998), chapter 6.

54. Sutton, *Western Technology*, pp. 161–3; Alexander B. Magoun, 'Adding Sight to Sound in Stalin's Russia: RCA and the Transfer of Electronics Technology to the Soviet Union', paper presented at SHOT annual conference, Amsterdam, 2004. See also *http://www.davidsarnoff.org/index.htm*.

55. See Santiago López García, 'El Patronato "Juan de la Cierva" (1939–1960), part I', *Arbor*, No. 619 (1997), p. 207.

56. Michael Adas, *Machines as the Measure of Men: Science, Technology and Ideologies of Western Dominance* (Ithaca: Cornell University Press, 1989). The later part of the book has a lot of material on lack of western self-confidence, especially around the Great War, but not all is related to a contrast with the non-western world.

57. S. C. Gilfillan, 'Inventiveness by Nation: a note on statistical treatment', *The Geographical Review*, vol. 20 (1930) p. 301.

58. M. Jefferson, 'The Geographic Distribution of Inventiveness', *The Geographical Review*, 19 (1929): 649–64, p. 659.

59. Venus Green, 'Race and Technology: African-American women in the Bell System, 1945–1980', *Technology and Culture*, Vol. 36 Supplement, pp. S101–S144.

60. Kathleen Franz, ' "The Open Road": Automobility and racial uplift in the interwar years', in Bruce Sinclair (ed.), *Technology and the African-American Experience: Needs and Opportunities for Study* (Cambridge, MA: MIT Press, 2004), pp. 131–54.

61. Karen J. Hossfeld, ' "Their logic against them": contradictions in race, sex and class in silicon valley', in Alondra Nelson and Thuy Linh N. Tu (eds.), *Technicolor: Race, Technology, and Everyday Life* (New York and London: New York University Press, 2002), pp. 34–63. The study reports data from the 1980s.

62. From his *Cahiers d'un retour au pays natal* (first published in part in 1938), quoted in David Macey, *Frantz Fanon: a Life* (London: Granta, 2000), p. 183.

63. Eduardo Galeano, *Las Venas abiertas de América Latina* (Mexico: Siglo XXI, 1978, first published 1971), p. 381.

64. G. A. Tokaty, 'Soviet Rocket Technology', republished in *Technology and Culture*, Vol. 4 (1963), p. 525.

65. These are my not wholly reliable estimates from the lists available from the Nobel Museum website. The Nobel Foundation do not provide ethnic data.

66. Rudolf Mrázek, *Engineers of Happy Land: Technology and Nationalism in a Colony* (Princeton: Princeton University Press, 2002), p. 10.

67. Ibid., p. 17.

68. Ibid., p. 239, n. 94.

69. J. P. Jones, 'Lascars in the Port of London', *Port of London Authority Monthly*, February 1931. Transcribed in *http://www.lascars.co.uk/plafeb1931.html* (20 April 2004).

70. 'A Pattern of Loyalty' by "Lighterman" (first published December 1957). Reproduced by kind permission of the author and the editor of Lloyd's List. This article was transcribed from the *P.L.A. Monthly*, December 1957. *http://www.lascars.co.uk/pladec1957.html*, 20 April 2004.

71. David Omissi, *The Sepoy and the Raj: Politics of the Indian Army, 1860–1940* (London: Macmillan, 1994).

72. See Daniel R. Headrick, *The Tentacles of Progress: Technology Transfer in the Age of Imperialism, 1850–1940* (New York: Oxford University Press, 1988), especially chapters 3 and 9.

73. Christopher Bayly and Tim Harper, *Forgotten Armies: the Fall of British Asia, 1941–1945* (London: Penguin, 2004), pp. 228–9.

## 6. War

1. For an exhaustive survey of this literature in its academic and non-academic versions, see Barton C. Hacker, 'Military institutions, Weapons, and Social Change: Toward a New History of Military Technology', *Technology and Culture*, Vol. 35 (1994), pp. 768–834.

2. J. F. C. Fuller, *Armament and History* (New York: Scribners, 1945).

3. Van Creveld, for example, is clear that there are differences: 'since technology and war operate on a logic which is not only different but actually opposed, the conceptual framework that is useful, even vital, for dealing with the one should not be allowed to interfere with the other'. Martin Van Creveld, *Technology and War: from 2000 BC to the Present* (London: Brassey's, 1991), p. 320.

4. Bernard Davy, *Air Power and Civilisation* (London: Allen & Unwin, 1941), p. 116.

5. Ibid., p. 148.

6. H. G. Wells, *A Short History of the World* (Harmondsworth: Penguin, 1946), p. 308.

7. Ernest Gellner, *Conditions of Liberty: Civil Society and its Rivals* (London: Penguin, 1996; orig. 1994), p. 200. See also pp. 33 and 179. Thanks to Brendan O'Leary.

8. Orwell, 'Wells, Hitler and the World State', *The Collected Essays, Journalism and Letters of George Orwell* (edited by Sonia Orwell and Ian Angus) (Harmondsworth: Penguin, 1970), Vol. II, *My Country Right or Left, 1940–1943*, p. 169.

9. Quoted in V. Berghahn, *Militarism: the History of an International Debate* (Leamington Spa: Berg, 1981), p. 42.

10. Liddell Hart, 'War and Peace', *English Review*, 54 (April 1932), p. 408, quoted in John J. Mearsheimer, *Liddell Hart and the Weight of History* (Ithaca: Cornell University Press, 1988), p. 103.

11. Fuller, *Armament and History*, p. 20. Again he saw the key technical developments of the interwar years around the internal combustion engine and radio, but 'divorced from civil progress, soldiers could not see this' (p. 135). See Brian Holden-Reid, *J. F. C. Fuller: Military Thinker* (Basingstoke: Macmillan, 1987) and Patrick Wright, *Tank: the Progress of a Monstrous War Machine* (London: Faber, 2000).

12. Lewis Mumford, *Technics and Civilisation* (London: Routledge and Kegan Paul, 1955), p. 95 (first published 1934).

13. Mary Kaldor, *The Baroque Arsenal* (London: Deutsch, 1982). For an investigation as to whether, as Kaldor suggested, state arsenals were concerned

with the production efficiency, but were very conservative in terms of product development, see Colin Duff, 'British armoury practice: technical change and small arms manufacture, 1850–1939', MSc thesis, University of Manchester 1990.

14. Jonathan Bailey, *The First World War and the Birth of the Modern Style of Warfare* (Camberley: Strategic and Combat Studies Institute, Occasional Paper No. 22, 1996).

15. Gil Elliot, *Twentieth Century Book of the Dead* (London: Allen Lane, 1972), p. 133.

16. *'My Gun Was as Tall as Me': Child Soldiers in Burma* (Human Rights Watch, 2002).

17. Elliot, *Book of the Dead*, p. 135.

18. Olivier Razac, *Barbed Wire: a Political History* (London: Profile, 2002).

19. See T. N. Dupuy, *The Evolution of Weapons and Warfare* (New York: Da Capo, 1990), pp. 307–20 (first published 1984).

20. See John Campbell, *Naval Weapons of World War Two* (Greenwich: Conway Maritime Press, 1985).

21. Thomas Stock and Karlheinz Lohs (eds.), *The Challenge of Old Chemical Munitions and Toxic Armament Wastes*, SIPRI Chemical and Biological Warfare Studies, No. 16 (Stockholm: SIPRI/Oxford University Press, 1997).

22. Richard Overy, *Why the Allies Won* (London: Cape, 1995).

23. G. A. Tokaev, *Comrade X* trans. Alec Brown (London: Harvill Press, 1956), p. 287.

24. Jim Fitzpatrick, *The Bicycle in Wartime: an Illustrated History* (London: Brassey's, 1998), chapter 6.

25. For the United States, see in particular Michael Sherry, *In the Shadow of War: the United States since 1930* (New Haven: Yale University Press, 1995).

26. Gabriel Kolko, *Vietnam: Anatomy of War 1940–1975* (London: Pantheon, 1986), p. 189. See also, Neil Sheehan, *The Bright Shining Lie: John Paul Vann and America in Vietnam* (London: Cape, 1989), a brilliant study of a liberal technocrat at war.

27. Gabriel Kolko, *Century of War: Politics, Conflict and Society since 1914* (New York: New Press, 1994), p. 404.

28. Ibid., p. 432.

29. Sheehan, *Shining Lie*.

30. David Loyn, 'The jungle training ground of an army the world forgot', *Independent*, 10 March 2004.

31. Daryl G. Press, 'The myth of air power in the Persian Gulf war and the future of air power', *International Security*, Vol. 26 (2001), pp. 5–44.

32. George N. Lewis, 'How the US Army assessed as successful a missile defense system that failed completely', *Breakthroughs*, Spring 2003, pp. 9–15.

33. George Riley Scott, *A History of Torture* (London: T. Werner Laurie, 1940, republished 1994).

34. Ricardo Rodríguez Molas, *Historia de la Tortura y el orden represivo en la Argentina* (Buenos Aires: Editorial Universitaria de Buenos Aires, 1984), online version at *http://www.elortiba.org/tortura.html*.

35. See the documentary by Marie-Monique Robin, *Escadrons de la mort, l'école française*, first broadcast in France, 2003.

36. Carlos Martínez Moreno, *El Infierno*, trans. Ann Wright, (London: Readers International, 1988; first published in Mexico, 1981, as *El color que el infierno me escondiera*), p. 8. A. J. Langguth, *Hidden Terrors* (New York: Pantheon Books, 1978) also deals with Mitrione.

37. For a remarkable historical study of a torture centre using the *picana*, see Andrés Di Tella, 'La vida privada en los campos de concentración', in Fernando Devoto and Marta Madero (eds.), *Historia de la vida privada en la Argentina*, Vol. III (Buenos Aires: Taurus, 1999), pp. 79–105.

38. A. Rose, 'Radar and air defence in the 1930s', *Twentieth Century British History*, vol. 9 (1998), pp. 219–45.

39. Thomas Parke Hughes, *American Genesis: A Century of Invention and Technological Enthusiasm* (New York: Viking, 1989), chapter 8.

40. David A. Mindell, *Between Human and Machine: Feedback, Control and Computing before Cybernetics* (Baltimore: Johns Hopkins University Press, 2002). John Brooks, 'Fire control for British Dreadnoughts: Choices in technology and supply', PhD, University of London, 2001. Sébastien Soubiran, 'De l'utilisation contingente des scientifiques dans les systèmes d'innovations des Marines française et britannique entre les deux guerres mondiales. Deux exemples: la conduite du tir des navires et la télémécanique' (Université de Paris VII : Denis Diderot, 2002), 3 vols.

41. Paul Edwards, *The Closed World: Computers and the Politics of Discourse in Cold War America* (Cambridge, MA: MIT Press, 1996); Janet Abbate, *Inventing the Internet* (Cambridge, MA: MIT Press, 1999).

42. Merrit Roe Smith (ed.), *Military Enterprise and Technological Change: Perspectives on the American Experience* (Cambridge, MA: MIT Press, 1985) and David Noble, *Forces of Production: a Social History of Automation* (New York: Oxford University Press, 1985).

## 7. Killing

1. James R. Troyer, 'In the beginning: the multiple discovery of the first hormone herbicides', *Weed Science*, Vol. 49 (2001), pp. 290–97.
2. William A. Buckingham Jr, *Operation Ranch Hand: the Air Force and Herbicides in South East Asia 1961–1971* (Washington: Office of Air Force History, 1982), *http://www.airforcehistory.hq.af.mil/Publications/fulltext/operation_ranch_hand.pdf.*
3. William Boyd, 'Making Meat: Science, Technology, and American Poultry Production', *Technology and Culture*, Vol. 42 (2001), p. 648.
4. Edmund Russell, *War and Nature: Fighting Humans and Insects with Chemicals from World War I to Silent Spring* (Cambridge: Cambridge University Press, 2001), p. 199.
5. Edward D. Mitchell, Randall R. Reeves and Anne Evely, *Bibliography of Whale Killing Techniques, Reports of the International Whaling Commission*, Special Issue 7 (Cambridge: International Whaling Commission, 1986).
6. J. N. Tønnessen and A. O. Johnsen, *The History of Modern Whaling*, trans. R. I. Christophersen (London: Hurst, 1982), pp. 368–429.
7. Ibid., p. 429.
8. http://www.wdcs.org/dan/publishing.nsf/allweb/69E0659244AE593C80256A5E0043C5C6
9. Tønnessen and Johnsen, *Modern Whaling*.
10. J. J. Waterman, *Freezing Fish at Sea: a History* (Edinburgh: HMSO, 1987).
11. A. C. Sutton, *Western Technology and Soviet Economic Development*, Vol. III, *1945 to 1965* (Stanford: Hoover Institution, 1973), pp. 287–8.
12. Oddly enough Britain did not develop a large factory-fishing fleet; the majority of new trawlers from the 1960s froze whole fish at sea for processing on land; their number peaked at forty-eight in 1974, a year before the last one was built. Waterman, *Freezing Fish.*
13. On related matters, see Paul R. Josephson, *Industrialized Nature: Brute Force Technology and the Transformation of the Natural World* (New York: Shearwater, 2002).
14. George Gissing, *By the Ionian Sea* (London: Century Hutchinson, 1986), pp. 153–4 (first published 1901).
15. Upton Sinclair, *The Jungle* (Harmondsworth: Penguin Classics Edition, 1974), pp. 328–9 (first published New York, 1906).
16. Ibid., pp. 44, 45.
17. Ibid., pp. 376–7.
18. See Hans-Liudger Dienel, *Linde: History of a Technology Corporation, 1879–2004* (London: Palgrave, 2004).

19. The lorry-mounted refrigeration unit was developed in the 1940s by an African-American inventor, Fred Jones, and led to the creation of the enormous Thermo King company.

20. J. B. Critchell and J. Raymond, *A History of the Frozen Meat Trade*, second edition (London: Constable, 1912), Appendix VII.

21. M. H. J. Finch, *A Political Economy of Uruguay since 1870* (London: Macmillan, 1981), chapter 5. Hank Wangford, *Lost Cowboys* (London: Gollancz, 1995) has a chapter on Fray Bentos.

22. Hal Williams, *Mechanical Refrigeration: a Practical Introduction to the Study of Cold Storage, Ice-making and Other Purposes to which Refrigeration is Being Applied*, fifth edition (London: Pitman, 1941), pp. 519–24.

23. *http://www.cep.edu.uy/RedDeEnlace/Uruguayni/Anglo/marcoanglo.htm* for oral testimony.

24. Sinclair, *The Jungle*, p. 48.

25. Siegfried Giedion, *Mechanization Takes Command: a Contribution to Anonymous History* (New York: Oxford University Press, 1948; W. W. Norton edition, 1969), p. 512. For a contrast between Germany and the USA, see Dienel, *Linde*.

26. Williams, pp. 487–515.

27. Ibid., p. 504.

28. Sinclair, *The Jungle*, p. 46.

29. Henry Ford, *My Life and Work* (online Project Gutenberg version).

30. Lindy Biggs, *The Rational Factory: Architecture, Technology and Work in America's Age of Mass Production* (Baltimore: Johns Hopkins University Press, 1996), chapter one.

31. See *Observer Food Monthly* (March 2002).

32. The captive bolt was promoted in Britain in the 1920s by the Humane Slaughter Association, and was made compulsory for cattle in 1933.

33. Eric Schlosser, *Fast Food Nation* (London: Penguin, 2002), pp. 137–8.

34. Ibid., chapters 7 and 8. See also Gail A. Eisnitz, *Slaughterhouse: the Shocking Story of Greed, Neglect and Inhumane Treatment Inside the US Meat Industry* (New York: Prometheus Books, 1997).

35. Rick Halpern, *Down on the Killing Floor: Black and White Workers in Chicago's Packinghouses, 1904–1954* (Chicago: University of Illinois Press, 1997).

36. T. S. Reynolds and T. Bernstein, 'Edison and "the chair"', *IEEE Technology and Society*, 8 (March 1989).

37. *http://www.geocities.com/trctl11/gascham.html.*

38. Around the world execution practices followed the colonial power – British colonies hung people; in the Philippines the Spanish had the garrotte; the US brought the electric chair.

39. But murdering a white victim is still much likelier to lead to an execution than murdering a black victim.

40. See Peter Linebaugh, 'Gruesome Gertie at the Buckle of the Bible Belt', *New Left Review*, No. 209 (1995), pp 15–33 and Walter Laqueur, 'Festival of Punishment', *London Review of Books*, 5 October 2000, pp. 17–24. *http://www.deathpenaltyinfo.org/getexecdata.php*. This gives access to the ESPY database of all US executions back to 1608.

41. Around 1941–42, the majority of the Jewish population of Poland and the Soviet Union was forced into ghettoes; this in itself was a way of killing many through hunger and disease, and some 800,000 succumbed.

42. Interestingly enough, there is one report that the NKVD introduced slaughter machines at the height of the purges, because executioners were beginning to doubt what they were doing, not least because those to be executed would speak out before death. There's a suggestion that Buhkarin himself was killed in such a machine. See Tokaev, *Comrade X*.

43. Jean-Claude Pressac and Jan van der Pelt, 'The Machinery of Mass Murder at Auschwitz', in Yisrael Gutman and Michael Berenbaum (ed.), *Anatomy of the Auschwitz Death Camp* (Bloomington: Indiana University Press, 1994), pp. 93–156.

44. Errol Morris (producer and director), *Mr Death: the Rise and Fall of Fred A. Leuchter Jr* (1999). Thanks to Andrés Di Tella.

45. *http://www.angelfire.com/fl3/starke/hmm.html* – for Leuchter on execution techniques.

46. For the demolition of Leuchter's argument, see Robert Jan van Pelt Report. *http://www.Holocaustdenialontrial.org/nsindex.html* is the website with the judgement, transcript etc. See also Pressac and van Pelt, 'The Machinery of Mass Murder at Auschwitz', in Gutman and Berenbaum (eds.), *Auschwitz Death Camp*, pp. 93–156 and *www.nizkor.org*.

47. Particularly hard hit were urban and rural minority populations, including the Chinese, Vietnamese and Thai Ben Kiernan, *The Pol Pot Regime: Race, Power and Genocide in Cambodia under the Khmer Rouge, 1975–1979*, second edition (New Haven: Yale University Press, 2002), Table 4, p. 458. In East Timor, the same proportion (roughly 20 per cent) of the population was killed around the same time, by the Indonesian state. Ben Kiernan, 'The Demography of Genocide in Southeast Asia: the Death Tolls in Cambodia,

1975–79, and East Timor, 1975–80', *Critical Asian Studies*, Vol. 35:4 (2003), pp. 585–97.

48. David Chandler, 'Killing Fields' in *http://www.cybercambodia.com/dachs/killings/killing.html*.

49. Human Rights Watch, *Leave None to Tell the Story: Genocide in Rwanda*, March 1999. *http://www.hrw.org/reports/1999/rwanda/*.

50. Report of the Rwanda Ministry of Local Government, 2001; quoted in Linda Melvern, *Conspiracy to Murder: the Rwandan Genocide* (London: Verso, 2004), p. 251.

51. My reading of Melvern, *Conspiracy to Murder*, p. 56.

## 8. Invention

1. Hyman Levy, *Modern Science* (London: Hamish Hamilton, 1939), p. 710.

2. For the centrality of this point, see my analysis of Vannevar Bush's *Science, the Endless Frontier*, in David Edgerton, ' "The linear model" did not exist: Reflections on the history and historiography of science and research in industry in the twentieth century', in Karl Grandin and Nina Wormbs (eds.), *The Science–Industry Nexus: History, Policy, Implications* (New York: Watson, 2004), and Sven Widalm, 'The Svedberg and the Boundary between science and industry: laboratory practice, policy and media images', *History and Technology*, Vol. 20 (2004), pp. 1–27.

3. Edgerton, ' "The linear model" '.

4. From Alec Nove, *The Economics of Feasible Socialism* (London: Allen & Unwin, 1983).

5. See the wonderful article by John Howells, 'The response of Old Technology Incumbents to Technological Competition – Does the sailing ship effect exist?', *Journal of Management Studies*, Vol. 39 (2002), pp. 887–906.

6. Leslie Hannah, 'The Whig Fable of American Tobacco, 1895–1913', *Journal of Economic History* (forthcoming, 2006).

7. Ulrich Marsh, 'Strategies for Success: research organisation in the German chemical companies until 1936', *History and Technology*, Vol. 12 (1994), pp. 23–77, but see also the standard accounts, such as Leonard S. Reich, *The Making of American Industrial Research: Science and Business at GE and Bell, 1876–1926* (Cambridge: Cambridge University Press, 1985) and D. A. Hounshell and J. K. Smith, *Science and Corporate Strategy: DuPont R&D* (Cambridge: Cambridge University Press, 1988). (Note how in these titles 'science' is equated with research and R&D.)

8. Michael Dennis, 'Accounting for Research: new histories of corporate laboratories and the social history of American science', *Social Studies of*

*Science*, Vol. 17 (1987), pp. 479–518; W. Koenig, 'Science-based industry or industry-based science? Electrical engineering in Germany before World War I', *Technology and Culture*, 37 (1996), 70–101.

9. Lindy Biggs, *The Rational Factory: Architecture, Technology and Work in America's Age of Mass Production* (Baltimore: Johns Hopkins University Press, 1996), pp. 106, 110–11.

10. Ronald Miller and David Sawers, *The Technical Development of Modern Aviation* (London: Routledge and Kegan Paul, 1968), p. 266.

11. These figures come from the remarkable Brookings Institution study on Stephen I. Schwartz, *Atomic Audit: the Costs and Consequences of U.S. Nuclear Weapons since 1940* (Washington: Brookings Institution Press, 1998).

12. I am indebted to a draft paper by John Howells.

13. S. Griliches and L. Owens, 'Patents, the "frontiers" of American invention, and the Monopoly Committee of 1939: anatomy of a discourse', *Technology and Culture*, Vol. 32 (1991), pp. 1076–93.

14. Ernest Braun, *Futile Progress: Technology's Empty Promise* (London: Earthscan, 1995), pp. 68–9.

15. Joseph A. DiMasi, Ronald W. Hansen and Henry G. Grabowski , 'The price of innovation: new estimates of drug development costs', *Journal of Health Economics*, Vol. 22 (2003), p. 154.

16. Ibid., pp. 151–185.

17. Anthony Arundel and Barbara Mintzes, 'The Benefits of Biopharmaceuticals', Innogen Working Paper No. 14, Version 2.0 (University of Edinburgh, August 2004); Paul Nightingale and Paul Martin, 'The Myth of the Biotech Revolution', *TRENDS in Biotechnology*, Vol. 22, No. 11, November 2004, pp. 564–8.

## Conclusion

1. John B. Harms and Tim Knapp, 'The New Economy: what's new, what's not', *Review of Radical Political Economics*, Vol. 35 (2003), pp. 413–36.

2. P. A. David, 'Computer and Dynamo: the Modern Productivity Paradox in a not-too-distant mirror', in OECD, *Technology and Productivity: the Challenge for Economic Policy* (Paris: OECD, 1991).

3. *Economist*, 17 January 2004.

4. *Observer*, 8 April 2001.

5. Martin Stopford, *Maritime Economics*, second edition (London: Routledge, 1997), pp. 485–6.

# Select bibliography

## Books and articles

Janet Abbate, *Inventing the Internet* (Cambridge, MA: MIT Press, 1999)

Itty Abraham, *The Making of the Indian Atomic Bomb: science, secrecy and the postcolonial state* (London: Zed Books, 1998)

Michael Adas, *Machines as the Measure of Men: Science, Technology and Ideologies of Western Dominance* (Ithaca: Cornell University Press, 1989)

Michael Thad Allen, *The Business of Genocide: The SS, Slave Labor and the Concentration Camps* (Chapel Hill: University of North Carolina Press, 2002)

David Arnold, 'Europe, Technology and Colonialism in the 20th Century', *History and Technology*, vol. 21 (2005)

Jonathan Bailey, *The First World War and the Birth of the Modern Style of Warfare* (Camberley: Strategic and Combat Studies Institute, Occasional Paper No. 22, 1996)

— *Field Artillery and Firepower* (Annapolis: Naval Institute Press, 2004)

George Basalla, *The Evolution of Technology* (Cambridge: Cambridge University Press, 1988)

Arnold Bauer, *Goods, Power, History: Latin America's Material Culture* (Cambridge: Cambridge University Press, 2001)

Z. Bauman, *Modernity and the Holocaust* (Cambridge: Polity, 1989)

Tami Davis Biddle, *Rhetoric and Reality in Air Warfare: the Evolution of British and American Ideas about Strategic Bombing, 1914–1945* (Princeton: Princeton University Press, 2002)

Lindy Biggs, *The Rational Factory: Architecture, Technology and Work in America's Age of Mass Production* (Baltimore: Johns Hopkins University Press, 1996)

Sue Bowden and Avner Offer, 'Household appliances and the use of time: the United States and Britain since the 1920s', *Economic History Review*, Vol. 67 (1994)

William Boyd, 'Making Meat: Science, Technology, and American Poultry Production', *Technology and Culture*, Vol. 42 (2001)

S. Brand, *How Buildings Learn: What Happens after They're Built* (London: Penguin, 1994)

Ernest Braun, *Futile Progress: Technology's Empty Promise* (London: Earthscan, 1995)

Michael Burawoy, *The Politics of Production* (London: Verso, 1985)

Cynthia Cockburn and Susan Ormrod, *Gender and Technology in the Making* (London: Sage, 1993)

Hera Cook, *The Long Sexual Revolution: English Women, Sex, and Contraception, 1800–1975* (Oxford: Oxford University Press, 2004)

Caroline Cooper, *Air-conditioning America: Engineers and the Contolled Environment, 1900–1960* (Baltimore: Johns Hopkins University Press, 1998)

P. A. David, 'Computer and Dynamo: the Modern Productivity Paradox in a not-too-distant mirror', in OECD, *Technology and Productivity: the Challenge for Economic Policy* (Paris: OECD, 1991)

— 'Heroes, Herds and Hysteresis in Technological History: Thomas Edison and "The Battle of the Systems" Reconsidered', *Industrial and Corporate Change*, Vol. 1, No. 1 (1992)

Michael Dennis, 'Accounting for Research: new histories of corporate laboratories and the social history of American science', *Social Studies of Science*, Vol. 17 (1987)

Development and Planning Unit, *Understanding Slums: Case Studies for the Global Report on Human Settlements*, Development and Planning Unit, UCL. See *http://www.ucl.ac.uk/dpu-projects/Global_Report/*

R. L. DiNardo and A. Bay, 'Horse-Drawn Transport in the German Army', *Journal of Contemporary History*, Vol. 23 (1988)

T. N. Dupuy, *The Evolution of Weapons and Warfare* (New York: Da Capo, 1990; first published 1984)

David Edgerton, 'Tilting at Paper Tigers', *British Journal for the History of Science*, Vol. 26 (1993)

— 'De l'innovation aux usages. Dix thèses éclectiques sur l'histoire des techniques', *Annales HSS*, July–October 1998, Nos. 4–5. English version: 'From Innovation to Use: ten (eclectic) theses on the history of technology', *History and Technology*, Vol. 16 (1999)

— ' "The linear model" did not exist: reflections on the history and historiography of science and research in industry in the twentieth century', in Karl Grandin and Nina Wormbs (eds.), *The Science–Industry Nexus: History, Policy, Implications* (New York: Watson, 2004)

— *Warfare State: Britain, 1920–1970* (Cambridge: Cambridge University Press, 2005)

Gail A. Eisnitz, *Slaughterhouse: the Shocking Story of Greed, Neglect and Inhumane Treatment inside the US Meat Industry* (New York: Prometheus Books, 1997)

Gil Elliot, *Twentieth Century Book of the Dead* (London: Allen Lane, 1972)

Jon Elster, *Explaining Technical Change* (Cambridge: Cambridge University Press, 1983)

R. J. Evans, *Rituals of Retribution: Capital Punishment in Germany 1600–1987* (Oxford: Oxford University Press, 1996)

Claude S. Fischer, *America Calling: a Social History of the Telephone to 1940* (Berkeley: University of California Press, 1992)

Jim Fitzpatrick, *The Bicycle in Wartime: an Illustrated History* (London: Brassey's, 1998)

Sheila Fitzpatrick, *Stalin's Peasants: Resistance and Survival in the Russian Village after Collectivisation* (New York: Oxford University Press, 1994)

R. W. Fogel, 'The new economic history: its findings and methods', *Economic History Review*, Vol. 19 (1966)

Robert Friedel, *Zipper: an Exploration in Novelty* (New York: Norton 1994)

Rob Gallagher, *The Rickshaws of Bangladesh* (Dhaka: The University Press, 1992)

Siegfried Giedion, *Mechanization Takes Command: a contribution to Anonymous History* (New York: Oxford University Press, 1948; W. W. Norton edition, 1969)

Kees Gispen, *Poems in Steel: National Socialism and the Politics of Inventing from Weimar to Bonn* (New York: Berghahn Books, 2002)

Arnulf Gruebler, *Technology and Global Change* (Cambridge: Cambridge University Press, 1998)

John A. Hall (ed.), *The State of the Nation: Ernest Gellner and the Theory of Nationalism* (Cambridge: Cambridge University Press, 1998)

Daniel R. Headrick, *The Tentacles of Progress: Technology Transfer in the Age of Imperialism, 1850–1940* (New York: Oxford University Press, 1988)

— *The Invisible Weapon: Telecommunications and International Politics, 1851–1945* (New York: Oxford University Press, 1991).

C. Hitch and R. McKean, *The Economics of Defence in the Nuclear Age* (Cambridge, MA: Harvard University Press, 1960)

David A. Hounshell, *From the American System to Mass Production, 1800–1932: The Development of Manufacturing Technology in the United States* (Baltimore: Johns Hopkins University Press, 1984)

David A. Hounshell and J. K. Smith, *Science and Corporate Strategy: Du Pont R&D* (Cambridge: Cambridge University Press, 1988)

John Howells, 'The response of Old Technology Incumbents to Technological Competition – Does the sailing ship effect exist?', *Journal of Management Studies*, Vol. 39 (2002)

— *The Management of Innovation and Technology* (London: Sage, 2005)

Thomas Hughes, *American Genesis: a Century of Invention and Technological Enthusiasm* (New York: Viking, 1989)

John Kurt Jacobsen, *Technical Fouls: Democratic Dilemmas and Technological Change* (Boulder: Westview Press, 2000)

Erik E. Jansen, et al., *The Country Boats of Bangladesh: Social and Economic Development and Decision-making in Inland Water Transport* (Dhaka: The University Press, 1989)

Katherine Jellison, *Entitled to Power: Farm Women and Technology 1913–1963* (Chapel Hill: University of North Carolina Press, 1993)

J. Jewkes, et al., *The Sources of Invention* (London: Macmillan, 1958, 1969)

Paul R. Josephson. *Industrialized Nature: Brute Force Technology and the Transformation of the Natural World* (New York: Shearwater, 2002)

Mary Kaldor, *The Baroque Arsenal* (London: Deutsch, 1982)

Terence Kealey, *The Economic Laws of Scientific Research* (London: Macmillan, 1996)

V. G. Kiernan, *European Empires from Conquest to Collapse, 1815–1960* (London: Fontana, 1982)

Ronald R. Kline, *Consumers in the Country: Technology and Social Change in Rural America* (Baltimore: Johns Hopkins University Press, 2000)

Arnold Krammer, 'Fueling the Third Reich', *Technology and Culture,* Vol. 19 (1978)

George Kubler, *The Shape of Time: Remarks on the History of Things* (New Haven: Yale University Press, 1962)

Bruno Latour, *We Have Never Been Modern* (New York: Harvester Wheatsheaf, 1993)

— *Aramis, or the Love of Technology*, trans. by Catherine Porter (Cambridge, MA: Harvard University Press, 1996)

Nina Lerman, Ruth Oldenzeil and Arwen Mohun (eds.), *Gender and Technology: a Reader* (Baltimore: Johns Hopkins University Press, 2003)

J. E. Lesch (ed.), *The German Chemical Industry in the Twentieth Century* (Dordrecht: Kluwer Academic, 2000)

Samuel Lilley, *Men, Machines and History* (second edition) (London: Lawrence & Wishart, 1965)

Svante Lindqvist, 'Changes in the Technological Landscape: the temporal dimension in the growth and decline of large technological systems', in Ove Granstrand (ed.), *Economics of Technology* (Amsterdam: North Holland, 1994)

Erik Lund, 'The Industrial History of Strategy: re-evaluating the wartime record of the British aviation industry in comparative perspective, 1919–1945', *Journal of Military History,* Vol. 62 (1998)

Walter A. McDougall, *The Heavens and the Earth: A Political History of the Space Age* (New York: Basic Books, 1985)

D. MacKenzie and J. Wajcman (eds.), *The Social Shaping of Technology* (Milton Keynes: Open University Press, 1985)

D. MacKenzie, *Knowing Machines: Essays on Technical Change* (Cambridge, MA: MIT Press, 1996)

John McNeill, *Something New under the Sun: an Environmental History of the Twentieth Century* (London: Penguin, 2000)

T. Metzger, *Blood and Volts: Edison, Tesla and the Electric Chair* (New York: Autonomedia, 1996)

Birgit Meyer and Jojada Verrips, 'Kwaku's Car. The Struggles and Stories of a Ghanaian Long-distance Taxi Driver' in Daniel Miller (ed.), *Car Cultures* (Oxford: Berg Publishers, 2001)

Ronald Miller and David Sawers, *The Technical Development of Modern Aviation* (London: RKP, 1968)

David A. Mindell, *Between Human and Machine: Feedback, Control and Computing before Cybernetics* (Baltimore: Johns Hopkins University Press, 2002)

Arwen P. Mohun, *Steam Laundries: Gender, Technology and Work in the United States and Great Britain, 1880–1940* (Baltimore: Johns Hopkins University Press, 1999)

Ricardo Rodríguez Molas, *Historia de la Tortura y el Orden Represivo en la Argentina* (Buenos Aires: Editorial Universitaria de Buenos Aires, 1984), online version at *http://www.elortiba.org/tortura.html*

Gijs Mom, *The Electric Vehicle: Technology and Expectations in the Automobile Age* (Baltimore: Johns Hopkins University Press, 2004)

Lewis Mumford, *Technics and Civilisation* (London: Routledge and Kegan Paul, 1955; first published 1934)

— 'Authoritarian and Democratic Technics', *Technology and Culture*, Vol. 5 (1964)

— *The Pentagon of Power* (New York: Harcourt, Brace, Jovanovich, 1970)

Alondra Nelson and Thuy Linh N. Tu (eds.) *Technicolor: Race, Technology, and Everyday Life* (New York and London: New York University Press, 2002)

Michael J. Neufeld, *The Rocket and the Reich: Peenemunde and the Coming of the Ballistic Missile Era* (New York: Free Press, 1995)

David Noble, *America by Design: Science, Technology and the Rise of Corporate Capitalism* (New York: Oxford University Press, 1977)

— *Forces of Production: a Social History of Automation* (New York: Oxford University Press, 1985)

Robert S. Norris, *Racing for the Bomb: General Leslie R. Groves, the Manhattan Project's Indispensable Man* (Hannover, NH: Steerforth, 2002)

David Omissi, *The Sepoy and the Raj: Politics of the Indian Army, 1860–1940* (London: Macmillan, 1994)

Arnold Pacey, *The Culture of Technology* (Oxford: Blackwell, 1983)

—*Technology in World Civilisation: a Thousand Year History* (Oxford: Blackwell, 1990)

John V. Pickstone, *Ways of Knowing: a new history of science, technology and medicine* (Manchester: Manchester University Press, 2000)

John Powell, *The Survival of the Fitter: Lives of Some African Engineers* (London: Intermediate Technology, 1995)

Daryl G. Press, 'The myth of air power in the Persian Gulf war and the future of air power', *International Security* Vol. 26 (2001)

Jean-Claude Pressac and Jan van der Pelt, 'The Machinery of Mass Murder at Auschwitz', in Yisrael Gutman and Michael Berenbaum (eds.), *Anatomy of the Auschwitz Death Camp* (Bloomington: Indiana University Press, 1994)

E. Prokosch, *The Technology of Killing: a Military and Political History of Anti-personnel Weapons* (London: Zed Books, 1995)

Carroll Pursell, 'Seeing the invisible: new perceptions in the history of technology', in *ICON*, Vol. 1 (1995)

— *The Machine in America: a Social History of Technology* (Baltimore: Johns Hopkins University Press, 1995)

Olivier Razac, *Barbed Wire: a Political History* (London: Profile, 2002)

Leonard S. Reich, *The Making of American Industrial Research: Science and Business at GE and Bell, 1876–1926* (Cambridge: Cambridge University Press, 1985)

T. S. Reynolds and T. Bernstein, 'Edison and "the chair"', *IEEE Technology and Society*, 8 (March 1989)

Pietra Rivoli, *The Travels of a T-shirt in the Global Economy: an Economist Examines the Markets, Power and Politics of World Trade* (Hoboken, NJ: Wiley, 2005)

Nathan Rosenberg, *Perspectives on Technology* (Cambridge: Cambridge University Press, 1976)

— *Inside the Black Box* (Cambridge: Cambridge University Press, 1982)

— *Exploring the Black Box* (Cambridge: Cambridge University Press, 1994)

Edmund Russell, *War and Nature: Fighting Humans and Insects with Chemicals from World War I to Silent Spring* (Cambridge: Cambridge University Press, 2001)

Witold Rybczynski, *One Good Turn: A Natural History of the Screwdriver and the Screw* (New York: Simon & Schuster, 2000)

Raphael Samuel, 'The workshop of the world: steam power and hand technology in mid-Victorian Britain', *History Workshop Journal*, No. 3 (1977)

— *Theatres of Memory: past and present in contemporary culture* (London: Verso, 1994)

Charles Sabel and Jonathan Zeitlin, 'Historical Alternatives to Mass Production: Politics, Markets and Technology in Nineteenth-century Industrialization', *Past and Present*, No. 108 (1985)

Virginia Scharff, *Taking the Wheel: Women and the Coming of the Motor Age* (Alburquerque: University of New Mexico Press, 1992)

Eric Schatzberg, *Wings of Wood, Wings of Metal: Culture and Technical Choice in American Airplane Materials, 1914–1945* (Princeton: Princeton University Press, 1998)

— '*Technik* comes to America: changing meanings of *Technology* before 1930, *Technology and Culture*, vol. 46 (2006)

Eric Schlosser, *Fast Food Nation* (London: Penguin, 2002)

Ralph Schroeder, 'The Consumption of Technology in Everyday Life: Car, Telephone, and Television in Sweden and America in Comparative-Historical Perspective', *Sociological Research Online*, Vol. 7, No. 4

Ruth Schwartz Cowan, *More Work for Mother: the Ironies of Household Technology from the Open Hearth to the Microwave* (New York: Basic Books, 1983)

Stephen I. Schwartz, *Atomic Audit: the Costs and Consequences of U.S. Nuclear Weapons since 1940* (Washington: Brookings Institution Press, 1998)

Philip Scranton, *Endless Novelty: Specialty Production and American Industrialisation* (Princeton: Princeton University Press, 1997)

Neil Sheehan, *The Bright Shining Lie: John Paul Vann and America in Vietnam* (London: Vintage, 1989)

Haruhito Shiomi and Kazuo Wada (eds.), *Fordism Transformed: the Development of Production Methods in the Automobile Industry* (Oxford: Oxford University Press, 1995)

Bruce Sinclair (ed.), *Technology and the African-American Experience: Needs and Opportunities for Study* (Cambridge, MA: MIT Press, 2004)

John Singleton, 'Britain's Military Use of Horses 1914–1918', *Past and Present*, No. 139 (1993)

James Small, *The Analogue Alternative: the Electronic Analogue Computer in Britain and the USA, 1930–1975* (London: Routledge, 2001)

Vaclav Smil, *Energy in World History* (Boulder: Westview Press, 1994)

Anthony Smith (ed.), *Television: an international history* (Oxford: Oxford University Press, 1995)

Merrit Roe Smith (ed.), *Military Enterprise and Technological Change: Perspectives on the American Experience* (Cambridge, MA: MIT Press, 1985)

Merrit Roe Smith and L. Marx (eds.), *Does Technology Drive History? The Dilemma of Technological Determinism* (Cambridge, Mass: MIT Press, 1994)

Raymond G. Stokes, *Constructing Socialism: Technology and Change in East Germany 1945–1990* (Baltimore: Johns Hopkins University Press, 2000)

Anthony Stranges, 'Friedrich Bergius and the Rise of the German Synthetic Fuel Industry', *ISIS* vol. 75 (1984)

— 'From Birmingham to Billingham: high-pressure coal hydrogenation in Great Britain', *Technology and Culture*, Vol. 26 (1985)

A. C. Sutton, *Western Technology and Soviet Economic Development 1930 to 1945* (Stanford: Hoover Institution, 1971)

— *Western Technology and Soviet Economic Development 1945 to 1965* (Stanford: Hoover Institution, 1973)

Andrea Tone, *Devices and Desires: a History of Contraceptives in America* (New York: Hill and Wang, 2001)

J. N. Tønnessen and A. O. Johnsen, *The History of Modern Whaling* (trans. by R. I. Christophersen) (London: Hurst, 1982)

Colin Tudge, *So Shall We Reap* (London: Allen Lane, 2003)

Martin Van Creveld, *Technology and War: from 2000 BC to the Present* (London: Brassey's, 1991)

W. Vincenti, *What Engineers Know and How They Know it: Studies from Aeronautical History* (Baltimore: Johns Hopkins University Press, 1990)

P. Weindling, 'The uses and abuses of biological technologies: Zyklon B and gas disinfestation between the First World War and the Holocaust', *History and Technology*, Vol. 11 (1994)

Tony Wheeler and Richard l'Anson, *Chasing Rickshaws* (London: Lonely Planet, 1998)

Langdon Winner, *Autonomous Technology: Technics-out-of-Control as a Theme in Political Thought* (Cambridge, MA: MIT Press, 1977)

Peter Worsley, *The Three Worlds: Culture and World Development* (London: Weidenfeld and Nicolson, 1984)

Jonathan Zeitlin, 'Flexibility and Mass Production at War: Aircraft Manufacturing in Britain, the United States, and Germany, 1939–1945', *Technology and Culture*, Vol. 36 (1995)

## Journals

*History and Technology*
*History of Technology*
*ICON*
*Technology and Culture*

# Acknowledgements

This book is animated by a belief that putting a new and more adequate history of technology in global history would change both for the better. That project is hardly original. In 1935 Lucien Febvre and Marc Bloch, who had founded the *Annales* in 1929, published the first special issue of their journal and devoted it to the history of techniques which they wanted to see developed a part of general history. It is pleasing to record that many of the key arguments of *Shock of the Old* first appeared in the 1998 second special issue on the history of techniques of the *Annales*, edited by Yves Cohen and Dominique Pestre. Some of my many other intellectual debts are acknowledged all too briefly in the deliberately limited footnotes and or by a listing in the select bibliography, which is meant to serve in part as a guide to further reading. These listings underestimate my indebtedness to what I call 'historiography from below', for this account has depended on a range of non-academic material too.

I am grateful too for those scholars from round the world who saw the merits of my argument for avoiding the conflation of innovation and use, and the need for new global histories of both. I have benefitted from comments at seminars and lectures (in roughly chronological order) at the Universidad de la República, Montevideo, the École des Hautes Etudes en Sciences Sociales, Paris, the Institute of Economic Affairs, London, the Royal Institute of Technology, Stockholm; the following universities: Athens, Bath, Cambridge, Manchester, National Tsing Hua University (Taiwan), Cornell, MIT and Wisconsin-Madison. I have also learned from responses to many presentations conferences and meetings: the Anglo-American conference at the Institute for Historical Research, London, a Japan Society for the Promotion of Science Symposium at Churchill College, a meeting of the Catalan Society for the History of Science and Technology, the National Identities of Engineers: their past and present conference on Syros, the Society for the History of Technology meeting in Amsterdam, and a conference on Big Issues in the History of Science, Technology and Medicine at the University of Manchester. I have also benefited from a meeting at Imperial College on 'What is new in the history of technology', and particularly from the contributions of John Pickstone, Svante Lindqvist, Eric Schatzberg, and Pap N'diaye.

I am grateful to many other colleagues, particularly those in the Centre for the

History of Science, Technology and Medicine at Imperial College. The key ideas were first presented, over a decade ago, to masters students at Imperial College, and in more recent years have been tried out on undergraduates too. I am grateful to them all and particularly those whose research and experience have contributed to my own knowledge, among them Toby Barklem, Roger Bridgman, Benjamin Fu Rentai, Mohammad Faisal Khalil, Groves Herrick, Emily Mayhew, Neilesh Patel, Russell Potts, Andrew Rabeneck, Sarah Ross, Claire Scott, Brian Spear, James Watson, and the late Nick Webber.

For information and help of many sorts thanks to Jonathan Bailey, René Boretto Ovalle, Dana Dalrymple, Julio Dávila, Hans-Liudger Dienel, Andrés Di Tella, Jennifer Dixon, Sithichai Egoramaiphol, Mats Fridlund, Delphine Gardey, Roberto Gebhardt, David Goodhart, Leslie Hannah, John Howells, Terence Kealey, John Krige, Simon Lee, Shang-Jen Li, Svante Lindqvist, Santiago López García, José-Antonio Martín Pereda, Bryan Pfaffenberger, Lisbet Rausing, Irénée Scalbert, Eric Schatzberg, Ralph Schroeder, Adam Tooze, Clio Turton, Aristotle Tympas, Valdeir Rejinaldo Vidrik, Chyuan-Yuan Wu and Diana Young.

For their essential criticisms of earlier versions of the text I am grateful to doctoral students at Imperial College, especially Jessica Carter, Sabine Clarke, Ralph Desmarais, Miguel García-Sancho, Neil Tarrant, Rosemary Wall and Waqar Zaidi. Jim Rennie was a crucial critic of early drafts. Andrew Franklin, who commissioned the book and waited patiently for it, not only greatly improved it but exemplifies its argument by believing in the book, independent publishing and history. My warmest thanks to him, and also to others at Profile, especially Daniel Crewe.

# List of Illustrations

# Index